Dec '07 Poppa (Bezzy),

Good luck with the project...
Here's to many happy hours looking
at the Grand & enjoying the breeze!
Love/Bruuy/
Kelly & Zuke

Cottage Essentials

Cottage
THE EVERYTHING GUIDE FOR YOUR COTTAGE, CABIN OR CAMP
Essentials

WAYNE LENNOX

whitecap

Edited by Alison Maclean
Proofread by Lesley Cameron
Cover and interior design by Jacqui Thomas
Cover photograph by Troy and Mary Parlee / Alamy Images

Printed and bound in Canada

National Library of Canada Cataloguing in Publication Data

Lennox, Wayne
    Cottage essentials: the everything guide for your cottage, cabin or camp / Wayne
Lennox.

    Includes bibliographical references and index.
    ISBN 1-55285-527-9

    1. Vacation homes. 2. Outdoor life. I. Title.
GV191.44.L44 2004   796.5   C2004-900365-8

The publisher acknowledges the financial support of the Government of Canada
through the Book Publishing Industry Development Program for
our publishing activities.

We are committed to protecting the environment and to the responsible use of natural
resources. We are acting on this commitment by working with suppliers and printers to
phase out our use of paper produced from ancient forests. This book is printed by Friesens on
100% post-consumer recycled paper, processed chorine free and printed with vegetable-based
inks. We are working with Markets Initiative (www.oldgrowthfree.com) on this project.

Dedication

This book is dedicated to my late father-in-law, Morley Duncan Abbott, the ultimate cottager. Morley could build or fix anything, and understood nearly everything mechanical, electrical, hydrological, zoological, botanical, and even metaphysical.

The lake was his realm, and Morley was its well-known sage. His cottage was a veritable Mecca and many came seeking help or advice. But many came just for the visit, because talking was almost as satisfying as fixing or building. He was the best darned storyteller I ever met, and he had a bagful of great tales from his past on the farm, in the army, and from life in general.

When Morley died, our family and his friends lost someone incredibly special. I am thankful that I learned so much from him; he was indeed one of a kind.

Acknowledgements

I wish to thank my editor, Alison Maclean, for her encouragement to move ahead with this project; without her, I would never have written this book.

My wife, Lynn, has always been the first to read my work, and I am grateful for her many useful suggestions, and her unflagging encouragement and optimism.

When I think about this book, I am frankly somewhat astonished at the help so many people were willing to provide, and the time they were so willing to give. I have steadfastly held that most people are genuinely generous; this belief was reinforced by the work I did on this book.

Contents

Introduction

EITHER YOU ARE OR YOU AREN'T A COTTAGER. It's that simple. People who aren't don't even understand those of us who are. And even those of us who are cottagers, though we share a special love for the life, often define "the cottage, camp, or cabin" quite differently. Our family's version is a place we built on the southern shore of Lake Wah-Wash-Kesh in Ontario.

Even though I was raised in the north, I had never really been a cottage—or camp—person until I visited my future in-laws' place. My experience with the outdoors had most often involved a canoe and a tent and I was frankly suspicious, and perhaps even scornful, of those who preferred the wilderness outside while they remained secure within four walls. When my girlfriend (who would later do me the great and lasting honor of becoming my wife) brought me out on our first date to meet her folks at their cottage, my opinion changed; I was hooked. Sure, I fell for a terrific woman, but from that moment I also began to develop a love for this life, this rather difficult to rationalize life, that has grown deeper every year.

Like my wife, Lynn, and I, our children value the cottage above all else. There is a real sense of tradition as well as attachment; when they stand on our shore they can see the cottages their father, grandfather, and great-grandfather built. If they look across the lake, they can even distinguish the roof of the place their great-great-grandfather constructed at the turn of the twentieth century. This is the place that binds us as a family. I cannot even reckon the number of hours that we have played board and card games together, and the experiences we have shared: treasure hunts, the first time they could swim to Miller's Point, Camp Mia-Kon-Da, the Great Storm of '95, learning how to shoot, how to split wood, how to build a fire in the stove, games with cousins, the Jumping Rocks, our dog and his relentless pursuit of chipmunks, water skiing, tubing, lying on the dock watching the Northern Lights, fires down by the lake, Thanksgiving weekends with family and neighbors, and a thousand other memories that make the cottage that place we can never replace.

I value every moment I spend at the lake, and this book is a lot about what I do know, have needed to know, or have wanted to know—some essential stuff (well, maybe even some whimsical stuff too!). I hope that, as the owner—or renter—of a cottage, camp, or cabin, you will not only enjoy this book, but also that you will find something useful among its pages. Perhaps you will disagree with me on some things. Since we are cottagers, some difference of opinion can be expected.

CHAPTER 1

Going for a Little Walk in the Woods?

MUCH OF THE APPEAL OF THE COTTAGE, CAMP, OR CABIN is the forest environment that surrounds us. Though the woods are a pretty thin illusion in some places, other cottages and shoreline communities are actually situated in the "bush." In these areas, many cottagers never wander far from the safety of the lights, though most—when the flies aren't bad—will at least take short hikes along known trails or roads. However, there is a segment of the deep-woods cottage population with a much greater sense of adventure.

Hikers enjoy trekking through familiar—or unfamiliar—wilderness territory. Amateur photographers, geologists, or field naturalists may venture well off the beaten path. In blueberry country, scores of cottagers head into the bush every year in the hopes of harvesting a tasty bounty. A snowmobile or an ATV can take you virtually anywhere when the conditions are right. Of course, any canoe trip, even a short one, may lead into unknown surroundings; for a few, mountain biking or back-country skiing are regular expeditions. And there is still a significant number of cottagers who hunt or regularly tramp though the bush to secret angling locations. For these groups, becoming disoriented, or suffering an injury are very real possibilities (the "Wait a minute…where the heck am I?", or "S__t…that looks bad!" scenarios). Getting lost is an extremely stressful and potentially life-threatening event, and even a minor mishap can have serious consequences when you're far from help. So, if you include yourself in one of these groups, it is important to evaluate just how well you're prepared for emergencies.

Setting Out

There are fundamental, conventional procedures that should be followed, regardless of a trip's duration or destination. Quite likely, most adventurous readers know and practice these procedures, and can probably add to the routines outlined in this chapter. For the less qualified though, this information might prevent, at the very least, a disagreeable experience.

1. You need to inform someone of your destination. Once you have determined a route, you have an obligation to stick with that trip itinerary unless you have some way of relating the change in plans to your contact. It might be a tad more difficult to find you if no one knows where you went! Experts also recommend that you never travel alone; if you get lost, or an accident happens, a companion can be your most important asset.

2. Provide your contact with a definite time frame: you'll be gone for two hours, two days, or two weeks. Be relatively generous with your estimation; if you think a particular trip will last X amount of time, try to factor in unexpected difficulties. When I'm mountain biking, I will tell my contact that I will be gone for two hours, but not to send the troops unless I'm not back in four. If I have a major mechanical problem, I figure I can walk out in the specified time.

3. Even when traveling in known wilderness territory, carry a map, know how to use it, and store it in a waterproof container such as a zip-lock bag. This seems obvious, but many people have only a very limited knowledge of map use. The most common map used for travel in the bush is the topographic map—scale 1:50,000. You should be able to determine your exact heading using a compass (basic orienteering—see end of chapter), be familiar with the military grid system, be able to determine approximate distance (on a 1:50,000 map, 1 cm on the map represents .5 km on the ground), recognize symbols and features, and understand and interpret contour information. Certainly, GPS (Global Positioning System) electronics can make navigation much easier, but batteries do fail so you could be in some trouble if you rely exclusively on these instruments.

    In the event that you get turned around—an ironic euphemism—there are several natural directional aids at your disposal. The sun is the most obvious for rough estimates during the day, and at night, the North Star could be used as a directional beacon. It's the brightest star that lines up with the two stars at the end of the Big Dipper's pan; face the North Star, and you're facing north. Remember that travel at night is both dangerous and difficult; use the stars to determine direction, but travel only in the day. Other clues include the direction of the tops of white pine trees which tend to lean toward the southeast, the melt line around dark objects on the surface of the snow (because of the sun's angle, the south side of the object will absorb more heat, thus creating a melted half-circle on the south side), and many others. The shadow stick is an alternative way to determine direction, as explained in the accompanying diagram.

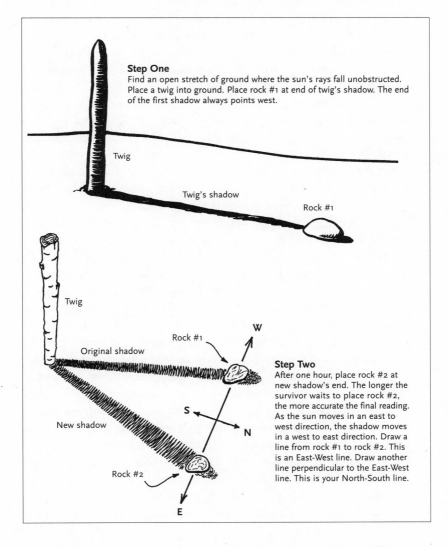

Step One
Find an open stretch of ground where the sun's rays fall unobstructed. Place a twig into ground. Place rock #1 at end of twig's shadow. The end of the first shadow always points west.

Twig

Twig's shadow

Rock #1

Twig

Original shadow

Rock #1

W

S

N

New shadow

Rock #2

E

Step Two
After one hour, place rock #2 at new shadow's end. The longer the survivor waits to place rock #2, the more accurate the final reading. As the sun moves in an east to west direction, the shadow moves in a west to east direction. Draw a line from rock #1 to rock #2. This is an East-West line. Draw another line perpendicular to the East-West line. This is your North-South line.

4. Dress properly for the activity and the season; some suggest that you should always dress for the possibility of an overnight stay. In the spring and fall (you can get downright nasty weather in April and October), and especially in the winter, practice the layering technique. Wear at least three layers of clothing: for example, an undershirt, a heavier wool or polyester fleece sweater or anorak over top, and a good quality jacket as the final layer. Dead air is trapped between layers of loosely fitting clothes; more layers provide more trapped air and that in turn creates more insulation. By dressing in layers, you can remove one or more as you warm up, or add layers as you cool down. Avoid cotton as it tends to retain moisture and thus keeps you perpetually cold. Traditionalists believe that wool is still the best material for sweaters, and their trust in this natural fabric is well-founded; however, most now opt for popular polyester fleece (often made from recycled plastics). It comes in a wide range of weights and styles to suit the activity and season.

Consider investing in a first-class outer jacket made of Gore-Tex® or a similar moisture management system (and unless you're a hunter, those bright colors are not only fashionable, but could make you easier to spot in an emergency). It should be long enough to cover the cold-sensitive kidneys, have a flap to seal the zipper to reduce wind penetration, have some means of fastening or closing the wrist part of the sleeve, have a high collar, and possess a proper hood. Though generally rather expensive, these coats can be used year round and often eliminate the need for rainwear.

Stay away from jeans; they take forever to dry, and they restrict movement when wet. In good weather, military trousers—the real polyester kind—or pants made of a quick-dry material are good selections (cargo pockets should also be considered: you can put a lot of stuff in them). Whoever designed military pants must have been a veteran of the bug wars, because they all feature a drawstring at the cuff to keep the bugs—and dirt—out. In colder weather, layer wind-resistant, water-resistant, or repellant pants over long underwear. Newer materials promise superior moisture management, but do a little research before you buy; today's long johns can set you back a few bucks. Outdoor stores sell bib-style outerwear that is an ideal cold-weather lower-body garment: it virtually covers the chest area—another prime heat loss zone—has suspenders rather than a belt, permits freer movement and better ventilation, and it reduces the likelihood of snow getting down your pants if you fall.

Good-quality waterproof boots or hiking shoes are absolutely essential. Because most of my outdoor experience is in rattlesnake country, I prefer boots. Boots also provide support to minimize ankle injuries and their greater height reduces the likelihood of wet feet. Some suggest sock layering as well: a thin technical-type sock close to the skin, and a heavier sock over top. Since the feet cannot be ventilated properly, you should also carry at least one change of dry socks. In winter, wear proper boots.

The head is the greatest heat-loss zone (60% to 75% of body heat loss is through the head), and a good hat or wool or fleece toque is necessary in cool or cold weather. In bug season, a wide-brimmed hat deters the deer flies and protects the head from sunburn.

Finally, in cold weather, choose mitts over gloves because gloves separate the fingers, making them cold. Mitts can also be layered: a good-quality fleece mitt works well inside a long-cuffed outer mitt (preferably water-resistant).

5. Do you have any idea what the weather will be like for the next 24 hours? You should listen to the weather forecasts before setting out, and you should pay attention to weather signs when you're out there. Expect bad weather if: a) cumulus clouds (the white puffy ones) grow taller and darken; b) the sky darkens with a gray or dark layered cloud with no definition; c) winds blow from the north-east, east, south-east to south; d) winds shift in a counter-clockwise direction (i.e. a west wind shifting to the south then the east); e) there are sudden gusting winds; f) bug activity is unusually high.

6. You should always carry a basic survival kit. Opinions vary as to what is essential, and outdoor stores will sell you a pre-packaged collection. Dr. Gino Ferri, director of Survival in the Bush Inc. and author of *The Psychology of Wilderness Survival*, recommends that wilderness travelers carry the following:

- Top-quality pocket knife.
- Compass.
- Waterproof container with matches, and an alternate fire-starting instrument (such as a lighter or metal firestarter).
- Space blanket; 2 large orange garbage bags.
- 10 adhesive bandages.
- Insect repellant.
- Safety pins / needle and thread.
- Small steel signaling mirror.

- Water bottle and a small metal cup.
- Cereal bars, trail mix, couple of packages dried soups, tea bag, etc.
- Good whistle.
- Light wire and string (a few meters of each).
- Survival book (in waterproof container), and small notebook and pen, perhaps stored with book.
- GPS.
- Personal medicines (if required).

I would add a wilderness first aid booklet, a small roll of duct tape, a canister of repellant in bear season (ensure active ingredient is capsicin), a small container of water purification tablets, and a small flashlight, and I would substitute adhesive dressing strips for the bandages (stored in a small zip-lock bag, the strips can be cut to any length). Dr. Ferri maintains that all of these items can be carried in a multi-pocketed vest and a good pair of army or cargo pants, and he suggests that survival gear should be carried on your person rather than in a pack. While I acknowledge the risk that a pack can be lost, I still prefer the pack because it is much more convenient; you can add a camera, a bird book, or a few tools, and you can hang it up, ready for the next adventure. Naturally, snowmobile and ATV enthusiasts should carry an extra plug and a selection of tools, while mountain bikers and skiers also need an assortment of emergency equipment (patch kits, link pins, ski tips, etc.). I generally tailor my gear to the activity and season. Bug repellant may seem a bit super-fluous in March, but you can never be absolutely sure!

Matches should be the strike-anywhere type, and dipped in paraffin to make them waterproof (for storage, an empty 35 mm plastic film canister is ideal). The notebook and pen can be used to note your observations or feelings; this activity can help to calm you down. The survival book provides reading material, which keeps the mind occupied and may even offer some worthwhile advice; it can also become fire-starter or toilet paper! You can sleep in one garbage bag, or use it as rainwear; the other—split open—can become a roof for a shelter, or a ground sheet. You could boil water in a metal cup for hot soup or tea.

7. Are you physically prepared for the planned activity? You need to know your limits, and you must travel within them. Exhaustion can hamper decision making, and injuries are more likely to occur if you're worn out. It is important to recognize when you must turn around and head back.

You're Lost! What to Do

1. The most important first step, and sometimes the most difficult, is to admit that you have no idea where the heck you are. That admission may require an enormous effort, but you must STAY CALM. This is especially critical if you sense that bad weather is imminent or it is late in the day. You need to assess your situation and make preparations. Any normal person will feel panicky, and may want to start running, but this isn't the end of the world; you must understand that the vast majority of lost persons are found.

2. Remain where you are. Most people are found relatively close to where they got lost, so don't make finding you a more difficult task by continuing to travel (no, the cottage is not likely just over that next ridge). This does not necessarily mean staying rooted in one place. You need to evaluate your surroundings and choose the best spot to possibly spend the night, or maybe even a couple of nights. Is water nearby, are there materials for shelter and a fire, am I overly exposed, do my surroundings present a physical danger (e.g. avalanche), etc?

3. Your priorities are: SAFETY, SHELTER, FIRE, WATER. Food is lowest on the list; you should have your emergency rations. Forget about foraging for edible plants; unless you've been trained, eating unknown species could cause more harm. Do your surroundings provide naturally existing shelters, such as hollow trees, blow-downs with up-ended root systems, caves, or hanging rock outcrops, or the materials to build one? Keep it simple and as weatherproof as possible. The following diagrams have been borrowed from Dr. Ferri's book and illustrate some basic structures.

Canoe Shelter

Prop the canoe on a 45-degree angle using a Y-shaped stick to hold it up (brace the canoe against a tree or a rock). Lean additional sticks against the exposed side and cover them with boughs (spruce, fir, cedar, etc), plastic, or a poncho. The exposed side

should face away from the prevailing winds. Add mud or rocks at top and bottom to keep covering in place. To prevent billowing, cover plastic with additional boughs or branches. Insulate sleeping area with a generous layer of boughs; this is not a time to worry about the environmental consequences of defoliation.

A-Frame Shelter

Find a 6- to 10-foot (2-3-meter) ridgepole. Wedge one end into the ground and support it at the entrance with two Y-shaped sticks. Prop additional "ribs" against the ridgepole. Cover the entire structure with boughs, plastic, poncho

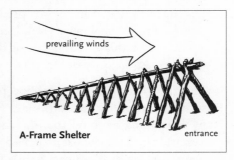

or a tarp (if using a tarp, allow enough covering at the entrance to make flaps). Line the sleeping area with an ample layer of boughs.

Winter Shelters

Building a shelter in late fall or winter presents a much greater challenge. Deep snow and freezing temperatures make for daunting conditions. The traditional snow shelter, such as the quinzhee, is one type. Essentially, snow is mounded up, and then hollowed out to provide a sheltered area. Begin by piling snow (snowshoes, pots, or hands can be used as shovels) about 6 feet (2 meters) high and 6 to 10 feet (2 to 3 meters) in diameter. Let the mound "sinter" for a couple of hours (the snow's structure becomes stronger). Tunnel into the mound and hollow it out. Keep the walls about 8 to 12 inches (20 to 30 cm) thick. You can maintain this thickness if you insert small sticks of this length through the mound from the outside; when you touch the end of the stick from the inside, then you have achieved the correct thickness. Leave an elevated sleeping area, and cover this with a very generous layer of boughs. To provide ventilation, poke a hole through the side of the roof. Once inside, cover up most of the tunnel.

Keep in mind that building a quinzhee may require several hours of wet, back-breaking work; you could become soaked from perspiration or melting snow. The problems this creates are obvious and, in my opinion, limit the quinzhee's potential as a suitable winter shelter (however, it could be better than nothing). Quinzhees are effective if suitable sleeping gear is available and, regardless of how cold it is outside, the temperature inside will not dip much below freezing.

An effective structure can be a combination of snow, sticks, and boughs. Shape a compact rectangular snow room with walls about 3 feet (1 meter) high; make the roof by laying "rafters"—sticks—across the top. Cover with boughs, plastic, and a layer of snow. Place a thick layer of boughs on the floor. Build your fire near the entrance; construct a reflector wall behind it to direct heat into the structure. Obviously, you will need a relatively large quantity of wood (collect more than you think you'll need) to feed the fire during the night, and you won't likely enjoy long periods of comfortable slumber. Don't build the fire so close that embers could ignite the boughs.

An A-frame shelter is another possibility. Keep it small, and cover with a thick layer of snow. Build a fire near the entrance (see previous page).

Finally, heated stone shelters offer another option. Ideally the right rock should be 6 to 10 feet (2-3 meters) long, flat on the sleeping side, and about 3 feet (1 meter) high. To heat the rock, clear the snow, and build a big fire close to the wall; continue heating the wall for at least three hours (remember to remove all snow from the rock, as melting water will cool it). The longer the wall is heated, the longer it will give off heat (up to three times as long). While the fires are burning, gather more wood, collect boughs and saplings for roofing and bedding, and perhaps dry out your clothes. Once the walls have been heated, allow the fire to die down; remove remaining live coals with a stick (no live coals can be left!). Cover the ashes with about 2 inches (5 cm) of soil (it will have been thawed by the fire). Place a thin layer of boughs on this soil and cover with a poncho—to prevent steaming—or sleep directly on the warm soil. Quickly erect the roof structure against the heat wall (see diagram, though a simple lean-to system would suffice), and layer with a thick blanket of evergreen boughs. Keep the walls as windproof as possible. A small conifer tree could act as a doorway to the shelter. Crawl in, and the heat radiated from the ground and rock will keep you relatively warm.

Timing is crucial for the final phase of construction, and no more than 20 minutes should elapse from charcoal removal to the finished structure. The survivor should also work into the

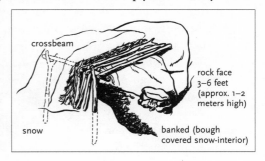

crossbeam

rock face 3–6 feet (approx. 1–2 meters high)

snow

banked (bough covered snow-interior)

night, say beginning at 3:30, and working until 8 or 9 o'clock, thereby ensuring a good night. All materials have to be collected during the day. As Dr. Ferri points out, this is no easy cottage construction project.

4. The seven enemies of the wilderness survivor are: pain, cold, thirst, hunger, fatigue, boredom, and loneliness. They can endanger your ability to survive, and must be recognized and dealt with. In an emergency, pain can weaken your will to survive, even if it's not serious or prolonged: keep your hopes up; help will arrive. Getting cold is no big deal when you can return to a nice heated cabin to warm up. But if you're lost and cold, then you have a serious problem; cold is an insidious enemy that seriously impairs thought processes. Thirst is the hidden enemy of survival, because it is often forgotten in stressful situations. Force yourself to drink (fresh water is always the best choice, but take what you can find—and remember those purification tablets!). Hunger lowers your ability to think rationally, and food helps ward off the effects of cold, pain, and fear (a few packed rations are a lot better than nothing). Fatigue makes you careless. When you must stay alone in one place, boredom and loneliness can set in; keep busy by building a shelter, gathering wood, constructing signaling systems, etc.

5. Start a fire. Fires provide warmth, light, a boost to morale, a means to boil water (or melt snow) and dry clothes and equipment, and a way to signal rescuers. You should be able to build a fire in almost any condition. Natural tinders include: dried grasses, cattail fluff, shredded birch bark, bird nests, dried pine needles, or pages from your survival books or notebooks. The lower dead branches of conifer trees (spruce, pine, fir, cedar) provide the best kindling in emergency situations because they will burn in all conditions. Larger pieces should be relatively dry, and dead—but not rotten—hardwoods (maple, birch, beech, oak) make the longest-lasting fires. If you find a good piece that is too big to break into manageable pieces, feed the piece in whole. Note: In extreme fire conditions, exercise extreme caution!

If the conditions turn wet, you can protect your fire by layering a row of closely packed larger pieces on top; in this way the fire will continue to burn from underneath, while the top layer will shield the coals from most of the rain. You can of course build a fire-pit, and cover the fire with a large flat stone (see illustration).

6. Devise a means to signal for help. The international distress code is three signals of any kind: three blasts on a whistle, three gunshots, three flashes of a signal mirror, and any group of three: three fires, three piles of rocks, etc.

    Signal fires can be constructed and ready for use, and should be erected in such a way as to provide maximum smoke value.

Built off the ground and covered with boughs, this fire signal burns very rapidly. Fanned by an incoming supply of oxygen, flames force the resulting blanket of smoke high into the air. The thick covering of boughs also helps to keep tinder dry at all times. The same effect could be created by piling a supply of timber and kindling under a solitary coniferous tree.

Orienteering for Beginners

If you have a map and a good compass, then orienteering is relatively straightforward.

Step 1: Draw a line on the map from where you are to where you're going. Because the accompanying photo is in black and white, it is a bit difficult to read, but you should be able to identify two lakes, Spence — X—and Keiller—Y—(the line is a luxury; if you don't have a pencil, simply set the edge of the compass along the intended route as in Step 2).

Step 1

Step 2: Lay the edge of the copass along the intended route of travel.

Step 3: Rotate the compass housing until the black lines on the bottom of the compass housing line up with the vertical blue grid lines on the map. The indicator on the housing now reads your bearing: in this case, about 78°.

Step 2

Step 4: Pick up the compass and orient it so the red end of the needle lines up with north. Travel in the direction of your bearing. Check your heading often.

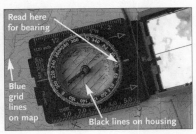

Step 3

Of course, there is the matter of **declination** (the deviation between magnetic north and true north), and this must be accounted for if you are traveling long distances to a very specific destination. If the distance is short, and it would be very difficult to miss your destination (eg. a large lake, road, hydro line), then don't bother to calculate.

Step 4

TMAW applies here ✓
(true to magnetic add if declination is west)

Here's the math: east of an imaginary line through Thunder Bay, Ontario, magnetic north is west of true north, while west of Thunder Bay, it is east (MN is what the compass arrow actually points to, while TN is the map's orientation; on that imaginary line, there is little or no variation between MN and TN). Magnetic north is not constant. Fortunately, topographic (topo) maps provide the deviation, generally in the right-hand margin.

There is a catch. You must also ascertain the date of the map's publication, because MN moves incrementally every year. This variation is provided with the map, but must be calculated.

The map used in this demonstration covers an area east of Thunder Bay. It was printed in 1975. The variation between TN and MN at the time of printing was about 9°. The annual increase was noted as .1° per year. Therefore, we can calculate the total variation: 9 + (25 x .1) = 11.5° (I rounded off the number of years between 1975 and the present). Since we took a map reading and we are applying it to the field, our bearing should read 78 + 11.5 = 89.5°. Rotate the compass ring a bit further until it reads the corrected bearing. If the topo map covered an area west of Thunder Bay, then this value would have to be subtracted from the bearing you worked out on the map.

or ↓
MTSW
or
TMSE
TTAE

Orienteering is a skill that needs practice, and if you've never attempted to follow a compass this precisely, perhaps you should experiment in an area that's relatively safe.

Three to remember:

1. Tell someone where you're going.

2. Carry a survival kit.

3. If you're lost or injured, stay calm, stay in one place, stay safe.

A follow up:

Recently, I attended a Search and Rescue Seminar in Toronto. Some Rescue personnel suggested that Personal Locator Beacons (406 MHz with GPS) should be considered for those who spend longer periods of time in the wilderness (currently, they sell for about $800 Cdn). A PLB requires registration and this can be done on-line <www.nss.gc.ca>. Others indicated a preference for satellite phones in areas where cell phones won't work. These can be purchased (about $1200 Cdn) or rented.

For search information, the military, coast guard, and police would rather receive latitude and longitude coordinates.

In Ontario, the Ontario Provincial Police should be contacted first in the event of a lost person: 1-888-310-1122; they will contact the Military and the Coast Guard should that be necessary (911 will work on a satellite phone, but not all of the province is covered by 911 service).

CHAPTER 2

First
Aid at
the Lake

OUR NEIGHBORS REGULARLY RENT THEIR COTTAGE to close acquaintances and family. We came to know and befriend one family in particular, the Courtads from Ohio. One summer morning during the construction of our place, Sandy Courtad ran into the yard. As soon as I saw her I knew that something was very wrong. When she had caught her breath, she told me that her dad, Marvin, had had a heart attack. Could I help? How could I not! I dropped my tool belt, and sprinted (that was 13 years ago) the 300 meters to their place. I was relieved to find that Marvin was very much alive; in fact, he was in the bathroom, shaving. Marvin was a real country gentleman, and when I asked him why he was performing this particular morning ritual—especially considering the circumstances—he said that he wouldn't be going to any hospital with a day's growth.

Even though I had no idea of the signs and symptoms of a heart attack, much less any treatment regimen—beyond the general knowledge gained from TV—from what Marvin told me I was convinced that he had in fact suffered some serious medical event. I asked Dorothy, his wife, if they had phoned the ambulance and she said no, they hadn't, because Marvin didn't want any fuss. I considered this only very briefly, and then decided there would be a call for emergency help. (In deference to Marvin's concerns, I asked them not to have the siren wailing when they met us.) Both Dorothy and Sandy looked relieved and later told me that they were glad that I had taken charge of the situation (I later learned that this is taught as part of any first aid course). I ran back to my place, brought my truck around, and helped the patient in. We met the ambulance halfway to Parry Sound. Marvin was quickly transferred and spent two weeks in the hospital, making a full recovery.

For me, that incident was the motivation to take a first aid and CPR course (and to upgrade when needed). So far, I have not had occasion to use this training (thank God), but I do know that I will be better prepared than I was that day 14 years ago. I believe that every cottager should have first aid and CPR instruction. The seclusion that we crave at the cabin means that emergency response times will be, generally, far slower than the norm.

It's also worth a discussion with your cottage neighbors to seriously consider forming mini emergency response teams. This could be especially valuable in the case of heart attack, when every second counts. Currently, there are reasonably priced Automated External Defibrillators that can be used, with instruction, by the layman. In essence, these machines tell you what to do, and can mean the difference between life and death. Even though knowledge of CPR is a great asset, in reality, very few lives are saved by this procedure alone.

This chapter is in no way intended to take the place of formal first aid education; it will merely cover some of the most important features of any good first aid course.

Accident-Scene Management

In truth, you are most likely to have to administer first aid to someone you know at your own home or camp. However, you may at some time in your life happen upon, or be called to, an accident scene (it is important to consider these steps even if the accident occurs at home). You need to ensure your own safety before attending to the injured; you don't want to become a victim yourself.

- Relax (obviously, somewhat easier said than done), take a deep breath and maintain your composure before approaching the scene.
- Assess the surroundings and check for hazards: GAS, GLASS, FIRE, WIRE. Dangerous conditions must be dealt with first.
- Protect yourself! Wear the proper barrier devices such as latex gloves, and use a breathing apparatus if giving artificial resuscitation or CPR.
- Send for help; call 911 if this hasn't been done already. If there are bystanders, clearly instruct one person to call and report back to you.

⚐ Determine who needs help most and deal with him/her first (life-threatening injuries obviously require priority treatment).

Do you, or will you, have the necessary protective equipment in the case of an emergency? Administering first aid without it to a stranger, or even a neighbor, might be a tough call. Legally, you are not required to give help, but if you begin you are obliged to continue until someone else can take over, or medical help arrives. If the victim is conscious you must get verbal consent.

Remember, if you don't have gloves you can substitute a towel, shirt, whatever to protect yourself from direct contact when dealing with a bleeding victim. And even if you have gloves, carefully remove and dispose of them, and wash your hands thoroughly as soon as possible.

ABC's

When assessing an unconscious casualty, the following are considered the ABC's of first aid. Remember, take several deep breaths to get control.

Airway—Does the victim have an open airway? To ensure that he/she does have an open airway use the head tilt/chin lift (see illustration).

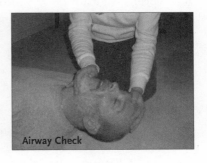

Airway Check

Breathing—Is the victim breathing? Having opened the airway, you can better determine whether or not the victim is in fact breathing. Put your ear close to his/her mouth; listen and feel for breathing. Face the chest while listening; look for a corresponding rise or fall of the chest. Assess for no more than 10 seconds.

Circulation—Does the victim have a pulse or signs of life? Feel for a pulse on the carotid artery along the neck.

Breathing Check / Pulse Check

Artificial Respiration (AR) and Cardiopulmonary Resuscitation (CPR)—

(for persons 8+ years old)

If, based on your ABC assessment, you determine that the victim is not breathing but has a pulse, then the victim is in respiratory arrest and **AR** is required. Here are the steps:

1. Maintain the head tilt/chin lift.
2. Pinch the nose.
3. Take a deep breath (this is the procedure before every breath).
4. Make a seal over the victim's mouth (either with your own mouth or a breathing apparatus).
5. Give a slow breath. If the breath does not go in, reposition head and try again. Gauge the amount of air needed based on victim's size.
6. If victim vomits, clear airway and continue with AR.
7. Watch the chest rise, and allow for exhalation.
8. Repeat—1 breath every 5 seconds—until the victim begins to breathe on his/her own, or until medical help arrives.
9. Check regularly for pulse; if victim does not begin to breathe on his/her own relatively quickly, then CPR will likely be required.
10. If victim recovers, place in recovery position—victim on his/her side, upper leg raised slightly, head on arm (in case of vomiting)—and wait with him/her.

If, based on your ABC assessment, you determine that the victim is not breathing and does not have a pulse, then the victim is in cardiac arrest and **CPR** is required. Here are the steps:

1. Maintain the head tilt/chin lift.
2. Pinch the nose.
3. Take a deep breath (this is the procedure before every breath).
4. Make a seal over the victim's mouth (either with your own mouth or a breathing apparatus).
5. Give a slow breath.
6. Wait a few seconds and give another slow breath.
7. Check for carotid pulse (if pulse resumes, but no breathing, continue with AR).
8. If there are no signs of circulation, landmark and administer 15 chest compressions—1½–2 inch (3–5 cm) depth.
9. Give 2 slow breaths.

10. Continue for four sets of 15/2—about 1 minute.
11. Re-assess for signs of circulation—no more than 10 seconds.
12. If no signs, continue with sets of 15/2.
13. Re-assess every few minutes until medical help arrives.
14. If victim begins to breathe, place in recovery position.

Chest Compression Notes

To landmark, determine the midpoint on an imaginary line between the two nipples. Position yourself directly above the casualty, using straight arms. Make sure he/she is on firm, flat surface. Interlock fingers, and place heel of hand on chest.

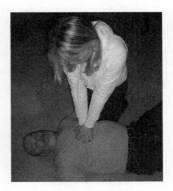

If dealing with a child (1–8 years of age), AR is 1 breath every 3 seconds, while CPR is 5 chest compressions followed by 1 slow breath (i.e. sets of 5/1).

Choking

Choking can be a scary situation for both the victim and those attending. If you suspect that someone is choking follow these steps:

1. Always ask first: "Are you choking?" "Can I help?"
2. If the person can speak, breathe, or cough, do not interfere. Encourage him/her to keep coughing. Do not slap on the back. Reassure.
3. If the person cannot speak, breathe, or cough, proceed with abdominal thrusts (chest thrusts for pregnant or obese persons).
4. Continue with thrusts until object is dislodged, or person becomes unconscious.

   If the person becomes unconscious:

5. Call 911.
6. Look in mouth for obstruction; if you can locate it, try to remove.
7. Provide assisted breathing—2 slow breaths.
8. If airway still obstructed, begin CPR.
9. After a set of 15/2 for adult, or 5/1 for child, check in mouth for obstruction; remove if possible.
10. Repeat assisted breathing—2 slow breaths.
11. If no luck, continue with CPR until medical help arrives.

When dealing with a choking infant (0–1 year of age), give up to 5 back blows and 5 chest thrusts. Continue with back blows/chest thrusts until object is dislodged or infant becomes unconscious. Proceed as above in the case of unconsciousness.

Full Body Assessment

A full body assessment is performed after treating any life-threatening injuries to determine the presence of any other injuries. It should be done if medical help will be delayed more than 20 minutes, or if you have to transport the victim to medical aid, or if you suspect the victim has more than one injury.

Step One: History
Ask the victim the following questions:
1. How is he/she feeling and where does it hurt?
2. Allergies or medications?
3. Previous injuries or illnesses?
4. How the injury occurred?

Step Two: Check Vital Signs
Monitor constantly.
1. Pulse.
2. Level of consciousness.
3. Breathing.
4. Skin color/temperature.

Step Three: Examination
Examine:
1. The head—blood, bruising, pain, swelling, bumps, depressions.
2. The eyes—bruising, pupil size, response to light.
3. The mouth and lips—bleeding, discoloration, odor.
4. The ears and nose—blood or fluid, swelling.
5. The neck—deformities, medical alert necklace.
6. The shoulders, arms, and hands—compare one side to the other: deformities, blood pain, nail bed refill, medical alert bracelet.
7. The chest, abdomen, and hips—bleeding, pain swelling; feel around the back (with as little movement as possible) for pain, deformities.
8. The legs, ankles, and feet—pain, deformity, swelling, lack of movement.

Step Four: Treating Any Other Injuries

Provide treatment for any injuries found during the assessment. Monitor vital signs and reassure victim. If you can, keep notes and pass them along to the medical team.

Shock

Shock is caused by a lack of oxygen to the brain and other body tissues or organs. Shock is a life-threatening situation, so you should always suspect, and treat for, shock with any injury or illness.

Common causes include: severe bleeding, severe burns, severe allergic reactions, crush injuries, spinal cord or nerve injuries, and heart attacks.

Symptoms include: pale, clammy skin; irregular breathing; bluish lips; tongue; earlobes, or fingernails; nausea or vomiting; weak, rapid pulse; anxiety; change in level of consciousness; confusion; thirst; dizziness.

Treatment:
1. Treat the injury; if there is bleeding, try to stop it as quickly as possible.
2. Keep the patient warm (not hot) and as comfortable as possible; loosen clothing around the neck, chest, and waist.
3. If casualty is conscious and head or spinal injury is not suspected, elevate legs 12 inches (30 cm).
4. If casualty is unconscious, and head or spinal injury is not suspected, place in recovery position.
5. Monitor ABC's, reassure patient, and give nothing orally.

Wounds and Bleeding

R... Rest the patient to reduce pulse rate, and prevent possible fainting.
E... Elevate the injured limb above the level of the heart (if possible) to reduce blood flow to the injured area.
D...Direct pressure should be applied to the wound to stop bleeding.

Severe External Bleeding
1. R, E, D. Direct pressure should be applied with a sterile dressing.
2. Monitor circulation below injury site.
3. Continue to apply dressings as needed, and NEVER REMOVE A BLOOD-SOAKED DRESSING.
4. Treat for shock and monitor ABC's. Seek medical attention.

Impaled Objects
1. DON'T REMOVE THE OBJECT.
2. Apply pressure around the object with a sterile dressing.
3. Cover the object gently and stabilize it using a ring pad or padding.
4. Secure ring pad with bandage.
5. Elevate if possible.
6. Treat for shock, and monitor ABC's. Seek medical attention.

Amputation
1. R, E, D.
2. Wrap amputated part in a clean, moist dressing and place in a waterproof plastic bag. Put this bag in a second bag with ice.
3. Don't clean amputated part.
4. Treat for shock, and monitor ABC's. Seek medical attention.

Internal Bleeding
1. Have patient rest on his/her back with feet and legs elevated about 12 inches (30 cm) if injury permits, and no spinal damage is suspected.
2. Treat for shock, and monitor ABC's. Seek medical attention.

Sucking Chest Wound
1. Immediately cover the chest wound with casualty's hand, your own, or a bystander's.
2. Place casualty in a position of comfort (usually semi-sitting), and lean toward injured side.
3. Seal wound on three sides with an airtight dressing.
4. Treat for shock, and monitor ABC's. Seek medical attention.
5. AR and CPR may need to be administered.

Impaled Object in the Eye
1. Instruct casualty not to rub the eye, or try to remove the object.
2. Stabilize object by padding around it with sterile dressings.
3. Place a cover over the object, and secure in place with tape.
4. Cover both eyes, so eye movement is minimized; stay with victim and provide reassurance until help arrives.
5. Treat for shock, and seek medical attention.

Burns

Burns are categorized as 1st, 2nd, and 3rd degree (see box).

1ST DEGREE BURNS	2ND DEGREE BURNS	3RD DEGREE BURNS
⬇	⬇	⬇
only the top layer of skin is damaged (epidermis)	both layers of skin are damaged (epidermis & dermis)	both layers plus tissues under skin are damaged
⬇	⬇	⬇
* skin is pink or red * slight swelling * mild to severe pain * skin is dry	* skin is red and raw * blisters * extreme pain * skin is moist	* skin is charred black, gray/white * may see blood vessels/bone * little or no pain

When treating burns remember:
1. Burns are highly susceptible to infection.
2. Never use butter, lotions, or ointments on a burn (except sunburn lotion on minor sunburn).
3. Never break blisters.
4. Never remove clothing that is stuck to the burned area. However, remove or loosen anything that is not.
5. Never use fluffy material, such as cotton, to dress a burn.
6. Never apply adhesive dressings to a burn. Use only a lint-free sterile dressing.
7. Once burn has been cooled, monitor the victim to ensure he/she stays warm.
8. Immerse the burn in cool water—about 15 minutes—unless it is a chemical burn that can be aggravated by water.
9. Electrical burns should be covered at the entrance and exit wounds.
10. Treat for shock, and seek medical attention.

Bone and Joint Injuries

R... (Rest) Stop the activity and rest the injured part.
I... (Ice) Apply cold to the injury as soon as possible, once the injury has been immobilized; 15 minutes on / 15 minutes off; do not put ice directly against skin.

C... (Compression) Using a bandage, apply compression to limit swelling; check circulation every few minutes.

E... (Elevate), if possible, the injured part above the heart.

Do not use ICE if there is an open fracture, the skin is being pushed up by a fractured bone, if the victim is sensitive to the cold, or if the casualty has diabetes or a disease of the blood vessels.

Fractures

1. Prevent movement.
2. If it is a closed fracture, immobilize the injured limb above and below the fracture site, as well as above and below the joints of the fracture site (e.g. if one of the lower leg bones is fractured, then knee and ankle need to be immobilized).
3. If it is an open fracture (i.e. broken bone protrudes through skin), cover the wound with a sterile dressing (treat like an impaled object—use a ring pad or padding to support the protruding bone).
4. Monitor circulation below the injury, elevate if possible, and treat for shock. Seek medical attention.

Dislocations

1. Immobilize the limb according to the most comfortable position for the casualty (do not attempt to put the limb back into position yourself).
2. Support and stabilize the injured limb with padding; use a sling if possible.
3. Apply cold, monitor circulation below injury site, and treat for shock. Seek medical attention.

Hypothermia

1. Prevent further heat loss.
2. If possible, remove casualty from cold and wind.
3. Remove wet clothing and cover casualty with something warm and dry.
4. Make sure head is well insulated, and any exposed skin is covered.
5. Seek medical attention and, if transporting, place in recovery position.
6. Do not give any alcohol, or drinks with caffeine.
7. Do not rub casualty.

Hyperthermia

Heat Exhaustion
1. If casualty is conscious, move to a cool place, have him/her lie down in the shock recovery position (i.e. legs elevated); provide water to drink, unless vomiting.
2. If casualty is unconscious, place in the recovery position, seek medical attention, and monitor ABC's.

Heatstroke
1. Immediately move casualty to a cool, shaded place.
2. Cool casualty with available resources:
   - cool bath
   - place in shock recovery position and cover with wet sheets
   - apply cool compresses to the head, groin, armpits, and chest.
3. Once casualty feels cool to the touch, cover with a dry sheet and place in shock recovery position.
4. If unconscious, place in recovery position.
5. Monitor ABC's and seek medical attention immediately.

Concussions

A concussion is a temporary disturbance of brain function as a result of a blow to the head. If the victim shows any of the following signs, even after several days, he/she needs medical help immediately:

- Decreasing level of consciousness.
- Difficulty seeing properly.
- Headache, becoming increasingly severe.
- Vomiting.
- Shallow breathing.
- Stronger, slower pulse.
- Seizures or convulsions.
- Unequal pupil size.
- Memory loss.
- Complains of seeing stars.
- Changing personality.

FIRST AID FOR POISONS

Determine the following:
- ♦ **how the poison was taken**
- ♦ **how much was taken**
- ♦ **how the poison entered the body**
- ♦ **when the poison was taken**

1. **If the casualty is conscious, immediately call the Poison Control Centre and follow their advice for first aid.**
2. **If the casualty is unconscious, immediately call 911 or emergency medical number and place in recovery position. Monitor ABC's.**
3. **Be prepared to provide artificial respiration, but be sure to check for any poisonous material in or around the mouth.**

INGESTED POISONS	INHALED POISONS
* never induce vomiting or give anything by mouth unless directed by Poison Control Centre.	* immediately get the casualty to fresh air, away from poison.
ABSORBED POISONS	**INJECTED POISONS**
* flush away the poison from the affected area with cool water for approx. 15 min. * wash with soap & water	* ask casualty if they carry an Epi-Pen * keep affected area below the level of heart * rest

Neck and Head Injuries

Always suspect a head / spinal injury when a casualty:

- ⚑ Is found unconscious and the history is unknown.
- ⚑ Has fallen from a height.
- ⚑ Has been in a car accident.
- ⚑ Has straw-colored fluid or blood coming from the mouth, nose, or ears.
- ⚑ Has received a blow to the head, back, or pelvis.
- ⚑ Dived into shallow water.

Symptoms can include:

- ▲ Numbness or tingling in the legs or arms.
- ▲ Pain with movement.
- ▲ Disorientation/confusion.
- ▲ Dizziness/drowsiness.
- ▲ Loss of movement.
- ▲ Swelling/bruising.

If you suspect a head or neck injury, seek medical attention immediately. DO NOT MOVE the casualty unless he/she is not breathing, and you need to relocate to administer CPR. Treat for shock, and monitor ABC's.

Severe Allergic Reactions

1. Once you have identified a severe allergic reaction, send for medical help immediately.
2. Have casualty rest and place in the position most comfortable for breathing.
3. If casualty has medication for any allergies, help him/her take it (often anaphylaxis medication is in the form of an Epi-Pen which is very user friendly; however, if the casualty cannot give him-/herself the injection, you may have to do it; use according to directions).
4. If swelling occurs around the neck, apply ice to reduce swelling.
5. Reassure casualty, and monitor ABC's until medical help arrives.

NOTE: If a stinger is present in the case of bee stings, remove by gently scraping downward.

First Aid for:

Animal Bites
1. Examine the wound to see if the skin is broken.
2. Allow the wound to bleed moderately to help cleanse the bite.
3. Wash the bite with antiseptic soap and apply a sterile dressing.
4. Seek medical attention if the skin was broken.

NOTE: Rabies should be suspected if the bite was from a wild animal or a domestic animal that behaved unusually. Rabies is fatal if left untreated; seek medical help immediately.

Snakebites

1. Have casualty rest in a semi-sitting position; keep the affected limb below the level of the heart to minimize spread of venom.
2. Wash wound with an antiseptic soap.
3. Immobilize the limb and seek medical attention immediately.

NOTE: Do not apply ice or cold, and do not try to suck the poison out of the wound.

Diabetes

Diabetes is a condition in which the body is unable to maintain proper blood sugar levels. In a healthy individual, insulin is released in response to sugar intake while a diabetic must control his/her blood sugar levels by either diet or insulin, or both. There are two conditions associated with diabetes:

Insulin Shock (Hypoglycemia)

- Develops quickly because victim has an elevated insulin level, has exercised too much, or has not eaten enough.
- Pulse is rapid and strong, and breathing is abnormal.
- Victim is often sweaty, pale, cold, confused, shaky, dizzy, weak, or lightheaded.
- Victim needs sugar.

Diabetic Coma (Hyperglycemia)

- Develops over hours or days because the victim has decreased insulin level, has eaten too much, or has exercised less than usual.
- Pulse is rapid and weak, and breathing is abnormal.
- Victim is dry, flushed, has warm skin, is drowsy, thirsty, nauseated, needs to urinate frequently, or breath has a "nail polish" smell; victim could be unconscious.
- Victim needs insulin.

Treatment

1. Ask the casualty if you can help him or her.
2. Seek medical attention immediately.
3. Give casualty some sugar or fruit juice but do not give insulin.
4. Place in the recovery position and monitor ABC's.

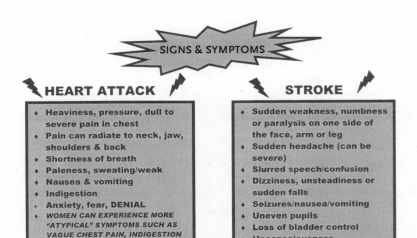

SIGNS & SYMPTOMS

HEART ATTACK

- ◆ Heaviness, pressure, dull to severe pain in chest
- ◆ Pain can radiate to neck, jaw, shoulders & back
- ◆ Shortness of breath
- ◆ Paleness, sweating/weak
- ◆ Nausea & vomiting
- ◆ Indigestion
- ◆ Anxiety, fear, DENIAL
- ◆ *WOMEN CAN EXPERIENCE MORE "ATYPICAL" SYMPTOMS SUCH AS VAGUE CHEST PAIN, INDIGESTION*

STROKE

- ◆ Sudden weakness, numbness or paralysis on one side of the face, arm or leg
- ◆ Sudden headache (can be severe)
- ◆ Slurred speech/confusion
- ◆ Dizziness, unsteadiness or sudden falls
- ◆ Seizures/nausea/vomiting
- ◆ Uneven pupils
- ◆ Loss of bladder control
- ◆ Unconsciousness

CALL 911 IMMEDIATELY

Basic First Aid Kit

Naturally, opinion will vary on what should be included in a cottage, camp, or cabin first aid kit. Here, after some research, is my version:

- ⚴ Adhesive dressings.
- ⚴ Fingertip and knuckle bandages.
- ⚴ Assorted safety pins.
- ⚴ 2 rolls of adhesive tape 1 inch x 8 foot (2.5 cm x 2.3 m).
- ⚴ Sterile gauze pads, 3-inch (7.5-cm) square.
- ⚴ Rolls of 1- (2.5-cm), 2- (5-cm) and 4-inch (10-cm) gauze bandage.
- ⚴ Compress bandages, 4- (10-cm) and 6-inch (15-cm) square.
- ⚴ Triangular bandages.
- ⚴ Splint padding.
- ⚴ Assorted wooden splints.
- ⚴ Bottle of liquid antiseptic.
- ⚴ Assorted sterile butterfly closures.
- ⚴ Antiseptic toilettes.
- ⚴ Cold packs.
- ⚴ Eye-wipes in sterile solution.
- ⚴ Tube first aid cream.
- ⚴ Several pairs latex gloves.
- ⚴ Surgical scissors.

⬧ Tweezers.

⬧ Couple of pre-made donut-style compression rings.

⬧ Disinfectant hand soap.

⬧ First aid booklet.

First aid websites worth a visit:

a) General
<www.sja.ca>
This is a St. John's ambulance site.

b) Kids
<www.kidshealth.org/parent/firstaid_safe/>

c) Epilepsy
<www.epilepsyontario.org>

d) Canines
<www.ckc.ca/scoop/aid/>

e) First aid products

Three to remember:

1. Take an approved first aid / CPR course, or get an upgrade if your first aid certificate is more than 3 years old (it is strongly recommended that CPR training be renewed yearly).

2. Don't endanger yourself.

3. Remember the ABC's.

CHAPTER 3

The King of Cottage Country —The Black Bear

I love mountain biking, and there are some good trails near my cottage. I try to get out every other day, and for years I rarely saw a bear. In the past couple of years, though, these encounters have grown more frequent (I came upon 6 last summer). I am not terrified by *ursus americanus*, but meeting one on the trail does unnerve me a bit…okay, maybe more than a bit (especially when I'm doing about 12 m/h [20 km/h], and flush one out of the brush). Because it is purported by the experts to work, I carry a can of bear spray. Thankfully, I have never yet had to determine whether or not the experts are correct. On every occasion, the bear has made his exodus at top speed. One time, I was riding on a snowmobile trail that I use regularly. I was traveling downhill, and had just glanced down at my speedometer (it registered 19 m/h [30+ km/h]) as I rounded a corner. When I looked up, a young bear was sitting nonchalantly in the middle of the course, minding its own business. It obviously hadn't heard me coming, but its head snapped up as I careened around the curve. I opened my mouth to yell some command like "scram"—or possibly something more erudite—but before I could utter a word, it was gone. Curiously enough, the bear took off straight away from me, down the trail. That little bugger made me look like I was standing still; at that moment, I certainly gained a real appreciation of a bear's tremendous speed (for short distances, they have been clocked at speeds of 35 m/h [55 km/h]). Bears are also excellent swimmers, and amazing climbers.

Black bears are very large, omnivorous animals, and they are found

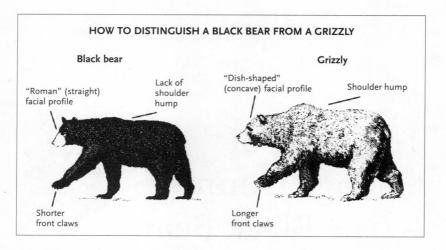

HOW TO DISTINGUISH A BLACK BEAR FROM A GRIZZLY

Black bear

Grizzly

"Roman" (straight) facial profile

Lack of shoulder hump

"Dish-shaped" (concave) facial profile

Shoulder hump

Shorter front claws

Longer front claws

in cottage country across Canada (except, apparently, on Prince Edward Island, in southern Saskatchewan, or in southern Alberta). Adult males can weigh 250 to 600 lbs (120 to 280 kg) while adult females can weigh 100 to 400 lbs (45 to 180 kg).

Female black bears can begin to reproduce when they are about 6 to 8 years of age (but only every second year, at best). A litter will consist of 1 to 4 cubs born during the winter (late December to early February), while mama is still denned up. Cubs will weigh in at a mere ½ lb (225 grams), on average (compare this to a normal newborn child who will tip the scales at about 6½ lbs [3 kilograms]).

Of course, by one year, a cub will have gained a bit of weight—28 to 59 lbs (13 to 27 kg). Young bears will stay with the sow for about a year and a half before striking out on their own. Male bears continue to grow until their seventh year, while females stop growing somewhat sooner. They have a life expectancy of about 10 years in the wild, if they can escape predation (occasionally cubs are killed by older bears, wolves, or lynx), starvation, injury, or hunters. Male bears travel more widely than females, and are thus more likely to get shot during hunting season (currently, in Ontario, this season is restricted to the fall; controversy still rages over whether a spring hunt should be reinstated).

Bears are not true hibernators, though they exhibit some of the traits of hibernators (e.g. greatly reduced heart rates). During the time bears are denned up (around October to April), they do not have to eat or eliminate waste; they subsist entirely on stored body fat, losing up to 30% of their weight (now if only some diet guru could devise a similar regimen for humans, he/she would make a fortune; lots of northerners would gladly sleep away winter to awaken a hundred pounds lighter!).

Unlike true hibernators, bears can be awakened; in fact, during exceptionally warm spells, bears may emerge from their dens for short periods.

Black bears will eat anything: twigs, leaves, shoots, buds, berries, roots, insects, grasses, nuts, fish, small mammals, and occasionally moose calves or deer fawns. Beech trees are abundant in our area, and the bark of each and every one shows signs that bears have climbed up to feast on nuts. Acorns and hazelnuts are also prized. Carrion is a gourmet delight for bears, and the greater the decomposition, the better. Because bears are highly intelligent, some discover that garbage dumps provide the bear equivalent of fast food takeout (hey, Ma, no need to fix dinner tonight, we'll just head to McDump's!). Other bears also learn that cottages and campsites can provide tasty treats. And this is where most human-bear problems develop.

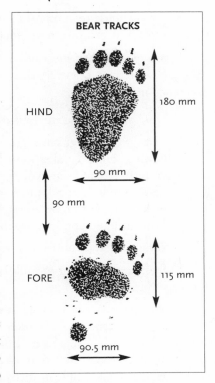

BEAR TRACKS

HIND — 180 mm, 90 mm

90 mm

FORE — 115 mm, 90.5 mm

You can generally prevent bear problems at your camp if you follow a few simple rules:

- ▲ Put all garbage in a tightly sealed metal container or, preferably, bear-proof garbage cans (we have a really heavy duty model that I have chained to the cabin; the top is also chained down). Wash your garbage receptacles regularly.

- ▲ Take your garbage to the dump frequently. If you have garbage collection, put it out just before pick-up, and not the night before.

- ▲ Do not fill birdfeeders during bear season (mid-April to late fall).

- ▲ Clean your barbeque (I believe that traditional barbeques—the ones that use real charcoal—are better in bear country because the coals burn long after you're finished and cremate meat residue; when we are done with the propane models, we just turn them off and meat residue often remains).

- ▲ Never leave pet food outside.

▲ If you choose to compost (though a compost pile could be a possible attraction), never include meat, fish, or sweet food.

If you meet a bear, most often—as in my experience—the bear will beat a hasty retreat, but every situation is unique. What should you do if you encounter a bear?

▲ Avoid approaching the bear to get a better look.

▲ If a bear shows signs of aggression (clacks its teeth, makes explosive blowing sounds, makes short lunges or bluff charges, slaps the ground), yell and wave your arms. Blow a whistle; air horns are also useful. You need to adopt an aggressive posture, but remember that the bear needs to have an escape route; if you have him/her cornered, then you increase the risk of attack.

▲ Never turn and run from a bear; slowly back away.

▲ If you are near a car or building, obviously it would be wise to get inside.

▲ Bear spray, as I mentioned, has also proven to be an effective deterrent, especially at close range (test your spray annually, and replace it when suggested. I once tested mine, having safely determined the wind direction, but the wind shifted slightly and I was given a small sample of the spray's potency—it was not pleasant!).

▲ Keep dogs away from a bear; a dog may excite or annoy a bear, and could lead the bear back to you.

Actual bear attacks are extremely rare (you're more likely, statistically, to be terminated by lightning, a bee sting, or a canine). Between 1907 and 1993 only 37 human deaths were attributed to black bears in North America (6 of those incidents have happened in Ontario in the last century). Though nuisance bears (those that frequent dumps, cottages, and campsites) can become dangerous because of their familiarity with people, it is thought that the so-called predacious bear, generally an older male, has usually not been in contact with humans. Moreover, these fellows may not adopt the "normal" behavior of an anxious or annoyed bear; instead of swatting the ground or bluff charges, they may simply press closer and closer to assess the success of attacking their intended prey—you.

In the event of a black bear attack, you should remember the following.

⚠ NEVER TURN AND RUN, though the temptation may be enormous.

⚠ DO NOT PLAY DEAD; this may work for grizzlies but is not the way to deal with black bears. FIGHT BACK, and use whatever is at your disposal as a weapon, even your bare hands.

Seeing a bear can be the highlight of a visit to the cottage, but good sense will prevent those sightings from becoming a problem. The Ontario Ministry of Natural Resources provides some great posters that can be downloaded from their website; these could be laminated and posted in your cabin to remind you and your guests how to avoid unpleasant encounters. An example is included to the right.

BEAR-PROOF YOUR RESIDENCE

- KEEP GARBAGE IN GARAGE OR SHED OR IN BEAR-PROOF CONTAINERS
- PUT GARBAGE OUT ON DAY OF PICK-UP
- CLEAN YOUR BARBECUE
- REMOVE BIRDFEEDERS UNTIL NOVEMBER
- NO SWEETS, MEAT & FISH IN COMPOSTER

Ⓥ Ontario

Three to remember:

1. Bear-proof your cottage environment.

2. If you encounter a black bear, never turn and run.

3. Invest in a can of bear spray.

CHAPTER 4

The Chainsaw

THE "RED GREEN SHOW" HAS LONG BEEN A FAVORITE OF MINE (I, too, am a duct tape disciple). About 10 minutes into the first episode I ever watched, I gradually became aware of a barely discernible background noise with which I am intimately familiar. A smile, then a chuckle. It was the less-than-harmonious drone of a chainsaw, and for the remainder of the show it labored away, just at the edge of the audio track. It was an appropriate comic backdrop for the program's setting.

Throughout at least three seasons—spring, summer, and fall—that sound must be all too familiar to virtually every cottager. For most, it is probably less than comic, and more of an annoying distraction (especially if some nitwit starts working with the dawn). However, I must confess that the sound of a chainsaw conjures up fond memories for me of the seven years I spent logging in northern Ontario. Well, maybe not every memory is fond, but during that time I learned a great deal about a tool that seems about as ubiquitous to cottage life as a rake. All of my neighbors own one. At the lake, somebody, somewhere, always seems to be cutting wood. Useful it is, but the chainsaw is one cottage tool that needs special attention.

Care and Maintenance

Actually, there are occasions when the sound of a chainsaw does put me on edge; even from a distance, I can tell when a saw is in need of adjustment. The din of a chainsaw is infinitely more acceptable to me if the engine is at least running at maximum efficiency. When I worked in the woods, we were always playing with the high- and low-speed settings, trying to achieve maximum cutting performance. But I recently learned that high-speed adjustment in particular should really be set in the shop. Tinkering with the high-speed jet can cause the saw to exceed its maximum rpm, leading to engine burnout, and tuning "by ear" is not a reliable procedure. Most new saws only permit minimum adjustment to the high- and low-speed settings, or simply feature fixed jets. This development is also a reflection of clean-air legislation (mostly in the U.S.) as improper adjustment of the fuel-air mixture can increase harmful exhaust emissions. So the tune-ups should really be left to the pros. At least get it done once in a while, please.

However, there is still essential, regular chainsaw maintenance that you should attend to. For the most part, this consists primarily of removing the chain and guide bar at regular intervals and cleaning the debris that builds up between the bar guide rails, in the lubrication holes, around the housing of the saw, and on the clutch shield (a compressor makes this job a breeze). When reassembling the guide bar and chain, remember to draw the slack out of the chain (that's what the tension adjustment screw is for) before tightening the nuts. If the guide bar has a sprocket nose (most newer saws are equipped with these), there should be little if any gap between the chain and the bottom of the guide bar. (To determine proper tension, you can perform the **snap test**: grasp the chain along the bottom of the bar, pull down, and let go; the chain should snap back to its original position, contacting the bottom of the bar.) The old solid-nose bars require some gap—about ⅛th of an inch (.3 cm)—between the bottom of the guide bar and the chain. Regardless, the chain should move freely, but it shouldn't be so loose that some obstruction will make it jump off the bar. Check chain tension regularly, and adjust it when necessary (**do not, however, set the tension when the cutting chain is hot!**). Remember to hold the nose of the bar up when adjusting the tension (gloves will protect your hands).

In addition, the breather screen should be cleaned regularly, and the spark plug should be examined at least once a year. Use only clean gas, the correct fuel to mixing oil ratio, and proper bar-and-chain oil.

Filing

Obviously, a chainsaw's cutting performance depends on how well the cutting teeth are filed. Most loggers—at least the ones I know—file freehand. However, the casual operator is rarely accomplished at freehand filing because that level of competence requires one heck of a lot of practice. When I started cutting, my stepfather would sharpen the saw for me, and then I would try to duplicate his expertise whenever it got dull. Every fourth or fifth occasion, he would intervene and correct my mistakes, always taking the time to explain to me exactly what I had been doing wrong. It was at least six months before I could do it well on my own, and I was operating that saw every day, five or six days a week. Fortunately for the average cottager, there are filing guides available that, though they can never duplicate an experienced logger's skill, will provide a journeyman's results in achieving sharp, uniform cutting teeth.

Figure 1 illustrates the parts of a cutter. From the diagram, it is evident that there are actually two main parts to the cutter: the **cutter** itself and the **depth gauge**. The depth gauges determine just how deep the teeth will cut. If they are too high, the chain will cut at less than maximum efficiency. If they are cut too low, the chain will try to cut more than it is designed to, and this will often result in grabbing or jamming and possibly even a broken chain or **kickback** (kickback will be explained later in the chapter). All chains have a recommended depth-gauge setting (Figure 2). The depth gauges should be inspected about every fourth or fifth filing and trimmed with a flat file if necessary. A specific depth-gauge tool is available for this task (they come in different settings, generally measured in thousands of an inch). It fits over a section of the cutting chain and exposes each depth gauge in turn. A few careful file strokes will generally do the trick (Figure 3). Remember to round the shoulder of the depth gauge after filing (Figure 4). If you have an older saw, and do not know the recommended

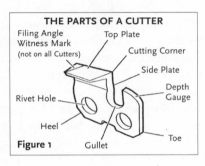

THE PARTS OF A CUTTER

Filing Angle Witness Mark (not on all Cutters)
Top Plate
Cutting Corner
Side Plate
Depth Gauge
Rivet Hole
Heel
Toe
Figure 1
Gullet

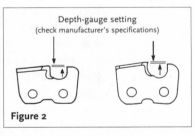

Depth-gauge setting (check manufacturer's specifications)

Figure 2

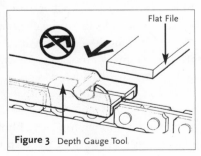

Flat File

Figure 3 Depth Gauge Tool

depth-gauge setting for your chain, then .025" is most likely best; in other words, the rider should be 25 thousands of an inch below the top plate of the cutter.

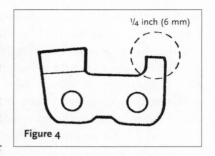

Figure 4

When filing the actual cutters, it is important to first have the correct file and guide for your chain. Sharpen the cutters on one side of the chain first, and file from the inside of each cutter to the outside. Maintain an even **top-plate angle** on both sides of the chain (Figure 5). The top-plate angle determines the width of the **kerf** or cut: the greater the angle, the wider the cut. Filing guides provide common top-plate angles stamped right on them; keep the **filing angle line** on your guide parallel with your chain (Figure 6). There is a recommended filing angle for every chain, but if you don't know the recommended filing angle, then 25 degrees will probably suffice.

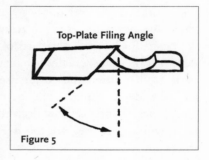

Figure 5

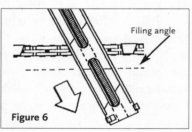

Figure 6

Turn the saw around and repeat the process. Keep all cutters the same length. It is generally easier to file on the forehand stroke than on the backhand; if you are not conscious of this tendency, then after several filings you will note that the cutters on the forehand side of the chain are shorter in length—this can lead to the chain cutting crookedly. An extra stroke on the backhand side each time you file will often compensate for this.

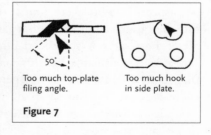

Too much top-plate filing angle.

Too much hook in side plate.

Figure 7

Avoid too much top-plate filing angle and too much hook in the side plate (Figure 7). Both of these conditions can be dangerous.

If one or more cutters become damaged by a rock, try to file away most of the damage, and then file the other cutters to length. Finally, you'll know that some kind of chain maintenance is necessary—depth gauges shortened or cutters filed—if you are producing mostly sawdust. A well-sharpened chain should generate nice, large chips.

(Note: a good source for more information on chain filing and maintenance is available at <www.oregonchain.com>).

Safety

A chainsaw is a dangerous tool. Even when it is not running, those teeth are lethal. One time, it seems so long ago now, I was a competitor at a Logging Sports event at the Canadian National Exhibition. My saw was off and sitting on the ground near me. I stumbled over something, and fell on the chain, sustaining a gash to my hand that needed five stitches to close.

It is imperative to wear protective gear at all times when operating a chainsaw:

- If you are felling trees, then a hardhat is absolutely mandatory.

- Eye—better yet, face— and ear protection are also necessary.

- If you won't purchase protective clothing, then at least always wear good, heavy duty, dry leather work gloves and proper-fitting long pants (the pros are required to wear special pants and gloves).

- Steel-toed boots are a must.

Most new saws are provided with a protective chain scabbard; use it. Do not walk more than a few yards with the chainsaw motor running. Shut it off. The proper way to carry a saw is by the handle with the bar pointing back, and the exhaust manifold pointing away from you. Keep the handles dry, and always hold the saw firmly with both hands when cutting—left hand on the front handle, thumb wrapped over the fingers. Never use a saw one-handed (avoid those little saws small enough to be operated with one hand—they're downright scary!).

Generally, it is advisable to start the saw on the ground, with one foot on the rear handle (the newer saws are designed with this in mind), and the left hand on the front handle. Some manufacturers suggest that you should also engage the chain brake when starting the saw.

Finally, remember that chainsaw kickback is one of the most common causes of serious chainsaw injuries. Kickback is the lightning-fast backward/upward motion of a chainsaw that can occur when the cutting chain near the nose of the guide bar contacts any object (somewhat less common, kickback can also occur if the cut closes in and pinches the cutting chain). The top of the nose of the guide bar is often referred to as the **kickback danger zone** (Figure 8).

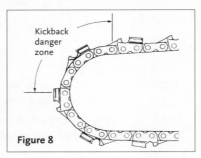

Kickback is a particular hazard when cutting limbs or small brush. In general, avoid cutting anything with the nose of the chainsaw; virtually all cutting should be started with the main body of the guide bar contacting the wood. To decrease the danger of kickback, newer saws are equipped with chain brakes. Some are activated by left hand/arm contact with the guard at the front of the saw, while more advanced chain brakes are automatically triggered by the sudden jolt of the saw under kickback conditions. The theory is that the brake will stop the chain's momentum before it can hurt you.

You know, sometimes you are aware of certain technical aspects of tools, especially newer ones, but you somehow don't internalize them. When I finally broke down and jettisoned my old professional Homelite that had no chain brake, I bought a new, smaller Stihl that did. About the third time I used it, I could not for the life of me figure out what the heck was wrong with the chain: it wouldn't turn on the guide bar. I took the saw apart, examined it, and finally, after denouncing it in a somewhat colorful manner, I decided that it was simply defective. Since my brother-in-law Duncan was heading into town that day, I asked him to take it into the local shop and have it fixed. Later that afternoon he returned to tell me that the mechanic had examined the saw and pronounced it perfectly functional. Duncan went on to say that the mechanic had suggested that perhaps I had inadvertently tripped the chain brake. Duncan claimed that he had quickly dissuaded the mechanic of such a notion, pointing out that, after all, his brother-in-law had been a professional lumberjack, and would certainly have been able to correct something as simple as that. Without uttering a word, I grabbed the saw, spun on my heel, and headed back to my place. Really, it's sad how some people seem to find other people's errors in judgment a source of amusement weeks, even months, later!

Your chainsaw manual—the one in the cupboard drawer—will provide more maintenance, operating, and safety tips. Take the time to read it.

Three to remember:

1. Dress and work safely.
2. Clean the guide bar and inspect the chain regularly.
3. Use the right files and guides.

Finally, for the truly technical reader, a special illustration just for you!

HOW A CUTTER WORKS

As the saw chain enters the cut, it is the depth gauge that first touches the wood. It sits just in front of the cutting surface of the cutter and regulates how deep the cutter can bite into the wood.

The working corner of the cutter digs into the wood to a depth equal to the depth gauge setting. It slices across the grain of the wood severing wood fibers.

The top plate of the cutter, meanwhile, feeds itself into the cut and slices out a chip of wood.

As the cutter is slicing into the wood, the chip starts to lift up and is chiseled out and thrown clear of the cut.

The next cutter will repeat the process, removing another chip of wood.

As the chain continues to move at high speed through the cut, chips are chiseled out and thrown clear at a rate of thousands per minute. The final cut through a log will be the cumulative total of all of these tiny, individual cuts made one at a time by the cutters on the chain.

CHAPTER 5

Tree Felling— The Good, the Bad, and the Ugly

REALLY, IT'S AN IRRESISTIBLE SIREN CALL. If you buy or even inherit a chainsaw, then eventually, some morning, you will be compelled to cut a tree down; it could be any tree. Maybe that scraggly balsam up the drive is just begging to be felled, or that dying maple near the outhouse. Whatever, you're going to finish that second cup of coffee, pull on your boots, and head out into the soft warmth of early morning sunshine knowing that this is the day (perhaps strains from "The Good, the Bad, and the Ugly" parade through your head, but you resist the temptation to whistle the tune—it's a friggin' tree after all!).

The night before you had some premonition that this was going to happen, because the saw is all gassed up and ready to go. Hefting its unfamiliar weight, out you go, only then realizing, as the spectators gather (oh yes, and there will be spectators—there's the disaster voyeur in all of us), that you have only a very dim idea of what's actually required. As you get closer to the intended victim—how'd that yellow birch get so much bigger in the last 24 hours?—a bit of anxiety begins to build, but what the heck, there has to be a first time for everything. But marvel of marvel, all goes well and you actually get the darned thing down. A smattering of applause erupts from the gallery. You smile broadly. This ain't so hard!

Maybe it isn't so hard or maybe you simply got lucky, because tree felling can be a very tricky and sometimes dangerous undertaking. A friend of mine was nearly killed up at his cottage near Buckhorn Lake a number of years ago when a maple he was cutting "barberchaired"; his shoulder was crushed by the impact and his leg was seriously injured. Year after year, the unwary succumb to accidents because they do not have the experience or the knowledge, or an appreciation of the risks.

Before introducing cutting chain to wood, you must first assess the tree to determine its direction of fall, and "down" is not what I mean. Unless you don't really care about the power lines, workshop, or pickup, you probably want the tree to fall in a certain place—preferably a relatively open area. Sight the tree from two directions, at least 90 degrees apart. There are certain elements that will affect direction of fall (Figures 1a, b, c). Most trees have some lean—essentially, a vertical deviation from the perpendicular. Of course, there will be some with virtually no discernible lean, and this does make determining direction of fall a bit of a challenge. Trees, especially hardwoods, with very pronounced leans should be avoided by the amateur lumberjack because of their tendency to barberchair. Wind direction can also affect direction of fall, particularly if the wind is strong, and/or the tree has little natural lean. A greater density of limbs or branches on one side of a tree will affect its balance and thus tend to pull the tree to the heavy side. Sometimes, more than one element must be considered: the tree has the right lean, but the wind is blowing the wrong way, or the tree has the wrong lean but the wind is blowing the right way. Making the correct call becomes more difficult in these circumstances.

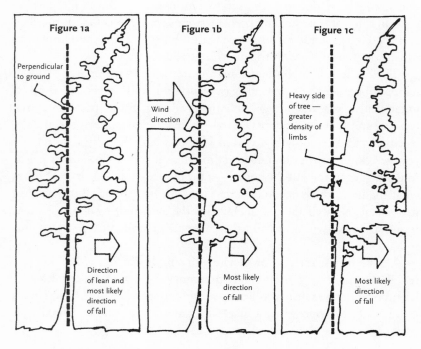

Figure 1a

Perpendicular to ground

Direction of lean and most likely direction of fall

Figure 1b

Wind direction

Most likely direction of fall

Figure 1c

Heavy side of tree — greater density of limbs

Most likely direction of fall

Regardless of whether or not the gods have smiled on you and the tree's direction of fall suits your intent, or you have to help it down, the next step is cutting the **notch**. A proper notch allows the tree to fall in a safe, controlled manner: with the piece of wood cut out, there is nothing holding the tree up on the notch side. The conventional notch is the most common. It should be cut about one-third of the way through the trunk (Figure 2a). Aim the notch where you want the tree to fall (or at least where you believe it will fall). Make the horizontal cut first, then the angled cut (about 45 degrees). Do not overcut the notch; if this happens then you must correct it (Figure 2b). The felling (cut) or back-cut should be started about 2 inches (5 cm) above the bottom cut of the notch (Figure 2c), and it should be executed in a three-stage or triangular fashion, rather than just straight in from the back (Figure 2d). We referred to this as "cutting the corners," and though not always necessary, this practice reduces the possibility of barberchair. The felling (cut) or backcut should be parallel to the notch. Never cut completely through to the notch. There should always be a couple of inches of wood fiber between the back of the cut and the notch (the technical recommendation is ¹⁄₁₀th of the tree's diameter). This strip of wood, known as the **hinge** secures the falling tree to the stump (Figures 2c and 3a).

The hinge provides a great deal

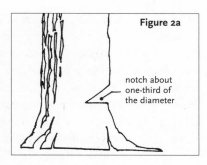

Figure 2a

notch about one-third of the diameter

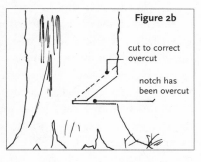

Figure 2b

cut to correct overcut

notch has been overcut

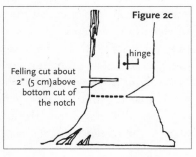

Figure 2c

hinge

Felling cut about 2" (5 cm) above bottom cut of the notch

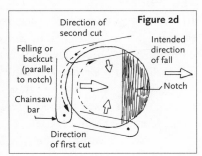

Figure 2d

Direction of second cut

Intended direction of fall

Felling or backcut (parallel to notch)

Notch

Chainsaw bar

Direction of first cut

of control over the tree's direction of descent; the hinge will resist sideways movement and it guides the tree in its direction of fall before it breaks off. The **snipe** (Figure 3b) prevents the tree from jumping back or slipping off the stump. If you cut through to the notch, the falling tree is fundamentally out of control as it falls.

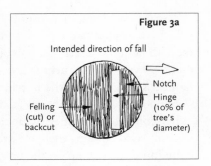

Figure 3a

Obviously, you should not only be worried about missing the cottage when felling a tree. Falling trees are unpredictable, and the unsuspecting can be bushwhacked by an amazing variety of nasty situations. Always plan and clear an escape route from the tree (generally, about 45 degrees from the angle of fall). When the tree first begins to fall, stop cutting,

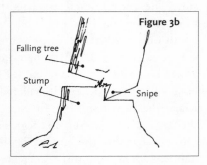

Figure 3b

engage the chain brake, and move quickly away along your escape route (if something unexpected happens, leave the saw). Keep a sharp eye on the sky; scary stuff can be suspended, wedged, or otherwise hung up there. Once safely away, turn and observe the tree's fall. Check the sky again before approaching the felled tree.

The more exotic holy-cripes-that-just-missed-me dangers earned their own special names among the lumberjacks I worked with. But, however fanciful the names were, the risks were not.

The Drunken Sailor

In an analogy to the legendary drinking habits of seafaring men, this term describes a fairly common felling occurrence. When a tree falls, especially in rather dense stands, often on its way down it will brush by other standing trees causing them to sway to and fro (ergo the allusion to drunkenness). This in itself is not dangerous, but if limbs are broken from the falling tree or the standing trees, the swaying can, on the rebound, hurl these projectiles toward the woodsman with what seems like unerring accuracy (Figure 4). On occasion, the whole top section

Figure 4

The Drunken Sailor

of a tree can be broken off and whipped at the feller.

The drunken sailor can happen in spite of good felling technique. However, look for an opening, cut the notch accurately, and try to place the tree where it will avoid contact with other trees on the way down.

The Barberchair

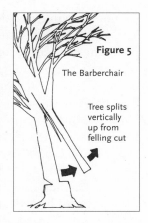

Figure 5

The Barberchair

Tree splits vertically up from felling cut

Hardwoods—i.e. maple, birch, etc.—are particularly susceptible to this phenomenon, especially those with a heavy lean. In essence, as you make the felling cut, the strain created by the lean causes the tree to split vertically up from the cut (Figure 5). The falling tree pivots on this huge upright slab, and the butt swings high into the air. When the top strikes the ground, the butt either bounces off its perch to come crashing down, sometimes with dire results, or remains precariously hung up, ready to fall at any moment. Cutting the corners is always, as mentioned earlier, a good practice to minimize the danger of the barberchair. The pros utilize a special technique when felling heavy leaners, but the amateurs should simply avoid them.

But barberchairs can happen, even with seemingly normal trees. What should you do? First of all, always stand to the side as you make the backcut so that if a tree does barberchair, it won't hit you; then, drop the saw and get the heck out of the way. If the butt remains hung up you've got a serious problem. Carefully get a rope or cable around the trunk and either winch it down with a come-along or hook the rope or cable to a vehicle trailer hitch and try to pull it down.

The Chicot

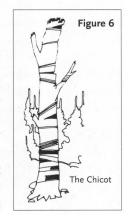

Figure 6

The Chicot

A constant menace to loggers, the chicot is a standing dead tree that is either completely or partly rotted through (Figure 6). Sometimes the tremors caused by a tree felled nearby can cause it to drop without warning. In my estimation, the worst chicots are dead birch; in many cases, the only thing that keeps the birch chicot standing is the bark casing—inside there is nothing but very heavy, rotten wood. Professionals are required to fell chicots before they start to work in logging operations. If there is a chicot in the vicinity of the tree you wish to fell then, for your own safety, take the time to dispose of it properly. Be particularly careful of any dead limbs that may still be connected to the trunk.

The Lodger

Lodgers are felled trees that don't quite make it to the ground, but instead get hung up in one or more standing trees as they fall (Figure 7a). The obvious but incorrect solution to this predicament would be to fell the tree or trees in which the lodger is caught. The reasons for not doing this are threefold: a) the lodger can become dislodged at any time and, because you have to position yourself practically under the lodger to cut the other tree(s) down, you are taking an enormous risk best avoided; b) the weight or stress that the lodger brings to bear on the standing tree or trees can cause them to barberchair when cut; c) when the supporting tree or trees are cut, you must scramble madly for safety as perhaps several trees come crashing down.

Figure 7a

The Lodger

Felled tree is suspended by standing tree

When I worked in the bush, I had the advantage of being able to call on the skidder to get me out of a jam. Nowadays, if I lodge a tree, I

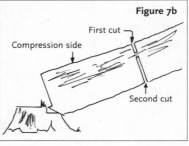

Figure 7b

First cut

Compression side

Second cut

must resort to other methods. Resist the temptation to cut the hinge (the guide bar can get pinched, or the butt can shoot back off the stump). Move up the trunk about 2 to 3 feet (60 to 90 cm) and cut a section off; make the first cut down a few inches through the compression side, and then up through the bottom side to meet the top cut (Figure 7b). This action may in fact dislodge the tree, as the trunk separates from the section holding it to the stump. If not, then use a canthook to twist the tree free of the branches holding it up.

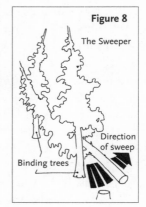

Figure 8

The Sweeper

Direction of sweep

Binding trees

The Sweeper

A falling tree can become a sweeper if it happens to slide down between two standing trees, causing the trunk to bend. When the butt eventually disengages from the stump, it can "sweep" violently sideways as it straightens out (Figure 8). Obviously, anyone in the path of the sweeper could be mowed down. Remember: always move back and away from the falling tree.

The Foolcatcher

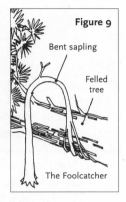

Figure 9

Bent sapling

Felled tree

The Foolcatcher

The foolcatcher or spring pole is rarely a fatal threat, but it can deliver a heck of a wallop. Sometimes a falling tree will bend and trap a smaller sapling under its greater weight (Figure 9). Even small ones, if undetected among the branches and brush, when inadvertently cut can spring back and catch the unsuspecting fool with stunning consequences. Stand on the inside of the foolcatcher's curve and saw outward at the top so that it will spring away from you.

Challenging Felling Situation

If Mother Nature is conspiring against you (i.e. you want the tree to fall north, but circumstances dictate that it wants to fall south), then you may be able to simply push it down by hand, or with a push pole (this will only work with smaller trees, and those with only a very moderate lean). A push pole should be about 12 to 16 feet (3 to 4 m) long with a Y-shaped top; set the pole against the trunk of the tree at about a 45-degree angle and push (applying force further up the trunk greatly increases leverage). But a **wedge** is probably the best tool for these situations. According to the experts, a 1-inch (25-mm) wedge driven into the backcut can move the top of a 75-foot (23-m) tree about six feet (2 m). A wedge is also useful for avoiding those iffy situations when you think that you have ascertained the direction of fall, but you aren't sure and you don't want the tree to sit back on the felling cut. If you are doubtful of the tree's inten-

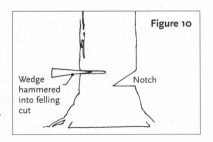

Figure 10

Wedge hammered into felling cut

Notch

tion, then it is always a good practice to insert the wedge once the backcut is far enough in so that the wedge will not contact the cutting chain (Figure 10).

Hollow trees and trees with a rotten center obviously lack solid hinge wood in the middle. In this instance, do not execute the 1, 2, 3 cut as in Figure 2d, but instead simply make the backcut straight in. The outer living shell then acts as the required hinge (leave a bit more than the recommended 1/10th suggested in Figure 3a).

Limbing and Bucking

Even when a tree has been safely felled, remember that limbing and bucking can still present some challenges and dangers. It is especially important to guard against kickback when limbing (see The Chainsaw chapter). The tree may be supported by the branches on the underside and, as you trim them off, it may roll. Limbs often get bent back when they hit the ground; they are under enormous tension, so when cut they can spring back (another version of the foolcatcher). The risk of tripping or falling on the saw is greatly increased when limbing.

When bucking (this has nothing to do with rodeos; it is the term used to describe cutting a tree up into the desired log or stove-wood lengths), you must be alert to several hazardous conditions. A tree can be under tension if it is wedged between two trees or stumps, etc. Cutting it can release this tension, and the trunk may shift suddenly. A section of the trunk may roll toward you when cut free. Kickback can occur, and the chain can be severely damaged if you cut through into the dirt and strike a rock, or the guide bar can be pinched and held securely in the cut.

Felling trees is not a job for the unwary, the unprepared, or the impaired.

Three to remember:

1. Direction of fall = notch.

2. Leave a healthy hinge.

3. Keep an eye on the sky.

CHAPTER 6

Firewood
and Wood Fires

THE SMELL OF WOOD SMOKE on a cool, crisp autumn afternoon, or a cold, clear winter morning, especially after a long invigorating walk or ski, has to be one of life's most pleasurable sensory experiences. I suppose that it must have some enduring link to our cave-dwelling roots, because we tend to associate the smell of wood smoke with shelter, security, a safe haven. We can sit and look at a wood fire for hours at a stretch, even if that fire is behind a woodstove glass door (the symmetrical blue flames of a gas fireplace do not seem to have the same effect). So it is that the time and effort to acquire the fuel for those wood fires is, generally, agreeably well spent.

Firewood

Most folks acknowledge that hardwoods make the best firewood because hardwoods produce a longer-lasting coal bed. However, not every cottager has access to hard maple, oak, or beech. In many parts of North America softwoods are the only fuel wood, and still people heat their places quite effectively. In fact, the energy content of dry wood per kilogram is actually almost the same regardless of species; softwoods and hardwoods burn differently because of differences in density (since the heat output of wood is proportional to its density, a stick of hardwood will produce more heat than a stick of softwood of similar size). My own experience has provided me with an appreciation for the value of heating with softwoods.

For a number of years, my wife and I owned a country home situated on 50 acres. The house was heated by a combination wood/oil furnace, and the property was well-treed, though most of it was poplar. I was less than convinced, but my father-in-law informed me that, properly dried, poplar burned rather well. As was most often the case, Morley was correct. I didn't split the blocks quite as fine as for hardwoods, and I built a shed of sorts to keep the poplar dry. The second year, I burned a lot of it, and though its BTU output was inferior to maple, it certainly provided plenty of heat. As would be expected, more wood was required to achieve the same results. What's more, there seemed to be less creosote build-up. And, even if you have access to a plentiful supply of hardwood, species like poplar can be a good choice for spring and autumn use when heat demand is lower.

Density of Common Firewoods

Here is a list of the tree species commonly used for firewood. Those at the top of the list are the hardest and those at the bottom of the list are the softest.

HARD

Ironwood
Rock elm
Hickory
Oak
Sugar Maple
Beech
Yellow birch
Ash
Red elm
Red maple
Tamarack
Dougas fir
White birch
Manitoba maple
Red alder
Hemlock
Poplar
Pine
Basswood
Spruce
Balsam

SOFT

Storing Wood

The moisture content of your firewood, regardless of species, should be your most important concern. Moisture content affects the rate at which wood burns, and the efficiency of combustion. When trees are cut, the moisture content ranges between 35% and 50% by weight. If you attempt to burn "green" wood, so much energy will be consumed in boiling the excess water, that the efficiency of combustion will be low. Firewood should be cut and split in the early spring to be ready for burning in the autumn (some believe that firewood should cure for a whole year). Properly seasoned firewood has a moisture content of approximately 20%; look for checks or cracks in the end grain as a sign of dry wood. Most authorities recommend that firewood should be piled outside, preferably under some kind of cover so the warm summer air can circulate through the pieces. On the other hand, some, like me, choose to put their wood in a shed; mine is open at the front—with a roll-down tarp, and well vented on both sides and at the back (plans can be found in The Woodshed chapter). The wood is certainly well seasoned, and it doesn't have to be dug out of a snow bank in the winter!

Note the way the sticks of wood are arranged at the end of a properly stacked wood pile.

Getting Wood

Firewood can be acquired in any number of ways. We don't have a big lot, but most of the trees are maple or birch. Every couple of years, a tree will die and need to be felled, and the quantity of firewood supplied by these fallen trees has been more than ample, so far. There's no doubt that when we spend more time up at the lake (retirement looms near), we will need a more plentiful source.

Some cottagers may have neighbors who would be willing to sell deadfalls or even standing timber; moreover, if that property owner has done, or plans to do, any logging, you might also be able to recover fuel wood from the discarded tops. These are generally of a size that does not require much splitting. In Ontario, at one time, you could also cut wood on Crown Land by acquiring a fuel wood permit. However, in many jurisdictions the Ontario Ministry of Natural Resources (OMNR) no longer grants these permits because they simply do not have the man-power to manage the process. If you currently cut firewood on Crown property, and you don't have a permit, you'd better check with your district office; you are probably breaking the law. Rules and regulations will vary, but wherever you cottage, you need to ascertain what is allowed before you cut a few blocks for the stove.

In some locations, you might be forced to buy firewood. Firewood is measured and sold in units called **cords**. A full cord measures 4 feet wide, by 4 feet high, by 8 feet long—128 cubic feet. Naturally, most cottage wood-burning appliances cannot accommodate a 4-foot piece of wood, so firewood is cut into shorter lengths. The most common is 16 inches, and a quantity of wood measuring 16 inches x 4 feet x 8 feet is often referred to as a **face cord**. If possible, avoid buying wood in units that cannot be related to the standard full cord, because you have no idea exactly how much you are paying for. That being said, many firewood dealers will deliver you a load of wood in log lengths, and this is far cheaper than buying firewood already cut and split (as usual, this is a good occasion to consult the locals for a trustworthy source). If it's a tandem-truck load, that might be too much for your needs, so you could consider getting together with your cottage neighbors to process the load cooperatively. Consider renting a splitter—it's worth it.

If you're near a sawmill, you may also be able to get cut-offs, slabs, or even cull logs for a reasonable fee.

Should you plan to reside at the cottage through the winter you will need to determine exactly how much wood you will need. Only experience can provide a definitive answer; cottage size, location, and severity of the winter season will factor into the equation. However, as a rule of thumb, a medium-sized modern home, if heated exclusively with wood, would need between three and five full cords for the year. But you can always cut a little extra because properly stored firewood won't go bad.

Splitting Wood

There are certain cottage tasks that are really quite enjoyable, and for some, believe it or not, splitting wood is one of them. Not only is it a superior fitness routine (forget the Tai-Bo), but it also affords the pleasure of providing a fundamental necessity for your family. It is essential for modern high-efficiency wood-burning appliances that pieces do not exceed 6 inches (15 cm) across the largest dimension. Granted, some woods are more satisfying to split than others. Ash, for example, splits beautifully and almost effortlessly, while elm can pose a threat to your immortal soul. Some woods split easier when green, while others are easier to split when dry (such as pine). Some seem to split easier in summer, while others seem to split easier in winter.

But to split wood properly, you must have the right tools (once again, we venture into territory that could generate some spirited discussion, or maybe even a difference of opinion!). Old-timers will assure you that "they don't make axes like they used to," and that could be true. An axe is not the necessary rural implement it once was, and those highly skilled in its use are rare indeed. Most modern buyers only want a passably good model anyway; after all, they won't be using it very often. Should you choose to split your wood with an axe, it should weigh at least three pounds. The face should not be too thin because the axe face needs to exert lateral force as it enters the block of wood. Both my stepfather and father-in-law also taught me to sharply twist the axe handle a little as the head contacts the block of wood; in this manner, you can increase splitting leverage. It is certainly an effective technique, but it requires a good deal of practice.

Like many others, I prefer a splitting **maul**. A maul is heavier than an axe—a six-pounder is a good choice, and it is characterized by a blunter profile.

A maul is less likely to stick in a block of wood, and it exerts much more lateral splitting force than an axe. Its greater weight does make it somewhat harder to wield, but each swing delivers more production value. In addition, if you miss the block and hit your leg, the maul is more likely to break it, while the axe will probably take a slab clean off! The accompanying photograph shows a three-pound axe to the left, and a six-pound maul on the right. Note the much thicker face of the maul. Specialty splitting tools are also available.

Experienced wood splitters will nearly always use a splitting block to work on, rather than simply setting the wood on the ground, except for the biggest, heaviest pieces. Usually, it just happens to be one with an equal or larger diameter than the wood to be split, and 12 to 16 inches (30 to 40 cm) high is about right (too much height will weaken the force

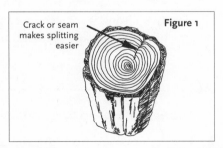

Figure 1

Crack or seam makes splitting easier

of the blow). Work on level ground, or slightly uphill from the block. Examine the block you're splitting, and look for cracks or seams (Figure 1). These make the chore a great deal easier, especially with larger pieces.

Obviously, try to work around big knots. If a large block does not show any weak areas, a couple of strategies may improve your splitting efficiency. Pattern your blows: strike near the edge of the block—not in the center—and work your way across (to maintain your accuracy, avoid changing your grip on the maul or axe, and your position). Once a split starts, work with it. Split more manageable slabs from the outer perimeter of a large block: this will quickly reduce the overall size of the block, and the slabs can be downsized quite easily later (see Figure 2).

For the hardest to split, try to start a crack big enough to insert a metal wedge; finish the job with a sledgehammer (wear safety glasses—

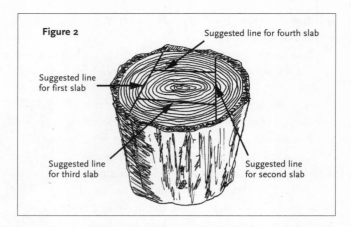

Figure 2

Suggested line for fourth slab

Suggested line for first slab

Suggested line for third slab

Suggested line for second slab

metal on metal). Or you can use your maul as a wedge. Drive it in, and give it a whack with the sledgehammer.

As a very last resort, some have been known (yes, perhaps even *moi*) to cut a slot in the top of a particularly obstreperous block with a chainsaw; this has to be deep enough to fit a metal wedge or your maul securely. As above, the sledgehammer will be required to make the unrepentant yield. However, this is a tricky and dangerous technique with a chainsaw: the block's short length makes it hard to control, and kickback is a very real possibility. Only experienced operators should ever attempt this. Otherwise, save that piece for a fall bonfire.

Finally, splitting wood can be dangerous. Start fresh, but stop when you get tired. Fatigue and inattention can lead to injury.

Three to remember:

1. Firewood needs to be seasoned for at least 6 to 9 months.

2. Protect firewood from the elements.

3. Wood should be split into pieces no bigger than 6 inches (15 cm) across the widest diameter.

The Wood Fire

Sometimes, we outdoorsy cottagers think that certain skills will come to us automatically: starting and maintaining a proper fire in a wood-burning appliance are among those we believe are somehow hereditary. Such is not the case, though many of us have, with trial and error, become reasonably proficient fire builders and tenders. However, a complete understanding of the wood-burning process might improve your ability and your appliance's efficiency.

What Happens When Wood Burns

As firewood burns, there are three phases to combustion. In the first phase water is evaporated: as the wood is heated in the firebox, water in the firewood is boiled off, consuming heat energy in the process. The wetter the wood, the more energy is consumed and the more it sizzles and hisses. Smoke emission constitutes the second phase: as wood heats up above the boiling point of water, it starts to smoke. Smoke consists of combustible gases and tar droplets; it will burn if the temperature is high enough and oxygen is present. When smoke burns, flames are produced. If smoke is not entirely burned in the firebox, it will exit the appliance into the chimney where it will either condense, forming creosote deposits, or be expelled as air pollution. Moreover, unburned smoke represents an efficiency loss because it contains a large part of the total energy in the wood.

In the charcoal phase, the fire has progressed, and most of the gases and tars have vaporized out of the wood. Charcoal is almost 100% carbon, and burns with a red glow and very little flame or smoke.

In reality, all three phases of wood combustion occur simultaneously: wood gases can be flaming and the edges of the pieces can be glowing red as charcoal burns, while water in the core of the piece is still evaporating. The challenge in burning wood effectively is to boil off the water content quickly, and make sure the smoke burns before it leaves the firebox.

Starting a New Fire

Effective fire-building requires that you have some idea of where air enters the firebox. The woodstove in our place has an inlet near the bottom of the firebox, just inside the loading door. Obviously, if that hole is obstructed by ash, then proper combustion is difficult to achieve.

Crumple several sheets of newspaper and put them in the firebox. The drier and finer the kindling, the less newspaper you will need, though some people make the mistake of using too little paper. Next, pile 10 to 15 pieces of finely split, dry kindling on top of the crumpled newspaper (cedar and pine make some of the best kindling). Set the air control to fully open, light the paper and close, but do not latch, the door (in some models, the door must be left ajar for as long as 10 to 15 minutes until the chimney has developed a strong draft— never leave the stove unattended during this time).

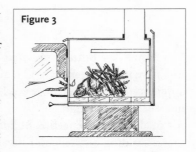

Figure 3

When the flames from the kindling load just begin to subside, add several small pieces of firewood, but do not smother the fire. Once the smaller pieces of firewood are fully engulfed, larger chunks can be loaded into the stove. Allow the wood to burn brightly for 15 to 30 minutes before reducing the air-control setting (reducing the setting in two or three stages reduces air pollution because the fire does not have to recover from a single, large reduction in air supply).

The most important rule is NEVER LET THE FIRE SMOLDER. As long is as there is solid wood in the firebox, there should be flames, or the smoke will escape unburned. With modern appliances, it is possible to achieve a reliable overnight burn while maintaining flaming combustion and having enough charcoal in the morning to rekindle a new load.

Remember, these are general suggestions only. They apply to most wood-burning stoves, but some appliances may require special firing techniques which will be explained in the owner's manual. Follow those instructions.

An Alternative... Building a Top-Down Fire

The top-down method of building a wood fire is quickly gaining converts among householders who heat with wood. To build a top-down fire, reverse the procedure described in "Starting a New Fire." That is, place two or three larger pieces at the back of the firebox, lean 10 to 15 pieces of kindling against the logs, then place several crumpled sheets of newspaper on and around the kindling. Set the air control to fully open, light the newspaper, and close the loading door.

You may not believe it until you see it for yourself, but most people report that the fire starts reliably and progresses through to the large pieces without needing any further poking or adjustment. The advantages of the top-down fire building method are:

🔥 minimal start-up smoke is visible at the top of the chimney;

🔥 no chance that the fire will collapse and smother itself: and

⚁ no need to open the loading door to add larger pieces once the kindling fire is established.

The top-down fire technique may not be appropriate for every type of wood-burning appliance, but it is effective in many cases. Why not give it a try?

Fuel Loading

A wood-burning appliance is not a gas furnace or a baseboard-heater, so don't expect perfectly steady heat output from the fire. Wood fires burn in cycles; each cycle should provide between 4 and 8 hours of heating, depending on how much wood was used, and how much heat is needed. For quick flash fires, a small load loosely arranged in the firebox produces enough heat to take the chill off in the spring and fall, but doesn't drive you out of the cottage (Figure 4). Stack several small pieces in a crisscross fashion on or behind the coal bed. Open the air inlet to produce a hot, bright fire; the air inlet can be reduced slightly as the fire progresses, but never enough to extinguish the flames. Once the fire has burned back down to coals, the air supply can be further reduced to preserve the coal bed.

Extended burns can be achieved by placing larger loads of bigger pieces compactly in the firebox. Placing the pieces close together prevents the heat and flame from penetrating the load, and saves the buried pieces for later in the burn cycle. Use the extended fire technique to achieve an overnight burn or a fire to last a cold winter day.

Figure 4

A Loosely Stacked Fuel Load
Good for short-duration or "flash" fires

A Thermometer
A stack thermometer tells you how hot the flue gases are. It is a good indicator of your stove's performance, and it is an important safety feature. Every wood-heating system behaves differently, and thermometers vary, so it is impossible to give exact operating temperatures. But, as a guide, the temperature should never exceed 850°F (460°C). With

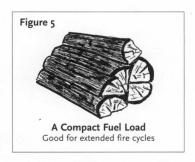

Figure 5

A Compact Fuel Load
Good for extended fire cycles

experience, you will be able to maintain a suitable temperature range that will give you the best performance from your appliance.

Most woodstoves require that the thermometer be mounted on the flue pipe. It should be installed about 18 inches (45 cm) above the stove. Some require a stovetop thermometer. The function is the same, but the temperature range will be different.

Signs of Efficient Wood-Burning

- Flames should be present until only charcoal remains.
- Firebricks should be tan, never black.
- Glass doors should be clear in appliances with airwash systems— hazy but not totally black in stoves without.
- Exhaust from the chimney should be clear or white, not blue or gray.
- Steel or cast iron parts in the firebox should be light to dark brown, not black or shiny.

Three to remember:

1. Use only seasoned firewood.

2. The fire should suit the time of year.

3. A thermometer is a good monitor of your stove's performance.

CHAPTER 7

Wood-Heating Appliances

WHY IS IT THAT COTTAGES BREED MORE STORIES than ordinary, everyday city homes? There is seldom anything unusual to relate about living in our house, yet in the 13 years since we built the cottage, we have already accumulated dozens of "Well, let me tell you about..." tales and anecdotes regarding the place on the lake. For example, there is the wood-stove experience!

In order for a structure to qualify as a cottage it must have a wood-stove or fireplace; that fact simply cannot be argued. We fully accepted that tenet, so, when the cottage was finished, we set out on our quest to find the right one, and what a quest it became (just ask my pal Brian)!

My brother-in-law Doug, ever the one to help another spend his money, clapped me on the back one day and suggested that we should have his—and, incidentally, my wife's—grandparents' old stove restored. In its time, the Good Cheer, a so-called parlor stove, must have been a thing of beauty: mica windows in the doors and lots of nickel plating. It had certainly fallen on hard times when we saw it, but Lynn had succumbed to her brother's insidious manipulation, and her own sentimentality and the Good Cheer was shipped off to a re-builder. He swore the old wood burner would be "as good as new." Oh, how the neophyte never wonders to ask, "Well... just how good was new?"

When it was returned, we did indeed marvel at its rejuvenation, and in no time it was installed in the cottage. That fall we didn't use it much, but around Christmas break of that year we spent a winter weekend up at the lake. Before retiring for the night, I filled the old-timer with well-seasoned hard maple—a standard loading for an extended burn. For some reason, the bliss of sweet dreams eluded me for about an hour. Gradually I became aware of a steady "click, click, click." It suddenly dawned on me that it was the sound of very hot metal expanding. I jumped out of bed and hurried downstairs. The flue thermometer's needle was buried deep in the danger zone. The Good Cheer was a beautiful old stove, but it had so many gaps and spaces around the viewing and fuel loading doors that there was no practical way to limit the draft. For the rest of the night, I sprayed water onto the wood to keep the fire from getting away. I won't say I cursed Doug during the time I squatted in front of the Good Cheer, but I will admit that I did harbor the occasional unkind thought.

Later that winter, Lynn found a beautiful modern stove manufactured in a European country that will remain nameless. The salesman judged that it would heat a place our size (come to think of it, I believe that *his* name was Doug). We bought it, and the next weekend Brian and I hauled it up to the cottage to replace the Good Cheer. We reasoned that moving the two would be relatively simple in the winter. Getting the new stove into the cottage was a cinch, but we hadn't bargained on the weight of the old one. The snowmobile couldn't pull the sleigh it was loaded on up the hill, so Brian and I had to carry it. "Carry" is perhaps a euphemism, because it took us the better part of an hour to manhandle it the 55 yards (50 meters) through the deep snow to the top of the grade (we were younger then, and didn't dwell so much on heart attacks and strokes). During that ordeal, I got one of those looks from Brian that suggested our long friendship could be in some jeopardy.

Soon after, Lynn and I spent another romantic winter weekend up at the lake. During the second night, the temperature outside fell to -20°F (-30°C), but the cute little cast iron foreign-built stove couldn't move the mercury over 60°F (15°C) inside, even with the draft thrown wide open (the cottage is fully insulated). I smiled at my dear wife, as I realized that we had purchased a second stove that still didn't meet our needs. Naturally, I waited until spring before I told Brian, and fortunately the sellers of the cute little cast iron foreign-built stove gave us our money back.

Eventually, our quest took us to the folks at Napoleon, and for a number of years now we have enjoyed the Model 1400's reliable operation. Brian grinned a lot during the job, but he still helped me take the second one away and replace it with yet a third stove (perhaps, cumulatively, the most expensive one in all of cottage country). That must say something about our friendship. It certainly says something about picking the right stove the first time.

Extended four-season use of cottages, especially by the snowmobile crowd, and conversion to full-time occupancy by an ever-growing number of retired cottagers has meant more intensive use for wood-burning appliances. Remarkably, nearly one million Canadian single-family dwellings—about 14%—use wood as a supplementary heating fuel, while more than 400,000—nearly 6%—use wood as the primary heating fuel. In cottage country, the number would have to be closer to 100%; I've never been in a cabin, camp, or cottage that did not include some sort of stove or fireplace, and I can't imagine that there would be such a thing. And of the two, the woodstove is by far the more common choice because it is the more flexible and inexpensive wood heating option. It can be located almost anywhere there is adequate space, and where a chimney can be routed.

Choosing a Woodstove

Woodstoves in general enjoyed a renaissance in the 1970s (because of the oil crisis) and models were produced by many different manufacturers (some good, some questionable). Eventually, concern for the amount of pollution produced by woodstoves, and consequently, tough new emission standards developed by the U.S. Environmental Protection Agency meant that woodstove makers (or at least those who wanted to distribute their wares in the U.S.) had to design more environmentally friendly products. Over the past 10 to 15 years technologies have been developed that greatly reduce woodstove pollutants, while improving efficiency and safety. Essentially, the goal for newer models has been to burn off the smoke before it leaves the firebox. Two technologies in particular have achieved this goal.

1. **Advanced combustion systems** create the conditions necessary to burn combustible gases (aka smoke) without the use of catalysts. In order to achieve this, these stoves are characterized by a) well-insulated fireboxes to keep temperatures high; b) devices to reflect heat back into the firebox to create gas turbulence and to give gases a long and hot enough route so they will be burned before they cool; and c) heated secondary air supplies to ensure that enough oxygen is present—usually fed to the fire above the fuel bed through ducts with small holes.

2. **Catalytic stoves** are equipped with a coated ceramic honeycomb through which the exhaust gas is channeled. The catalytic coating lowers the ignition temperature of the gases as they pass through.

This allows catalytic appliances to operate at low firing rates while still burning cleanly. However, according to some experts, catalytics are on the decline; they work really well for a few years but eventually the catalyst begins to break down and the replacement cost is generally quite high.

If you're buying your first stove, or need to replace the aging one currently in use, you should consider two other factors.

1. **Heat output:** Woodstoves range from very small units designed to heat a single room to large ones with enough capacity to heat a big house. A common problem is selecting a stove that is too large for the space to be heated (this over-sizing often results in extended periods of low firing that can be inefficient and problematic). An experienced retailer can match stove size to heating requirements and the location you have chosen for it.

2. **Design:** There are no clear performance differences between cast iron and plate steel construction, painted and enameled finishes, glass panels and solid doors, and so on. However, there is an important performance difference between **direct radiation** stoves and those that deliver their heat by **convective air flow**. Radiant woodstoves send their heat out in all directions (cast iron stoves and those with heavy steel plate are typical radiant stoves). Convection stoves heat air that flows between the stove body and a sheet metal casing. There are advantages to using one or the other, depending on the details of installation. Radiant stoves are particularly effective in a relatively open area, though the heat is more difficult to distribute, while convection stoves produce hot air, which can be more easily circulated. In fact, many modern stoves have incorporated both radiant and convection characteristics, and are suitable for most installations. Again, a good retailer will help you make this decision.

Some cottagers use a cookstove. While most cookstoves are not designed to heat a bigger, multi-room cottage, and generally cost more than most woodstoves, they might be suitable for small, open-concept cottages. A bonus is that during power outages you can still heat, cook, bake, and warm water. However, manufacturers have not yet been able to build advanced, clean-burning technology into their ranges, though cookstoves are noticeably more efficient than they were at the turn of the 20th century.

Whichever model you choose, safety, efficiency, and emissions should be the standards by which you evaluate a stove. You should also look for the following certification agencies as your assurance that an appliance has been tested and meets performance and safety criteria.

Location

Woodstoves should be situated in the part of the cottage you want to be the warmest; this is generally the main floor where kitchen, living, and dining rooms are located, and where your family normally spends most of its time. The cottage layout can have a direct bearing on appliance selection. If it is made up of several smaller rooms, then you may not be able to heat it entirely with a single appliance. Avoid the temptation to buy a large stove; instead select a small one and locate it in the common room. You can distribute some of the heat by installing grilles above door openings or a small room-to-room fan. Some rooms may have to be heated with supplementary devices, such as baseboard heaters. Open-concept cottages with fewer partitions can often be heated entirely by a larger woodstove strategically positioned. If the cottage has a cathedral ceiling, then consider installing a good ceiling fan to move the heated air back down into the living space. We did that in our cottage; we selected a plain commercial model—no lights or fancy rattan—and wired it to a rheostat.

When planning the location of the woodstove, consider where the chimney will be run. You should avoid, if you can, running the chimney up the outside wall of the cottage, because chimneys work more efficiently when they run straight up from the stove and through the house interior.

To get the best performance from a wood-burning appliance, and to be assured of its safety, you should get reliable advice from a trained professional and consider having the system professionally installed. In Ontario, professionals should be graduates of the Wood Energy Technical Training program (WETT), and should display the WETT logo.

That being said, many cottagers fancy themselves as highly competent do-it-yourselfers and will likely attempt the installation regardless of the above counsel. Almost all new woodstoves currently on the market in Canada have been safety certified. The manufacturer's guidelines for certified stoves specify minimum installation clearances and instructions. *Follow them.*

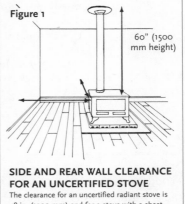

Figure 1

60" (1500 mm height)

SIDE AND REAR WALL CLEARANCE FOR AN UNCERTIFIED STOVE
The clearance for an uncertified radiant stove is 48 in. (1200 mm) and for a stove with a sheet metal jacket or casing the clearance is 36 in (900 mm). The clearances are large because they apply to all shapes, sizes and designs of stoves that have not been tested to determine the actual clearances.

Appliances that have not been tested have no such safety guidelines (these include used or antique stoves, or stoves that may have been constructed by small welding shops). Some insurance companies will only accept certified appliances, so before installing an unapproved wood-heating system, you should check with your agent. However, guidelines do exist for uncertified devices and are found in the Canadian Standards Association solid fuel installation code, CSA B365. These are summarized in Figure 1; clearances must be measured from the outer surface of the appliance to the combustible material. Sheet metal jackets must be spaced out from the stove at least 2 inches (5 cm) by non-combustible spacers, with provision for air circulation at the top and bottom.

Reducing Minimum Clearances

Most cottage owners want their woodstove installation to take up as little floor space as possible. As a result, the reduction of minimum clearances using special **shields** is very common (these must be permanent fixtures, not free-standing, folding panels). The first step in reducing clearances is to determine the minimum clearance, either from a certified appliance's label, or from the clearance specs for uncertified stoves. Then calculate the permissible clearance reduction for the type of shield you plan to use from the table on clearance reduction (see chart).

Shield construction rules are very specific, so be sure to obtain current standards.

The shield establishes an air space behind the shield material, and this space sets up a convection flow of air and prevents the stove's heat from reaching the wall behind.

Reducing Clearances With Shielding		
	Clearances may be reduced by these percentages	
Type of protection (shield)	Sides and rear %	Top %
Sheet metal, a minimum of 29 gauge in thickness spaced out at least 21 mm (7/8 in.) by non-combustible spacers	67	50
Ceramic tiles, or equivalent non-combustible material on non-combustible supports spaced out at least 21 mm (7/8 in.) by non-combustible spacers	50	33
Ceramic tiles, or equivalent non-combustible material on non-combustible supports with a minimum of 29 gauge sheet metal backing spaced out at least 21 mm (7/8 in.) by non-combustible spacers	67	50
Brick spaced out at least 21 mm (7/8 in.) by non-combustible spacers	50	N/A
Brick with a minimum of 29 gauge sheet metal backing spaced out at least 21 mm (7/8 in.) by non-combustible spacers	67	N/A
Source: CSA Standard B365-1991, Table 4, Page 27		

Ready-made commercial shields are also available, and these are tested to determine effective clearance reductions. Choose only **certified** commercial shields.

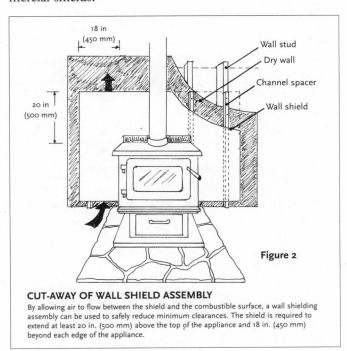

Figure 2

CUT-AWAY OF WALL SHIELD ASSEMBLY
By allowing air to flow between the shield and the combustible surface, a wall shielding assembly can be used to safely reduce minimum clearances. The shield is required to extend at least 20 in. (500 mm) above the top of the appliance and 18 in. (450 mm) beyond each edge of the appliance.

Protecting the Floor

Certified woodstoves have been tested, and will not overheat a combustible floor. However, the floor must be protected from live embers and sparks that might fall from the stove during loading or tending. The floor pad must be made of a durable non-combustible material such as sheet metal, grouted ceramic tile, or mortared brick (a continuous, non-combustible surface). We used granite fieldstone in our cottage. It was only ½ inch (2 cm) thick; we glued it to the plywood floor and mortared the space between the rock (it's quite attractive).

The protective floor pad must not be installed on carpet unless it is structurally supported so that it does not move or distort. Figure 3 provides minimum protective floor pad specifications.

The heat from the bottom of untested, uncertified stoves may overheat floors, and the rules for floor protection for uncertified appliances are complicated. Contact a qualified professional for floor protection details.

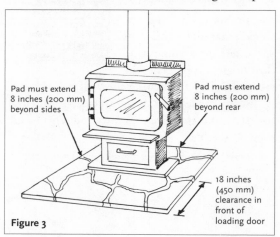

Pad must extend 8 inches (200 mm) beyond sides

Pad must extend 8 inches (200 mm) beyond rear

18 inches (450 mm) clearance in front of loading door

Figure 3

Flue Pipes

Flue pipes (commonly known as stove pipes) carry smoke from the woodstove flue collar to the base of the chimney. They have been referred to as the "weak link" in the wood-burning system because they are often improperly installed. The rules for installation of **single-wall flue pipe** are, in fact, very specific:

⚊ Minimum clearance from combustible material: 18 inches (45 cm); this may be reduced to 9 inches (23 cm) if suitable shielding is installed either on the pipe or the combustible surface.

⚊ Maximum overall length of straight pipe: 10 feet (3 m).

⚊ Maximum unsupported horizontal length: 3 feet (1 m).

- Maximum number of elbows: 2.

- Minimum upward slope toward the chimney: ¼ inch per foot (20 mm per meter).

- The crimped ends (male) of the sections must be oriented toward the stove.

- Each joint in the assembly must be fastened with at least 3 screws.

- 6, 7, and 8-inch diameter pipes must be at least 24 gauge in thickness.

- Galvanized flue pipes must not be used (the coatings vaporize at high temperatures, and release dangerous gases); use **black painted** flue pipes only

- The assembly must have allowance for expansion: elbows in assemblies allow for expansion; straight assemblies should include an inspection wrap with one end unfastened, or a telescopic section.

Figure 4

THE IDEAL SINGLE-WALL FLUE PIPE ASSEMBLY
When the flue gas path is straight, the system will produce stronger draft and will need less maintenance than if the assembly has elbows. The ideal flue pipe assembly rises straight from the appliance flue collar into the chimney. A straight single-wall flue pipe assembly needs an inspection wrap or telescopic section so it can be installed and removed without having to move the appliance. The wrap also allows some movement for expansion when the flue pipe gets hot.

Certified **double-wall flue pipe** systems are also available. There are two general types: sealed and vented. Though more expensive, the minimum clearances for double-wall flue pipes are much less than those for single-wall pipes, and the maximum length of an assembly may be greater than is permitted for a single-wall pipe.

The Chimney

The selection, location, and installation of your chimney is at least as important as the type of wood-burning appliance you choose. The chimney's function is to produce the draft that draws combustion air into the stove, and to safely exhaust the gases from combustion to the outside. The chimney must isolate nearby combustible materials from the flue

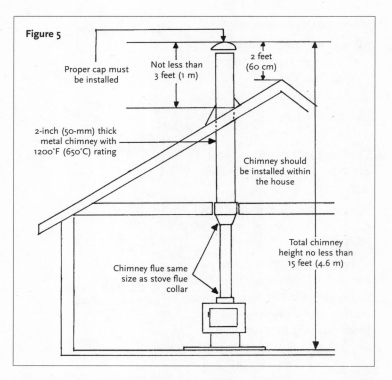

Figure 5

Proper cap must be installed

Not less than 3 feet (1 m)

2 feet (60 cm)

2-inch (50-mm) thick metal chimney with 1200°F (650°C) rating

Chimney should be installed within the house

Chimney flue same size as stove flue collar

Total chimney height no less than 15 feet (4.6 m)

heat, and be able to tolerate high temperatures that can result from a chimney fire. It must be able to conserve normal flue heat to promote a strong draft, and be resistant to corrosion on the inside and to the effects of weather on the outside. It must also be sealed to prevent leakage.

Figure 5 outlines the basic requirements for good chimney installation.

- The 2 feet (60 cm) chimney height requirement must be measured in relation to any roof, building, or other obstacle within a horizontal distance of 10 feet (3 m). This stricture is designed to place the top of the chimney higher than any areas of air turbulence. The chimney must also extend not less than 3 feet (1 m) above the highest point it exits the roof.

- According to the experts, when chimneys are run up outside walls, the chilling effect of the outside cold air can reduce stove draft. Keep the chimney inside, if possible.

- Taller chimneys usually produce stronger draft. The 15 feet (4.6 m) overall height from floor to top of chimney is a rule of thumb; most normal installations exceed this height, but installations in cottages with low-slope roofs may not. As a result, stove performance may not be optimal.

↟ Chimney flues that are bigger than stove flue collars are common, partly because people used to think that bigger is better. This is not the case. A given volume of flue gas flows faster and has less time to cool in a chimney that is sized according to the appliance.

↟ Developed in the 1980s, the 1200°F (650°C) metal chimney can withstand the heat of a chimney fire; it has more insulation and a stronger liner than the older 1 inch (25 mm) type.

↟ A proper chimney cap prevents water from leaking into the insulation, and keeps the critters out.

Type A Metal Chimneys—those manufactured before 1981—are not considered suitable for wood-burning appliances. These were available in both cylindrical and square sections, and featured a 1-inch (25-mm) wall thickness. You should seriously consider upgrading to a 1200°F (650°C) chimney if your current installation includes a Type A system.

Masonry Chimneys

Obviously, construction of a masonry chimney should be left to a mason, unless you are one heck of a do-it-yourselfer, and must be built according to national, provincial/state, and municipal building code specifications.

Hire a qualified chimney sweep to inspect your chimney immediately if you see any deterioration of the bricks or mortar joints near the top, or if there are dark stains on the brickwork. Old, unlined masonry chimneys, or those that are too large for the stove you want to connect, or chimneys that have been damaged by a chimney fire can often be relined with a certified stainless steel liner.

Bracket masonry chimneys are brick chimneys that are built on wooden supports, often within a wall, instead of on proper concrete foundations, and should not be used. Often found in older buildings, they cannot be upgraded to meet current building code requirements and should be replaced.

Creosote and Chimney Fires

Creosote deposits develop when wood is burned slowly, and the smoke condenses on the cool inner surface of the liner. Creosote from smoldering fires is black and tarry (creosote does develop even if you use proper firing techniques, but it is soft, flaky, and dark brown in color, and less combustible). If it ignites at the base of the chimney, this can result in a very dangerous chimney fire. Although 1200°F (650°C) chimneys can withstand chimney fire temperatures, the heat will still cause extreme stress to the components.

Chimneys require regular maintenance. If it is a new installation, it should be inspected frequently until you know how quickly creosote deposits build up in your chimney. Remove deposits if the build-up exceeds ⅛ inch (4 mm). Newer, low-emission woodstoves burn the wood so completely that when they are operated properly, their chimneys normally need cleaning only once each year. I clean mine annually—part of the opening-up ritual—whether it needs it or not. (I also invented a little device to scrape deposits from the stove or flue pipes as well: see Figure 6.)

Older chimneys should be inspected for corrosion or rust stains on the outer shell; check for bulges or corrosion in the liner (during cleaning, not during operation!). Generally, it is best to inspect and clean in the spring, as the warm, humid summer air together with deposits will hasten corrosion of steel parts. With proper firing techniques, seasoned firewood and regular inspection, you should never have to experience the trauma of a serious chimney fire. But if you do have a chimney fire, you should have the system inspected by a professional before using the stove again.

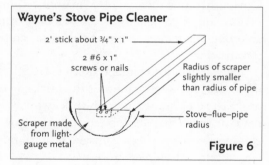

Figure 6

Installation Checklist

- Get a municipal building permit; some municipalities require one even if you are exchanging an older stove for a newer one.

- Contact your insurance agent regarding premiums; insurance company treatment of wood-heat installations varies widely.

- If you are installing the system yourself, get advice from a qualified professional.

- READ and FOLLOW the installation instructions carefully.

- If a pro is installing the system, satisfy yourself that the manufacturer's directions are being observed during installation.

- Check the installation to make sure that it meets code.

- Notify your insurance agent that installation is complete (they will probably want to inspect it themselves, or have their representatives inspect it); if your agent does not examine it, have the system inspected by your municipal building department, or WETT certtified inspector.

- Install smoke detectors, and replace batteries annually.

- Buy and install an approved ABC-type fire extinguisher near the installation. Follow the manufacturer's maintenance schedule.

Conventional Fireplaces

When you first imagined your cottage, you may have pictured it with a traditional fireplace. However, like most of us, you probably balked at the cost and installed a practical woodstove. But fireplaces are still quite common in lakeside retreats, even though, as a heating system, they are vastly inferior to the woodstove. Tests have shown that conventional fireplaces can produce a negative energy efficiency by drawing heated air out of the building while producing very little heat. We love fireplaces because we get the sight and sounds of the fire but fireplaces, unlike efficient woodstoves, do not incorporate the design features needed to convert wood fuel to useful heat. To improve the efficiency of a conventional fireplace, there are two options.

Fireplace Inserts

A fireplace insert is a specially designed woodstove intended for installation within the firebox of a masonry fireplace. An insert consists of a firebox surrounded by a convection shell through which air flows. This outer shell ensures that most of the heat is delivered to the room instead of being trapped behind the insert in the masonry structure. A faceplate

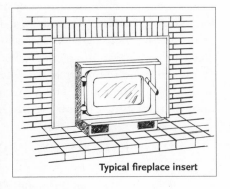

Typical fireplace insert

covers the space between the insert body and the fireplace opening.

Older inserts had a bad reputation for safety and efficiency because they simply allowed exhaust gases to exit the flue collar and find their way up the chimney. Now, installation codes require that a stainless steel chimney liner must be installed from the insert flue collar to the top of the chimney. Newer inserts are nearly as efficient as freestanding woodstoves. As always, verify that an insert has been tested and certified to Environmental Protection Agency (EPA) or CSA standards. If you already have an insert installed in a masonry fireplace, the addition of a stainless steel chimney liner can improve performance and safety.

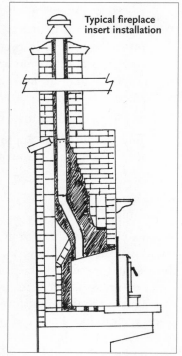

Typical fireplace insert installation

The installation of an insert is virtually permanent, and not a simple do-it-yourself job. The existing fireplace and chimney must be cleaned thoroughly, and the liner installation can be tricky. Make sure that all connections are secure, and that all materials are corrosion-resistant. Professionals know the potential trouble spots and how to avoid future problems.

Note that the hearth almost always needs to be extended to provide protection to the floor (at least 16 inches—20 cm—beyond the front of the appliance).

Hearthmounts

A hearthmount stove is an option to an insert for upgrading the performance of a fireplace. These are woodstoves that are mounted in front of, or inside, the fireplace and vented through the fireplace chimney/fireplace throat. Like an insert, they must also be vented through a full liner that is continous to the top of the chimney. Only certain woodstoves can be used as hearthmounts. The certification label and installation instructions indicate if the unit can be vented through the fireplace.

High-Efficiency, Factory-Built Fireplaces

High-efficiency, factory-built fireplaces—sometimes referred to as a "zero clearance" fireplaces—can be just as efficient for home heating as a good woodstove, and are certified as low-emission appliances. They use the same internal technologies as woodstoves, but heated air is delivered to the room a different way. Room air is drawn under the firebox, passed through a heat exchanger and returned to the room either through a wide grille at the top of the fireplace body or through ducts that can be routed to grilles above the fireplace or into other rooms beside or behind the fireplace. Many models also feature circulating fans.

These fireplace units can meet both aesthetic and heating objectives, but their installation is complicated. Because they are within and surrounded by combustible materials, great care must be taken during set-up. There are no general installation instructions for factory-built fireplaces; each one has its own distinct guidelines. The fireplace, heating ducts, chimney, and other components are safety tested as a unit. You can be assured of reliable performance only if you follow the manufacturer's instructions to the letter. Seriously consider hiring a trained pro.

During construction of our cottage, we thought about one of these models but, unfortunately, space and layout did not allow that option.

Three to remember:

1. Seek the advice of a qualified retailer/installer before installation or replacement of a wood-heating appliance; check for current specifications.

2. Have your installation (current or new) verified by your insurance agent.

3. Inspect and clean your wood-burning system regularly.

CHAPTER 8

Oil Lamps— Operation and Maintenance

AT THE LAKE, WE OFTEN DINE LATE, especially when it's just the two of us. On those wonderful, warm evenings in the summer, we always set the table in the screened-in porch; there we can feel the sultry breeze and hear the night sounds we love so much. Electric lights would only spoil the mood, so we invariably light a candle or two and the hurricane oil lamp that hangs close to the table. We all love candles, but there is something especially comforting in the glow of the light from an oil lamp (we have half a dozen). Besides, the relatively regular incidence of electrical power interruptus at the cottage makes ownership of alternative sources of lighting not only romantic, but practical as well. And the oil lamp is, quite simply, the logical candlepower option when the lights suddenly go out at the lake.

If you don't own one, then chances are you know many who do. Oil lamps of every description abound in cottage, camp, and cabin country, but generally include some variation of the flat wick, the Aladdin™, and even the round wick lamp.

The Light Output of Oil Lamps:		
A Comparison		
#1 flat wick lamp	=	4 – 7 foot (1.2 – 2.1 m) candles
#2 flat wick lamp	=	6 – 10 foot (1.8 – 3 m) candles
Rayo™	=	15 – 20 foot (4.6 – 6 m) candles
Aladdin™	=	48 – 50 foot (14 – 15 m) candles

Flat Wick Lamps and Burners

The flat wick oil lamp, fueled by kerosene or lamp oil, is the most common and the easiest to operate and maintain; however, it does not emit the best light (technically, the yellow flame is evidence of incomplete combustion). Flat wick lamp burners come in sizes, classified according to the burner collar.

The collar attaches to the lamp font or oil reservoir. Today, the most popular size is the No. 2 (a lamp with a No. 2 burner and one with a No. 1 burner are pictured below right). Operation is simple. Essentially, it is just a matter of filling the reservoir with oil, removing the chimney, raising the wick, and lighting (a new wick must soak awhile first). Light intensity is determined by the height of the wick; height can be adjusted by turning the wick raiser wheel. However, the wick should never be elevated above the deflector; this will produce smoke and a dirty chimney.

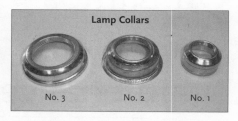

Lamp Collars

No. 3   No. 2   No. 1

Over time, a carbon residue will build up on the wick, and it will need to be trimmed; use a sharp pair of scissors and cut straight across (some purists nick the corners slightly). You will know you've got it right if the wick produces a nice, even flame with no tongues. At least once a season, you should also remove the burner assembly from the lamp and detach the deflector (see photo on facing page). Flies and other debris can build up under the deflector and restrict airflow to the wick, thus reducing the lamp's lighting efficiency.

Some soot build-up is unavoidable, so the chimney will require occasional cleaning too: when cold, wash in warm, soapy water and dry thoroughly before using the lamp. The burner assembly and font can also be cleaned by soaking in soapy water—in the ratio of 10 parts of water to 1 part detergent. My mother-in-law, who knows about flat wick lamps from experience, claims that newspaper is also an excellent cleaning agent for dirty chimneys.

Burner Assembly · Prongs · Deflector · Wick · Wick raiser wheel

To extinguish a flat wick lamp, lower the wick height, and blow into the chimney. You can also cup your hand above the chimney and blow into your hand; this deflects air down the chimney.

According to Stan Walker of Cottage Kitsch—a shop that specializes in oil lamps—you can use kerosene or lamp oil in any lamp (avoid scented and colored oils, as these can clog the wick). Stan

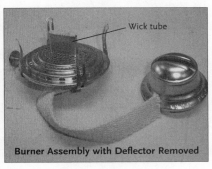

Wick tube

Burner Assembly with Deflector Removed

claims that paraffin-based lamp oils seem to be more stable, whereas kerosene will evaporate producing gummy varnish residues. The removal of these residues constitutes his number one repair intervention. He suggests that, if you use kerosene as a fuel source, you should empty your lamps and replace with fresh oil once a year (opening up would be a good time). Save the kerosene and clean your paintbrushes with it.

Stan also maintains that, generally, older lamp burners were better made; he easily substantiated this claim by demonstrating antique models in comparison to samples currently available in hardware stores. The quality of the older burners was unmistakably superior. He also noted that burner assemblies are available for $3 to $4 in a hardware or department store, while he stocks both the econo version and a better quality model that sells for about $15. His advice is to buy old lamps and burners in good condition.

Round Wick Lamps

Round wick, center draft lamps were very popular during the late 19th and early twentieth centuries (they were constructed on the principle of

Flame Spreader

supplying air to the flame through a center draft tube). They produced a much brighter light than the old flat wick lamps, though their fuel efficiency was considerably less. One of the most common models was the RAYO™, manufactured especially for the Standard Oil Company of New Jersey. Standard's motivation in marketing an oil lamp might have had something to do with selling kerosene.

These lamps, though they haven't been produced since the 1940s, are relatively common. The round wicks can still be purchased, but the critical flame spreader is more difficult to locate. Many round wick lamps were converted to electrical lights; consequently, the flame spreaders were often discarded.

Mantle Lamps

The mantle lamp was the last variation of the oil lamp to be developed before the widespread proliferation of the electric light bulb, and it marked an extraordinary leap in oil lamp technology. The Aladdin™ quickly became the leader in incandescent mantle lamps, and is the only lamp of its kind still in production today. It was popular in the U.S., Canada, Britain, Australia, and in many other countries around the world.

I am the proud owner of an Aladdin. It is a "Caboose" lamp, and it was used by railroad companies throughout North America. My Aladdin does indeed produce a bright light (about 60 candlepower), but it is a bit more technical to operate. The following illustrations have been selected from a manual for new Aladdin lamps to demonstrate the correct procedure for replacing a mantle, and proper lamp operation (obviously, if you buy a new Aladdin, then the complete booklet would be provided; only some illustrations have been used here). These operating instructions are *fundamentally* the same for every Aladdin ever made.

Figure 1

In Figure 1, the owner removes a new Lox-On® mantle assembly from the box. Extra care must be exercised when doing so, as the mantle is quite delicate and cannot be touched (the mantle fabric could fracture). Handle by the wire frame only.

Figure 2

In Figure 2, the mantle is fitted to the gallery; the gallery, the mantle, and the chimney form a complete unit. Again, handle the mantle by the wire frame only. Fit the mantle frame assembly (i.e. the bottom of the mantle) to the top of the gallery by turning to the right (clockwise) until locked.

A new mantle is coated with a special film to protect it. This coating must be burned off before the lamp can be used. Only the match **flame** can touch the top of the mantle and not the match itself (the match could damage the mantle fabric). The mantle coating burns off instantly. DO NOT BREATHE IN THE FUMES. Figure 3 illustrates this process.

Figure 3

Figure 4 illustrates the installation of the chimney onto the burner gallery. Newer Aladdins feature the heel-less chimney seen in this diagram. Adjust the gallery prongs to get a good *snug* fit (if particles of glass are scraped off during installation, or the chimney flops around like a dead rock bass, then you may not have it quite right!). Older Aladdins, like mine, are outfitted with the Lox-on® Chimney. These chimneys have glass cleats on the heel; the cleats mate with tabs on the gallery, and the chimney is locked to the gallery by turning it clockwise. The fit of this style of chimney can be improved by adjusting the gallery tabs. Be careful during assembly, as the cleats can be broken off rather easily.

Figure 4

With the gallery/mantle/chimney assembly removed, raise the wick about ⅛-inch (3 mm) above the outer wick tube and light (if the wick is new, allow it to soak in lamp fuel at least one hour before lighting). Allow the flame to form a complete ring. Carefully lower the gallery/mantle/chimney assembly onto the burner and lock it into place by turning clockwise (to the right), Figure 5.

Figure 5

Now comes the interesting part. You should raise the wick just enough so that the mantle begins to glow faintly. Allow the burner to warm up for about 10 minutes. As it does so, the mantle's glow will increase on its own (Figure 6). Now the wick can be raised, and the Aladdin will pour forth its uniquely bright light. There should be no black spots on the mantle (Figure 7). These are an indication that you are supplying too much fuel (i.e. the wick has been turned up too much). Turn the wick down, and the black spots will gradually dissipate. Stan made an interesting observation about this adjustment; he suggested that, once the lamp is warmed up, beginners should actually just over-fire the mantle to determine the maximum light output for their Aladdin. In this fashion, they will get a feel for the lamp's limitations and operating

Figure 6

idiosyncrasies. He added that you should keep an eye on it for the first 20 minutes or so, as it still may be too close to max; then, every half hour, glance at it to make certain that no black spots have appeared.

To extinguish the lamp, turn the wick down; all glow should be absent from the mantle. Cup your hand behind the top of the chimney, and gently blow across the top of the chimney. DO NOT BLOW DOWN INTO THE CHIMNEY, as this could damage the mantle (Figure 8).

Occasionally, the Aladdin wick will have to be trimmed because it develops a carbon "crust." A special wick trimmer is required for this job. The new ones are made of plastic, while the old ones were metal. The procedure is the same for both. Remove the flame spreader and place the trimmer over the wick tube; raise the wick until it engages with the trimmer's groove. Rotate the trimmer clockwise only to clean excess carbon buildup. Stan suggests that you should also trim any errant threads with small, sharp cuticle or embroidery-style scissors.

There are, as always, a number of safety tips included in the Aladdin manual, and I have incorporated the most noteworthy:

- ⚑ Use only good quality kerosene or good quality lamp oil, *never* gasoline.

- ⚑ Never leave the lamp unattended, or in the reach of children (that goes for any lamp or candle!).

- ⚑ Do not place the lamp under shelves or close to the ceiling *(must be 30 to 36 inches [75 to 90 cm] from the ceiling)*; Aladdins produce a great deal of heat, so should not be near combustible materials.

Figure 7

Figure 8

Wick trimmer

Finally, here's a reference guide for the most common oil lamps.

SIZES FOR READY REFERENCES

Burners	Required Collars	Chimney Base Sizes
No. 00 – Nutmeg or Acorn	fits 5/8" collar opening	1 1/8" chimneys
No. 0 – Horner	fits 7/8" collar opening	1 9/16" chimneys
No. 0 – Eagle	fits 7/8" collar opening	2 1/8" chimneys
No. 1 – Gem Arctic	fits 7/8" collar opening	1 5/8" chimneys
No. 1 – Burner	fits 7/8" collar opening	2 1/2" chimneys
No. 2 – Burner	fits 1 1/4" collar opening	3" chimneys
English Duplex Burner	fits 1 1/2" collar opening	2 1/2" chimneys
#14 Kosmos Burner	fits 1 1/2" collar opening	2" chimneys
No. 3 – Burner	fits 1 3/4" collar opening	3" chimneys
Aladdin-Type Burners	fits 2 1/8" collar opening	2 5/8" chimneys
Rayo Burner	fits 2 1/4" collar opening	2 5/8" chimneys
Central Draft Burner	fits 2 3/8" collar opening	2 5/8" chimneys

Three to remember:

1. Use only regular lamp oil or good quality kerosene.

2. Never leave an oil lamp unattended.

3. Practice regular lamp maintenance.

CHAPTER 9

Tools— You Gotta Have Them

AT THIS POINT IN MY LIFE, I have almost all of the tools I need. I say almost, because tool ownership is never a finite quest. Either you acquire some new gadget you never had but have always wanted (and new gadgets have a way of convincing you that you need them—even if it is only once a century), or you gradually replace the cheap stuff you could only afford when you were younger. And once you have collected enough tools, of course you have to store them somewhere. Like most folks, I can't afford a full collection for both home and cottage, so tools have to travel back and forth in something. Over the years I have tried using old toolboxes purchased at yard sales, plastic bins, and even fancy generic containers from the hardware store. They never really satisfied me. So, recently, I built a toolbox to house virtually every hand tool I own, or at least use regularly. Constructed simply out of ½-inch plywood, it isn't real pretty (in fact it's rather utilitarian, unlike some plans I have seen that transform toolboxes into works of cabinet-making art). But I took my time deciding what should go in it, and how it should be organized. During this process, I actually committed what could be considered an act of tool heresy: I threw some out! These were mostly duplicates, or even triplicates in some cases, so I know I can be forgiven. The layout required a seemingly inordinate amount of time to conclude, but I wanted to build this one to last awhile. I believe it will.

The plans that follow, and the tool inventory that accompanies the plans are in no way meant to cast aspersions on your particular toolbox or tool collection (I know how sensitive some people are about their tool stuff). I offer the plans as a possible solution to mobile hand-tool storage, and the inventory as my version of a suitable all-purpose collection for cottage and home. This is not meant to be the ultimate tool guide, as there could never be one list to cover every cottage.

Some of the tools I own did not make into the box. In a couple of cases, I decided that to include them would make the box size unmanageable: router, full-size circular saw, electric plane, etc. These travel up to the lake on opening day and travel back home on closing, as do the air compressor and chainsaw. When deciding not to include others, I did so knowing that I had one at home and one at the cottage: 2- and 4-foot levels, handsaws, planes, and squares for example.

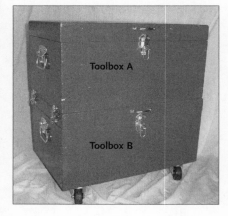

From the photograph, it is evident that I actually built two toolboxes. In the bottom box—we'll call it Toolbox B—I store larger, and/or not as frequently required items, while the upper one—Toolbox A—accommodates day-to-day gear. The two can be joined together with simple lockable draw catches but, in reality, this rarely happens. Both are also equipped with sturdy chest/trunk-style handles for ease of transportation and light hasps to secure the lids. Toolbox B has 2½ inch casters so the boxes can be rolled easily around the basement or workshop.

View of Inside of Toolbox A

View of Inside of Toolbox B

The actual construction job was relatively straightforward. I used G1S fir plywood and some scraps of ¾-inch maple from a previous project. The sides are simply nailed—1¼-inch finishing—and glued together (Figures 1 and 2 feature the layout for Toolbox A; the dimensions for B are the same—12 x 16 x 24 inches—but B does not have the built-in tool shelves). I did, however, rabbet the top and bottom panels to achieve greater frame rigidity, and added three-quarter round in the corners of Toolbox B for reinforcement (the shelving in A achieves the same result). Shelf A is secured to the main compartment in Toolbox A with three 1½ x 6-inch strips of ½-inch plywood (B1, 2, 3). They were nailed and glued to the shelf, and then I glued and screwed the strips to the box (#8 x ¾-inch screws). Parts C, D, E, F, H, and the brackets for the pop rivet gun and stapler were all fashioned out of ½-inch maple, and were glued and screwed to the box. I formed a simple bracket—I—out of 1⅜-inch slotted flat (general purpose metal strapping) to hang my 30-foot tape (see Figure 2). Pencils are stored in a 1- x 4-inch piece of ABS pipe—J—that I glued to the edges of D and E and to the bottom of the box (Figure 2). The hammer bracket—G—is designed to support the handle and is fashioned out of ½-inch plywood.

I have not provided an exact location for the tools listed in my inventory because differences in your collection and mine will require that you, too, invest some time in designing a custom layout. The photographs will give you a general idea of my arrangement.

In the lid of Box A, I located a pop rivet gun—how can you survive without one?—staple gun, simple drill index, safety glasses, flat file, and a set of precision screwdrivers. I had to consider the location of the other tools in the main compartment when positioning these so the lid would close without interference. I screwed the cases for the drill index and the precision drivers into the top, and secured them, the safety glasses, and the handle of the pop rivet gun with leather straps and dome fasteners

Figure 1

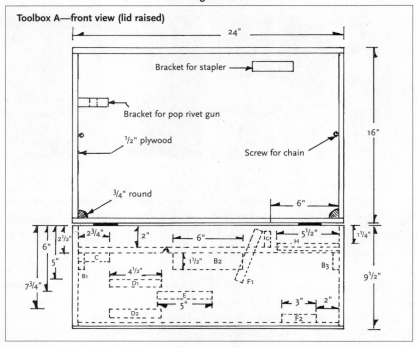

Toolbox A—front view (lid raised)

24"

Bracket for stapler

Bracket for pop rivet gun

Screw for chain

1/2" plywood

16"

6"

3/4" round

2 1/2"
6"
5"
7 3/4"

2 3/4"
2"
6"
5 1/2"

1 1/2"
B2
H

C
B1

4 1/2"
D1

E
5"

D2

F1

B3

F2

3"
2"

1 1/4"
9 1/2"

Figure 2

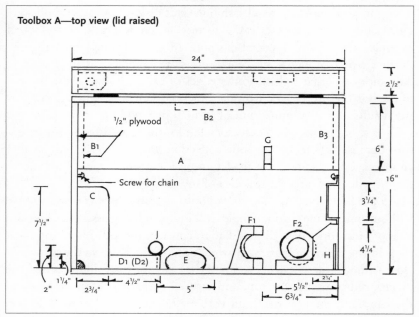

Toolbox A—top view (lid raised)

24"

1/2" plywood

B2

B1

G

B3

A

Screw for chain

C

I

7 1/2"

F1

F2

J

D1 (D2)

E

H

2"
1 1/4"
2 3/4"
4 1/2"
5"

5 1/2"
6 3/4"
2 1/4"

2 1/2"

6"

16"

3 1/4"

4 1/4"

(there was an old leather welding apron up at the lake). The barrel of the pop rivet gun nests in a hole in the bracket, while the stapler is held in place with a simple wooden turn-key (Figure 3). The flat file is located on the hinge-side of the lid; I bent a heavy-duty picture hanger into a flat U-shape and screwed it to the lid's back panel. The flat file is quite effectively wedged in place by this device.

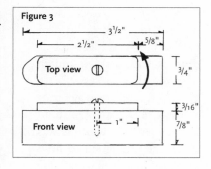

Figure 3

I managed to fit a lot of stuff into Shelf A.

The (+)s obviously represent my Tool Rating System. If I were buying my first tool collection, then those rated with four (+)s would definitely make it into the box.

- 4 Robertson screwdrivers (yellow, green, red and black) ++++
- 2 slotted screwdrivers (1 small, 1 medium) ++++
- Phillips screwdriver ++++
- Scratch awl ++++
- 2 nail sets (small and medium) +++
- 1 dry wall drill adapter ++
- Chalk line ++++
- Hammer (note the bracket—G—Figure 4) ++++
- Wire stripper ++++
- Round Surform tool +++
- 4 Marples chisels—¼", ½", ¾", 1" ++++
- Chainsaw tool (the one supplied with the chainsaw) ++++
- Putty knife ++++
- Aviation snips (straight, left, right) +++
- Adjustable auger bit ++
- Vise grips ++++
- Crescent (adjustable) wrench ++++
- Regular pliers ++++
- Needle-nose pliers ++++
- Utility knife ++++
- Drill bit extender ++
- Side cutters ++++

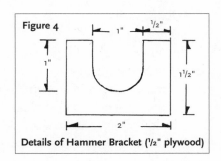

Figure 4

Details of Hammer Bracket (½" plywood)

I located a small block plane and pocket Surform tool in shelf C, as well as calipers and a small punch (the punch also serves as a hanger for my hearing protectors). D1 and D2 hold four auger bits, while E was specifically designed to hold a 300 mL bottle of wood glue (a piece of pipe strap would

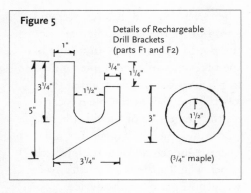

Figure 5

Details of Rechargeable Drill Brackets (parts F1 and F2)

(3/4" maple)

probably work as well). F1 and F2 are brackets made to hold my 14-volt rechargeable drill (Figure 5). A try square (note the slot for the blade, Figure 2), countersinks, and driver bits are all located in H. As mentioned earlier, my tape is stored on a bracket—I—while my pencils are easy to find in the ABS tube—J. Finally, a sliding bevel hangs from the screw used to secure the chain for the lid (near C, Figure 2).

Despite my best efforts to organize absolutely everything, more stuff than I wanted—but need—still ended up in the bottom of the box:

- Contact cement +++
- Extra blades for the utility knife ++++
- Twine +++
- Chainsaw file (I suppose I can still design a spot for it on the lid!) ++
- Rasp (ditto) ++
- Cheap set of Forstner-style bits in a wooden case +++
- Staples (¼" and ⅜") ++++
- Pruning shears ++
- Teflon and electrical tape ++++
- Assorted pop rivets in a plastic film cartridge ++++
- Sandpaper ++++
- Extra chalk ++++
- Wood putty ++
- Couple of rolls of light wire ++
- Assorted cable ties +++
- Assorted screws in a plastic container +++
- Assorted small wooden plugs ++
- An old roofing knife, a couple of hex keys and some other stuff +
- Hearing protectors ++++
- Stair gauge clamps ++
- Receptacle/circuit tester ++++

In the lid of Box B, I positioned a big 16-inch slotted screwdriver (it slides into a piece of ABS pipe screwed to the lid), metric and SAE hex sets (just essential sizes), and a hack saw (two small maple blocks were glued to the hinge side; two slots in the blocks hold the blade, while the handle is held in place with a good old leather strap and dome fastener).

In the main compartment, the following:

- Sabre / jig saw ++++
- Rechargeable 14-volt circular saw +++
- Rotary tool set ++
- Orbital sander and grinder ++
- Caulking gun ++++
- Multimeter ++++
- 2 "Boa Constrictors" (specialty tools for turning) ++
- Knee pads +
- Assorted clamps ++++
- Heavy-duty extension cord ++

When I decided to include this chapter, I also thought that it might be worthwhile to catalog the rest of my tool collection, including the stuff in the shed at the lake. As I reviewed the list—and it seems a long one—I could easily defend the purchase of each and every item (naturally, tool junkies like me can rationalize such things). Some get regular use, but all have been called on at one time or another to complete some cottage project (there is nothing more frustrating than the realization that if only you had had a "_____," you could have been finished this job 2 hours ago).

- Framing square ++++
- Pipe wrench ++++
- Crowbars ++++
- Rubber mallet ++
- Socket set (metric and SAE) ++++
- Wire brush ++
- Handsaws +++
- Propane torch ++++
- Electric spray painter (okay, so I bought it to paint the porch!) +
- Wet stone +++
- Router ++++
- Circular saw ++++
- Electric plane (it was given to me!) +

- ⚑ 2' and 4' levels ++++
- ⚑ Come-along +++
- ⚑ House jacks (you can always rent 'em) +
- ⚑ Saw horses +++
- ⚑ Bench grinder +++
- ⚑ Table saw ++
- ⚑ Radial arm saw ++++
- ⚑ Drill press +++
- ⚑ Air compressor ++++
- ⚑ Chainsaw ++++
- ⚑ Shop vac ++++
- ⚑ Straight-edge tool guide (used mostly with circular saw) ++
- ⚑ Tube cutter (indispensable for cutting copper pipe) ++++

Finally, there is the collection of garden, yard, and excavation tools just inside the shed door:

- ⚑ Rakes ++++
- ⚑ Shovels ++++
- ⚑ Hoe +++
- ⚑ Axes ++++
- ⚑ Splitting maul ++++
- ⚑ Sledgehammer ++++
- ⚑ Pry bar +++

In the big tools league, it's nice to have a table saw but I'm not sure, given the choice now, that I would buy one. A radial arm saw, on the other hand is definitely a wise big tool investment. In fact, when we built the cottage, I increased the mortgage enough to include a top-quality model (as well as a bunch of other neat toys… I mean, tools). The radial arm saw is much more versatile than the table saw, if perhaps not so precise; it can rip, cross-cut, and make miter and compound cuts. It remains up at the lake, getting regular use, while the table saw, at home, gets no use whatsoever.

Only recently did I finally acquire a compressor, and now I don't know what I ever did without one. I can't imagine not having a chainsaw, but it is perhaps the most lethal tool of all to own. I would never do without good-quality hand-power tools, and in the near future I intend to replace a standard-duty sabre/jig saw (if you've ever tried to cut 1½-inch stock with a regular sabre/jig saw, you will appreciate how poorly they perform) and my aging router. And for some time now, I've wanted a compound-miter saw. I aim to get one. Oh, and I'd really like a biscuit joiner, a belt/disc sander combo, and I've got a line on a full-size planer and a jointer. Just noticed a little accessory in a recent flyer: the Mitey Moe Angle Finder—might like that, too! Then, will I be happy? Yes, until something breaks, or I find another irresistible accessory, or the price is too hard to resist, or....

Three to remember:

1. Buy the best; buy once.

2. Wear eye and hearing protection.

3. Read the manual.

CHAPTER 10

Using a Water Level

OCCASIONALLY, AN ORDINARY LEVEL ISN'T LONG ENOUGH, even if you extend its reach by placing it on the edge of a board. Or, it isn't convenient to use a conventional level because of the situation (such as straightening and leveling piers under the cottage or tool shed). In these circumstances, a water level is a handy alternative. It is a simple device: a length of hose filled with water. The physics principle is beyond me to explain but, essentially, the water in the hose will stay level, providing the user with a reliable leveling tool (see diagram below).

We keep a length of clear plastic hose in our cottage workshop especially for those times when a level can't be used.

Step 1: Fill the hose with water, making sure that there are absolutely no bubbles. This is one benefit of the length of clear plastic pipe—you can easily determine whether or not there are any. You will need about 10–12 inches (25–30 cm) of free space at either end of the water level, so pour out a suitable amount of water (simply lower one end of the hose, and water will start to dribble out).

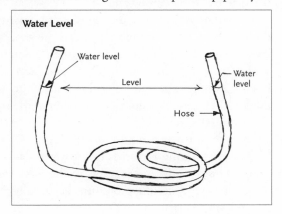

Water Level

Water level

Water level

Level

Hose →

Step 2: Hold both ends of the hose together, as in Figure 1. Obviously, you will have some initial reference mark to work from. Here we simply drew a line on a post. Move the hose ends up or down—in tandem—until the water level in both is on the mark.

Step 3: At the reference mark, draw a line across both hoses as in Figure 2.

Step 4: Secure one end of the hose to the project (for demonstration purposes, we'll call it hose B). It must not move up or down. Here we used a staple, see Figure 3, but duct tape, electrical tape, or some other contrivance would work. The end cannot be completely pinched off.

Step 5: Move the other end of the hose—A—to the location you wish to level with the original reference point (in Figure 4, we chose another post). It is important to remember that no water can be spilled

> **An ordinary garden hose will do;**
> you only need to purchase a male and a female hose fitting, and about 6 feet of clear plastic pipe big enough to be installed over the fittings.
> Cut the 6-foot length in half, and secure a 3-foot piece to each fitting. Screw the extensions to each end of the hose you'll need for the job, and you're in the water level business.

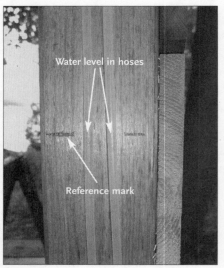

Water level in hoses

Reference mark

Figure 1

from the end of the hose during transit (consequently, you have to hold the hose end at a reasonably constant height; keep an eye on the water level as you move). If this happens, then you must go back and start over at the initial reference mark. Once you reach the location you want to level, move the hose end up or down until the water level aligns with the mark on the hose. When they are aligned, then you can make a mark on the object(s) you are leveling.

Any number of positions can be leveled in this manner; hose length is the only limiting factor. If it is a warm day, every once in awhile you should compare the water levels in the hose with the original reference mark during the leveling procedure; expansion could create an error factor that must be corrected.

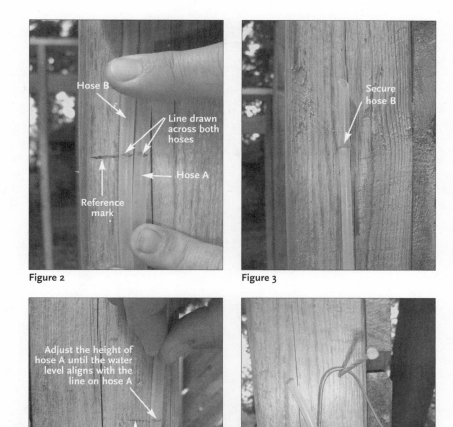

Figure 2

Figure 3

Figure 4

Figure 5

Finally, when you're working with a water level, you'll want to hang up the unsecured end of the hose. We simply tape a piece of wire to that end, bend it and hang it over a nail (Figure 5).

Three to remember:

1. Don't spill any water from the hose when moving from location to location.

2. Check the reference levels in the hose on hot days, and correct for possible expansion.

3. Don't pinch off the end of the stationary hose.

CHAPTER 11

The Deck

THE DECK IS OFTEN THE ENTERTAINMENT CENTER at the cottage. It's a great place to eat and drink (so what if something gets spilled!) and it generally accommodates a bigger crowd. Besides, it's outside, and where would we rather be on a beautiful day (unless the bugs are bad)?

A normal deck is a reasonably straightforward project, within the skill-set of the average cottager. However, before you give a deck even a modicum of consideration, you should consult your municipality's building/planning department and familiarize yourself with the requirements that you will have to meet. In all Ontario jurisdictions, the Ontario Building Code dictates that every structure over 108 square feet (9 square meters) will require a permit and must comply with the standards in the OBC (obviously, other provinces/states will have similar documents). Moreover, your municipality will likely have its own unique restrictions/conditions and your deck will have to conform to these as well. And remember, regulations change, so don't consider the guidelines outlined here—or in any text—as fixed in stone; check for the current standards.

Once you understand the local and provincial/state conventions, you can develop a design: this can be an original concept, or one gleaned from books, magazines, or other deck builders. Consider how your deck will be used, and its location: How big should it really be? Do you entertain a lot? Do you like sun or shade or a combination of both? Do you want a great view of the lake or is privacy more important? What are you going to do about that big pine tree or other natural obstructions? Does your planned deck meet construction and set-back standards? Will you opt for a conventional railing or tempered glass panels? Some suggest that a deck should act as a transition between cottage and surrounding landscape, and should therefore stay close to the ground. If this is not possible or practical, then perhaps you can screen the less-than-appealing underside—the view as you walk up from the lake—with lattice or cedar shrubs. A deck with more than one level is also very attractive, and may allow you to make the transition from terra firma to cottage level in a pleasing fashion (of course, that will complicate construction). Take some time at this stage. You'll have to live with your planned deck for 20 years or more.

A detailed plan must be submitted to the local building department and some municipalities require quite elaborate diagrams, perhaps including a lot plan. But a building official can be a real asset at this stage as he/she will be able to help you correct any structural or technical inconsistencies in your design.

You will need to choose which material you will use for construction. One of my wife's cousins built his deck out of maple (yes, it did make me wonder), but most deck builders will opt for one of three possibilities. Pressure-treated (PT) lumber—spruce-pine-fir—is the most common and the least expensive choice for decks and is used for the construction of most outdoor structures. However, it ain't pretty, and there have been health concerns (whether these are justified or not remains a topic of debate). Cedar is, of course, the best wood choice if you can afford it—cedar will set you back roughly twice as much as PT (if you must have cedar, you could cut costs by building the sub-structure—posts, beams, ledger boards, joists, etc—out of PT). Composite materials—a combination of wood and polymers—are making inroads but still constitute only a fraction of the decks built. They are relatively attractive, wear well, require little maintenance, and are a commendable environmental choice. However, they are even more expensive than cedar and cannot be used for structural components. In doing research for this chapter, I also learned of a composite available for cladding the surface(s) of tired, old PT decks (it can be difficult to find).

Design finalized, plan submitted and approved! Where should construction start?

Project Toolbox
- Wheelbarrow
- Shovel
- Pry bar
- Hoe
- Rake
- Hammer
- 3/8" drill and bits
- 4' level
- Circular saw
- Square
- String
- Socket set or adjustable wrench
- Safety glasses
- Clamps
- Crowbar
- Jig saw

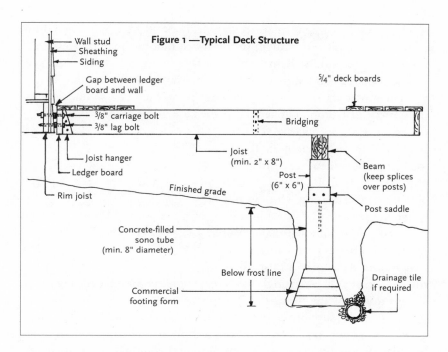

Figure 1 —Typical Deck Structure

Wall stud
Sheathing
Siding
Gap between ledger board and wall
$^3/_8$" carriage bolt
$^3/_8$" lag bolt
Joist hanger
Ledger board
Rim joist
Finished grade
Joist (min. 2" x 8")
Bridging
Post (6" x 6")
Beam (keep splices over posts)
Post saddle
$^5/_4$" deck boards
Concrete-filled sono tube (min. 8" diameter)
Below frost line
Commercial footing form
Drainage tile if required

Obviously, opinions will vary, but since most decks are attached to the cottage and the ledger board is the structural component that enables this, I think that it is the logical choice for a starting point (see diagram Figure 1—Typical Deck Structure).

You will need a level line along the cottage wall as a reference; some accommodation with true level may be required if you have horizontal siding and the wall no longer runs perfectly true. A good 4-foot level on the straightest piece of lumber will generally do, though a water level (see previous chapter) or a laser level is more accurate.

Attach the ledger board with lag bolts or carriage bolts—minimum $^3/_8$-inch in diameter—making sure to tie into a major structure such as the cottage rim joist. To minimize moisture damage, leave a $^3/_8$-inch to $^1/_2$-inch gap between the cottage wall and the ledger board—galvanized washers make good spacers—or cap the ledger.

Consult your plan to locate the piers that will support the main beam(s). In Ontario, an attached deck must have proper piers that extend below the frost line or sit on bedrock (you can sit your project on deck blocks if the deck is not attached to the cottage). The easiest way to create a pier is by using sono tubes with a diameter of 8 inches or greater. There are also a number of products that can be attached to the base of the sono tube to make an integrated pier/footing. Locate hole, dig, connect sono tube and footing form, place in hole, back fill while keeping plumb, trim to length, fill with cement (ready-mix is best for small projects), and install the post saddle. Remember to orient the post saddle so the post can be adjusted—as required—toward or away from the ledger board. If you encounter water when digging your piers, then you should seriously consider installing drainage tile at the base of footings.

Deck posts are usually 6" x 6"; they look more substantial. If you are using PT, remember to treat cut ends—as with all PT—with a suitable protective coating. Deck beams generally consist of 2" x 8" lumber or greater in a 3-ply laminate. Nail in from both sides, and make sure that splices occur over a post (drive

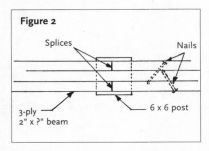

Figure 2

Splices

Nails

3-ply
2" x ?" beam

6 x 6 post

the nails in at a bit of an angle to increase holding power—see Figure 2). Keep the top of the beam flat. Temporarily secure the beam(s) to the posts (the main support beam(s) can be attached to the deck posts with galvanized commercial connectors or simply toenailed). Once the two outside joists are in place, square everything up, and secure permanently (for large projects such as a deck, to square it up remember the 3–4–5 or 6–8–10 rule: if one side of a right-angled triangle measures 3 feet and the other side 4, then the hypotenuse must measure 5; likewise for 6, 8, and 10).

In Ontario, deck joists must be 2" x 8" or greater. Joist hangers are used to attach the joists to the ledger board—every hole in the hanger must be used: 1½-inch deck screws or joist-hanger nails. Joist spacing cannot exceed 24 inches on center. If you install bridging between the joists—a good idea—then try to locate under a deck board (it should be easy to approximate the deck board layout to achieve this arrangement).

Decks are surfaced with 2" x 6" or 1¼-inch rounded-edge boards— a full 1 inch thick. This was the material I selected for my deck, and even at 2 feet on center, there is no springiness. Decking can be nailed or screwed to the joists. A ¼-inch gap between the boards is suggested. Check the distance from the leading edge of every fourth or fifth deck board to the

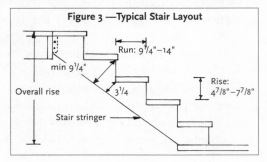

Figure 3 —Typical Stair Layout

Run: 9¼"–14"

min 9¼"

Overall rise

3¼

Rise:
4⅞"–7⅞"

Stair stringer

ends of the joists to determine whether or not you will have to adjust the gap; you will want the final board to come out even. Warped deck boards can be a real problem; special tools are available for aligning twisted ones, or you can use a simple bar clamp.

Stairs can be the most challenging aspect of deck construction, and ready-made stringers are available at construction centers if you don't think you're up to the task. If you are intent on building your own, Ontario Building Code dictums are illustrated in Figure 3. A good rule of thumb: rise + run = 18 inches. If stair height exceeds 24 inches then a guardrail must be installed.

Railings (or guardrails) are also mandatory on any deck 2 feet above finished grade (see insert: Railing specs). The guardrail must be non-climbable, and the vertical components cannot be spaced more than 4 inches apart. Unfortunately, a properly constructed guardrail often interferes with the view. Approved tempered glass panels are available; they eliminate the need for spindles and provide a much better view of the water (however, they're not cheap). While decking can be nailed or screwed, vertical details must be screwed or bolted, though I trust only in carriage bolts for key verticals. Avoid adding permanent deck seating; it may not meet code and it creates a static seating arrangement. In my opinion, mobile deck chairs and benches work much better.

> **Railing specs:**
> a) Deck 2'–5'11" above finished grade—railing must be not less than 2'11" in height
> b) Deck higher than 5'11" above finished grade—railing must be not less than 3'6" in height

The final consideration is finish. Frankly, I'm of the "less is best" school of deck finishes. There is, however, no denying that you may want to improve on PT green; the pros suggest that semi-transparent oil-based stains are still the best bet on either PT or cedar and that you should, generally, avoid solid finishes. I used this type of product on our deck; looks great and wears well, though it needs refreshing every 4 to 5 years.

Three to remember:

1. Check with your municipality about code requirements.

2. Consider your deck needs before you design.

3. Remember the builder's motto: plumb, level, and square.

CHAPTER 12

The Dock

A DOCK IS NOT AN ABSOLUTELY ESSENTIAL COTTAGE STRUCTURE, and there are cottage families that do without. However, a dock is more or less necessary for mooring most boats and makes swimming a safer, more enjoyable recreational experience since climbing up a dock ladder is generally easier than clambering over rocks or wading through loon poop and weeds.

I've always maintained that docks should be utilitarian. Those big, fancy, varnished structures have always struck me as a waste of money and an intrusive blot on the shoreline viewscape. Keep it simple, keep it only as big as necessary, and let Mother Nature take care of the finish. In the opinion of many, cedar is the only choice for the lumber to build any dock. Pressure-treated wood is often selected, mainly because it is less expensive, but there is growing debate about its suitability for use in lakes and rivers.

Flotation billets are one of the most common flotation systems used in dock construction, and for good reason. They are easy to handle and install, extremely buoyant, and quite durable (they won't waterlog or corrode, and they resist the attack of marine growths). We used these for our dock and since the day it was launched, over ten years ago, it has floated true. In this chapter, plans are detailed for an 8- x 10-foot dock section (see the illustrations that follow); different sizes will obviously require some modification.

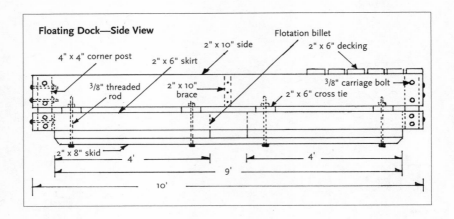

Floating Dock—Side View

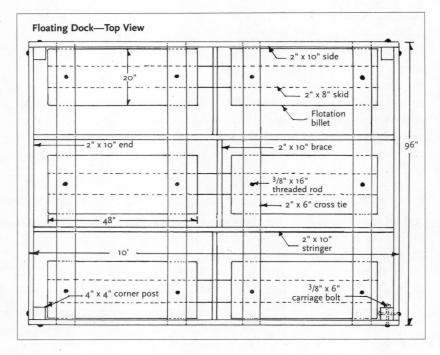

Floating Dock—Top View

Step 1: Cut the two 2- x 10-inch dock frame sides and ends to length: 120 inches and 93 inches respectively. Cut the four 4- x 4-inch corner posts to length—16 ½ inches. Bolt the sides and ends to the posts using ⅜ x 6-inch galvanized carriage bolts (4 per side, 4 per end); see both Side and Top Views.

Step 2: Cut the two 2- x 10-inch stringers to length—117 inches. Position about 32 inches in from the sides—as in diagram, Top View—

and secure to the ends of the dock frame (#8 x 3-inch deck screws or 3½-inch galvanized spiral nails). Cut the 2- x 10-inch braces to length; install with deck screws or nails (note that the middle brace is offset to permit easier installation).

Step 3: Cut the four 2- x 6-inch cross ties to length—96 inches. Check the dock frame for square (the length of the diagonals should be the same), and screw or nail the cross ties to the bottom edge of the 2- x 10-inch sides and stringers (layout the cross ties according to the position of the flotation billets—Top View).

Step 4: Cut the 2- x 6-inch dock frame skirting to length (the skirting protects the billets. Bolt the side skirts to the 4 x 4 posts (the side skirts sit on the cross ties). Bolt the end skirts to the posts (2 per end, 4 per side—⅜- x 6-inch carriage bolts).

Step 5: Cut the 8-foot flotation billets in half and lay the six pieces on top of the cross ties (as in Top View—remember that at this stage you are working with the dock upside down so, yes, the diagram is correct). Cut the three 2- x 8-inch skids to length—81 inches; taper the ends (i.e. trim to 45 degrees). Position them on top of the billets. Bore ⅜-inch holes through the skids, billets, and cross ties (temporarily secure the billets and skids to the cross ties with bar clamps or strapping to maintain accuracy). Since the holes measure over 13 inches deep, you will need a bit extension to drill all the way through. Secure the skids to the cross ties with ⅜-inch galvanized threaded rod cut to length (about 16 inches). Basically, the billets are sandwiched between the skids and cross ties so apply enough torque to do the job, but you don't have to crush the billets. The rod should be flush with the head of the nut on the skid side of the assembly. Sure as heck, some day, some kid is going to swim under that dock, and contact with the end of a bolt could mean a trip into town for medical intervention. And you know how much you love a trip into town! File the ends carefully to eliminate any sharp edges.

Step 6: Get some help. Flip the dock over onto the skids (carefully now!). Check the frame once again for square, though at this point addressing any major deviation will be a bit of a challenge.

Step 7: Cut the deck boards to length—96 inches—and nail or screw to the top of the sides, ends, stringers, and braces. Use a scrap piece of ½-inch plywood as a spacer. Check the distance from the ends of every third or fourth deck board to the end of the dock to make sure you are proceeding evenly; adjust the gap—slightly—if necessary.

Step 8: Get some help again. Lift, slide, carry, push the dock into the lake; the skids also protect the billets during this maneuver (naturally, if you built the dock some distance from the water—i.e. in your driveway at home—you will have considered some means of transporting the dock to its destination). Secure the dock to the shore in a manner appropriate to your circumstances.

In the photos that follow, I have provided the system we adopted for our dock, and it works very well but it won't be suitable everywhere.

In all likelihood, you will need to build some kind of ramp to get from the shore to the dock. The photos also depict our ramp and the manner in which we secured it to the dock.

Attach a ladder, and get the heck out of the way. The kids will be running by any minute now, and you're sure to get wet from that very first cannonball.

Materials List for an 8- x 10-Foot Dock Section

Part Name	Dimensions	Quantity Req.
Sides	2" x 10" x 10'	2
Ends	2" x 10" x 93"	2
Stringers	2" x 10" x 117"	2
Deck Brace	2" x 10" x 30"	3
Side Skirts	2" x 6" x 10'	2
End Skirts	2" x 6" x 93"	2
Cross Ties	2" x 6" x 8'	4
Decking	2" x 6" x 8'	20 (+ / -)
Skids	2" x 8" x 9'	3
Corner Posts	4" x 4" x 16 ½"	4
Carriage Bolts c/w Nuts and Washers	⅜" x 6"	28
Threaded Rod c/w Nuts and Washers	⅜" x 16"	12 (24 nuts)
Nails	3 ½" Galvanized Ardox	3 lbs.
Or		
Screws	#8 x 3" Deck type	200 (+ / -)
Flotation Billets	10" x 20" x 8'	3

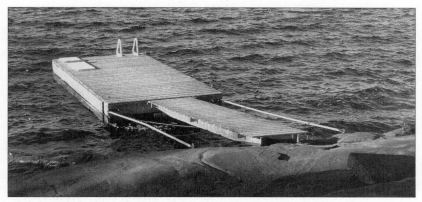

Figure 1

Figure 2

Figure 3

In Figure 1, note that the dock is anchored to the rock, and that racking is prevented by cables secured to the arms in an X pattern. In Figure 2, you can see that a hole was drilled into the rock, and an eyebolt was fitted into the hole (epoxy was used to hold it); a bolt was welded at 90 degrees to the end of the arm. In this fashion, the arm can be secured to the eyebolt.

In Figure 3, the cables are secured to the arms. Half pieces of chain link were welded to the arms, and cable was threaded through the links and then crimped with cable clamps.

In Figure 4, the arms have been attached to the dock: a clevis was welded to the other end of the arm and bolted to a bracket on the end of the dock. In Figure 5 the ramp is attached to the dock by means of four eyebolts: two are bolted into the end of the dock, and two are bolted into the end of the ramp (we mounted 4- x 4-inch blocks in the ends of the dock and the ramp to accept the eyebolts). The pipe can't slide out because it is held in place by a pin at one end and the other end is flared.

Figure 4

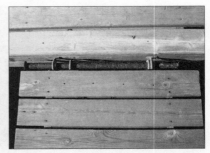

Figure 5

Three to remember:

1. Check with your municipality and/or the coast guard before you build.

2. Consider your needs; design accordingly.

3. Think of the lake; choose cedar.

Website of the Canadian Coast Guard:
<www.ccg-gcc.gc.ca/cen-arc/nwp-pen/index_e.htm>

This site will provide you with the Application Guide that is necessary for all structures to be located in navigable waters.

CHAPTER 13

The Woodshed

THE WOODSHED FEATURED IN THE PHOTOGRAPH (see next page) is a simple structure to build. It will hold almost two bush cords—more than enough for the spring and autumn and several winter weekends at the lake.

Step 1: See Figure 1. Use pressure-treated 2- x 6-inch lumber for the floor frame (remember to treat the ends of any cut pieces). I screwed the outside joists to the joist headers (#12 x 3½ inch screws), and then fastened the rest with joist hangers for greater load-bearing capability. The floor deck proper is full 1- x 6-inch pressure treated (sometimes referred to as ⁵⁄₄). I set the frame on four deck blocks, but patio slabs would do as a foundation.

Step 2: See Figure 2. Obviously, two side walls will need to be assembled. The outside of each was clad in ½-inch spruce plywood, and stained (other sidings could be used). Note that the plywood extends 1½ inches beyond the back edge—to cover the rear wall end studs, and 3 to 4 inches below the bottom plate—to secure the side walls to the outside floor joists. I am a big believer in the holding power of screws, so the frame is screwed together, and the sheathing is screwed to the frame. The 18- x 36-inch space in the wall plan accommodates a vent frame (Figure 6). Note: all wall framing materials (side and end walls) are 2 x 2-inch unless otherwise noted in diagrams.

Step 3: See Figure 3. I trust that the diagram is fairly straightforward. Once again, the outside was covered in ½-inch plywood, and the frame

was screwed together. The sheathing extends 3–4 inches below the bottom plate to secure the rear wall sheathing to the rear joist header.

Step 4: Once it has been built, stand the rear wall on the floor, and screw or nail the sheathing to the face of the rear joist header; screw or nail the bottom plate to the floor. You might want to use temporary bracing to hold the rear wall in place, but it should stand unaided (though it won't withstand gale-force winds!).

Step 5: Stand the side walls up, screw or nail the sheathing to the outside floor joists, and screw or nail the bottom plate to the floor. Screw or nail the back wall to the side walls; the side wall end studs butt up against the rear wall end studs, so secure through same. Nail the side wall sheathing to the rear wall end studs (this is the 1½-inch strip referred to in Figure 2 and Step 2).

Step 6: See Figure 4. Screw or nail a 2- x 6- x 72-inch header into the notches in the side walls (those depicted in Figure 2). Screw or nail two 2- x 4-inch braces to the header and to the side walls.

As you will note in the photo, I covered the braces with artfully sculpted 1- x 6-pine for a more aesthetically pleasing effect.

Step 7: See Figure 5. This diagram illustrates the layout for the rafters. The 92-inch length is a more-or-less measurement. Adept do-it-yourselfers could cut bird's-mouths in the rafters, but simply toenailing them to the front header and the top plate of the rear wall will suffice. The fascia, front and back, is 2 x 4 x 84 inches (again, note the 1- x 6-pine trim on the front). Nail 1- x 3-inch strapping to the rafters, and cover with steel or fiberglass roofing.

Step 8: See Figure 6. To guarantee maximum ventilation, install vent louver assemblies in the openings in the rear and side walls. The frames and louvers (eight of them) are made from inexpensive 1- x 3-inch spruce strapping. Nail an extra ½-inch piece to the bottom louver to act as a drip edge. Mount the assemblies flush to the insides of the walls. As you will note in the photo, each assembly was framed on the outside with 1- x 3-inch as well.

To keep the snow out in the winter, add a 6- x 8-foot tarp to the front (see photo). Use screws and wide washers to secure the tarp to the header, and screw a 2- x 4-inch board to the bottom to weight it down (I fashioned a couple of brackets for the two-by-four to sit in when the tarp is unfurled).

Roll it up, and screw the two-by-four to the side walls in good weather.

Plant some cedars around the sides and back, and the woodshed will blend in much better with its surroundings.

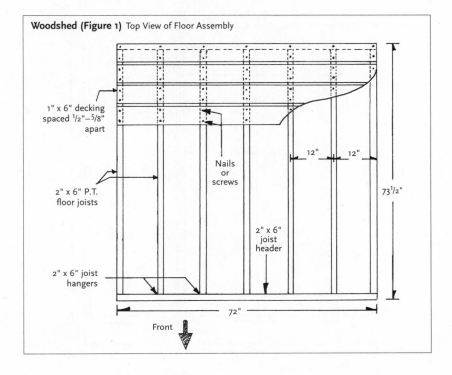

Woodshed (Figure 1) Top View of Floor Assembly

1" x 6" decking spaced ½"–⅝" apart

2" x 6" P.T. floor joists

2" x 6" joist hangers

Nails or screws

12" 12"

73½"

2" x 6" joist header

72"

Front

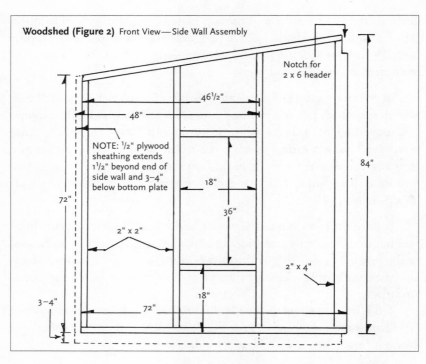

Woodshed (Figure 2) Front View—Side Wall Assembly

Notch for
2 x 6 header

46½"

48"

84"

NOTE: ½" plywood
sheathing extends
1½" beyond end of
side wall and 3–4"
below bottom plate

18"

36"

72"

2" x 2"

2" x 4"

18"

3–4"

72"

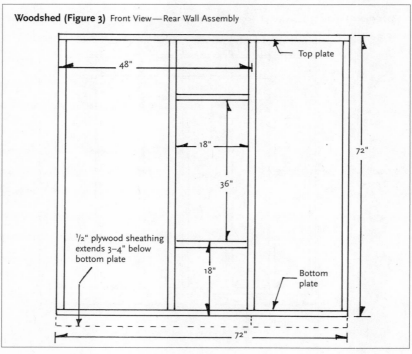

Woodshed (Figure 3) Front View—Rear Wall Assembly

48"

Top plate

18"

72"

36"

½" plywood sheathing
extends 3–4" below
bottom plate

18"

Bottom
plate

72"

Woodshed (Figure 4)
Front View—Side and Rear Wall Assembly featuring front header and braces

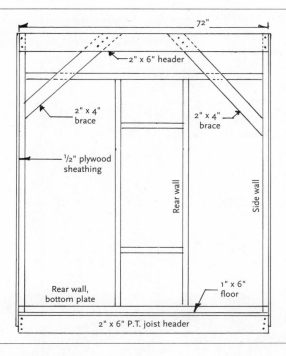

72"

2" x 6" header

2" x 4" brace

2" x 4" brace

1/2" plywood sheathing

Rear wall

Side wall

Rear wall, bottom plate

1" x 6" floor

2" x 6" P.T. joist header

Woodshed (Figure 5)
Top View— Rafter and Strapping Assembly

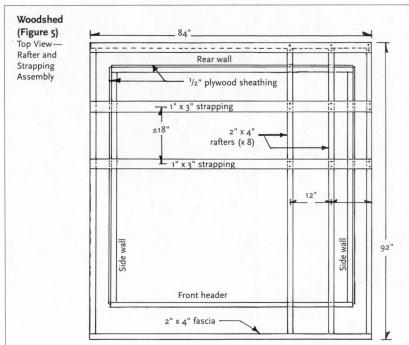

84"

Rear wall

1/2" plywood sheathing

1" x 3" strapping

±18"

2" x 4" rafters (x 8)

1" x 3" strapping

12"

Side wall

Side wall

92"

Front header

2" x 4" fascia

The photograph on this page is another version of the woodshed. Note that the diagonal boards are spaced about ¾ inch apart to allow air to flow through the structure. The fiberglass roof provides better light, and heat to speed drying.

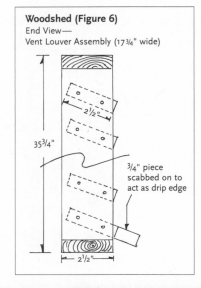

Woodshed (Figure 6)
End View—
Vent Louver Assembly (17¾" wide)

35¾"

2½"

2½"

¾" piece scabbed on to act as drip edge

CHAPTER 14

The Outhouse

WHEN WE BUILT THE OUTHOUSE at my in-laws' cottage, it was strictly a utilitarian structure, erected mostly for the menfolk and for winter weekends. In Morley's opinion, there was no need for the able-bodied males of the clan to be performing bodily functions indoors, and winter weekends were relatively few. As a result, no great care was taken in its construction. It was pretty much a slap-dash affair, and the only redeeming feature was the clear fiberglass roof we installed; it made for a rather bright environment in which to contemplate the mysteries of the universe as one engaged in more earthly business.

Remarkably, despite the growing preference for indoor plumbing and modern conveniences, many cottagers on our lake still maintain outdoor johns. For some, the outhouse is the only system, but for most it is a back-up resource. Privies often have a less-than-favorable reputation, despite their commonality. But a well-designed, well-built, and well-maintained outhouse—like the one in this chapter—can be a pleasure to visit. Besides being a sound choice environmentally as an alternative to or support for a standard septic system, a properly constructed privy won't have the problems of odor and creepy-crawlies that we often find in sub-standard editions.

While the venerable outhouse is most often a simple affair, the one in this chapter is a rather deluxe version: solid, comfortable, and classy enough for anyone (even fastidious guests). It's a privy that outhouse-goers (and with luck, outhouse converts) will actually enjoy visiting. The plans are somewhat elaborate, and it wasn't cheap (about a thousand bucks at the time of construction—1999). If you don't want to build an exact replica, the basic design can serve as inspiration for your own customized version. But I think the extra money required to build a biffy *par excellence* is worthwhile when you consider the time you'll spend there.

During the construction of this model, I took a few liberties with accepted building practices for the sake of convenience and common sense (e.g. not all studs are centered exactly on 16 inches). However, under no circumstances did I compromise its structural integrity. If you should build this outhouse, you can expect minor variations in measurement to occur. That's only normal. As with all construction, check your own building as construction progresses.

Building the Floor (Figure 1a and Figure 1b)

Step 1: The floor structure is constructed of 2- x 6-inch pressure-treated spruce (see the materials list on page 148). Cut all the pieces to length according to Figure 1a. Treat the cut ends with a suitable preservative. The inner frame consists of two 43½- and two 55½-inch pieces nailed together with 3½-inch galvanized spiral spikes to form an interlocking frame.

Step 2: Add the two 42-inch joists and the two 15-inch bridge pieces (note that the joists are not 16 inch o.c.).

Step 3: Construct the outer frame from the two remaining 46½- and two 58½-inch pieces. An extremely strong corner is achieved by not only nailing the outside corners together, but also nailing through the outer-frame corner into the inner-frame corner.

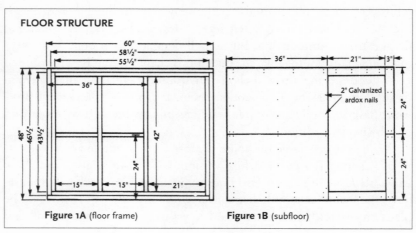

FLOOR STRUCTURE

Figure 1A (floor frame)   **Figure 1B** (subfloor)

Step 4: Part of the material package for this project includes two sheets of ⅝-inch spruce sheathing. The sheets should be cut to create two 4- x 6-foot and two 2- x 4-foot pieces. Rip three 3- x 24-inch strips from one 2- x 4-foot piece, and then trim to 24 x 36 inches. From the other 2- x 4-foot piece, rip one 3 x 24-inch strip, and then trim to 24 x 36 inches. A table saw is the best tool for this job, though a circular saw and a guide will do.

Step 5: Install the plywood floor according to Figure 1b (you will obviously need to cut two of the 3-inch strips down to a length of 21 inches). Use 2-inch galvanized spiral nails and nail the plywood to both inner and outer frames.

Step 6: If you didn't build the floor structure right on top of the pit foundation timbers in the first place, have someone help you move it there now (the foundation timbers should be resistant to rot, e.g. railroad ties, or 6- x 6-inch PT).

Framing the Side Walls (Figure 2)

Step 1: Cut eight 76½-inch studs from four 2 x 4 x 14 footers. The remaining pieces, as shown in Figure 2, are cut from two more 14 footers, as well as two 2 x 4 x 10 footers.

Step 2: Lay out, according to the diagram, the location of the studs on the two 60-inch bottom and two 60-inch top plates. Nail the studs to the bottom and top plates using 3½-inch spikes (two for the bottom and two for the top of each stud).

Step 3: The blocking, window frames, and the seat deck supports can be nailed or screwed to the studs (#8 x 3-inch screws).

Step 4: The double top plates for the side walls measure 53 inches, which leaves the right gap for the top plates of the front and rear walls. Nail in place (if you hammer 3½-inch spikes in at an angle, they won't stick through).

Step 5: Are the walls square? Check the measurement of the diagonals: they must be equal. The 1- x 3- x 8-foot spruce in the materials list is meant to be used as temporary wall bracing, which will let you move the walls without having them rack or twist. With your squared-up side walls lying flat, lay a 1- x 3-inch board across each—diagonally, then mark and cut so the bracing does not extend beyond the bottom or top plates. Attach with 2-inch nails (leave the heads sticking out a bit so you can remove the nails easily later on).

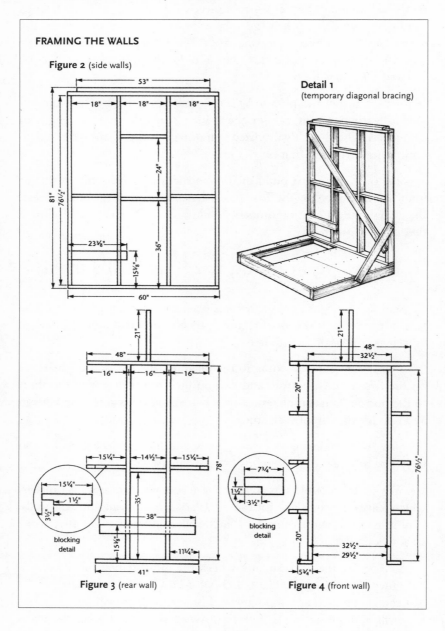

FRAMING THE WALLS

Figure 2 (side walls)

Detail 1
(temporary diagonal bracing)

Figure 3 (rear wall)

blocking detail

Figure 4 (front wall)

blocking detail

The Rear Wall (Figure 3)

Step 1: Like the sides walls, the rear wall is a very straightforward bit of framing. Note that the studs are 78 inches long because there is no double top plate. Lay out the location for the studs on the 48-inch top plate and 41-inch bottom plate as in Figure 3. Nail in place.

Step 2: Nail the 14½-inch blocking piece in place.

Step 3: The 15½-inch blocking pieces must be notched according to the detail drawings in Figure 3 (do not attach them at this time; once all four walls are in place, these are secured with screws to the rear and side walls to minimize racking). Likewise, do not attach the 21-inch gable stud, as it makes more sense to do so when assembling the roof structure.

Step 4: You can choose to attach the rear wall seat-deck support now, or wait until later to make sure if fits perfectly between the side wall seat-deck supports.

Step 5: Nail a piece of 1- x 3-inch bracing to the real wall to keep it square.

The Front Wall (Figure 4)

The front wall is similar to the rear wall, except that the studs are 76½ inches long (like the side wall studs). Note that the door header is laid flat and nailed to the top plate. Traditionally, it should be on edge, but the door opening is narrow enough to justify laying the header flat. Cut and notch the blocking pieces (blocking detail, Figure 4), but do not attach until the walls are in place (these too will be secured with screws).

Since the bottom plates on the front wall are so short, I suggest that you drill clearance holes and attach to the studs with #8 x 3-inch deck screws to prevent splitting.

Diagonal bracing is very difficult to install on the front wall at this time, so just skip it (just be sure to handle the wall section carefully). Put the gable stud aside until later.

Securing the Walls to the Floor
and to Each Other
(Figures 2, 3, 4, Detail 1, and Diagram 1)

Step 1: At this point it might be wise to look for a suitable helper. Position a side wall—brace in—on the floor. Additional short temporary braces can be nailed from the ends of the walls to the outer frame of the floor for support; you can fine tune for plumb once the bottom plate is nailed in place (see Detail 1).

Step 2: The side wall bottom plate should be flush with the outside edges of the floor. Nail in place (about eight 3½-inch spikes should be adequate, evenly distributed between inner and outer floor frames). In turn, leave each short brace attached to the floor frame, but remove it from the end of the wall; check for plumb and nail the brace back to the wall.

> **NOTE**
> The term "level" is a horizontal reference, while "plumb" is a vertical reference.

Step 3: Position the rear wall—brace in—on the floor. The top plate should fit in the gap that was provided in the side wall (Figure 2). Nail the rear wall top plate to side wall top plate (drive in at a slight angle so the nails won't stick through).

Step 4: The rear wall bottom plate should be flush to the outer edges of the floor and tight to the side wall bottom plate. Nail in place with six 3½-inch spikes.

Step 5: Position the remaining side wall on the floor—brace in. Nail to the floor and to the rear wall top plate. The wall should be plumb if the floor was leveled, and the walls were squared; however, you might have to make some minor adjustments.

Step 6: Carefully position the front wall on the floor. Nail the front wall top plate to the top plates of the side walls. The bottom plates of the front wall should be flush to the outside edge of the floor, and tight to the side wall bottom plates (make minor adjustments based on whether or not the studs for the door frame are plumb). Since they are so short, and might split if nailed, I suggest drilling two clearance holes in each bottom plate and screwing them to the floor with #8 x 3-inch deck screws.

Step 7: As in Figure 3, Detail 5, and Diagram 1, secure the two 15¼-inch blocking pieces to the rear wall studs and to the side wall studs with #8 x 3-inch screws.

Step 8: As in Figure 4, Detail 2, and Diagram 1, secure the six 7¾-inch blocking pieces to the front wall studs and to the side wall studs with #8 x 3-inch screws.

Step 9: Attach a temporary diagonal brace to the inside of the front wall, and remove the short outside braces from the side walls. The walls should all be square and plumb.

Installing the Siding (Detail 6)

The installation of the siding is easy if you can cut it to convenient 4- and 5-foot lengths. Since the front wall is mostly door opening, the 9¼-inch pieces for either side of the opening can be cut from leftovers. When ordering the siding, suggest to the staff at the lumberyard that you would prefer 10- and 16-foot lengths (you need twice as many 5-foot pieces as 4-foot pieces).

The bottom edge of the first run of siding should begin 4 inches from the bottom edge of the floor framing (i.e. from the bottom of the floor joist; see Detail 6). Use 2-inch galvanized ardox nails at the ends of each board (these will be covered by trim), and 2-inch galvanized finishing nails for the inner studs. Remember that **the groove is down, and the tongue up.** Check for level and check that each course is the same height. The last course of siding should be flush with the top edges of the top plates if you are using pine cove siding, as I did (this eliminates the need to rip the last course).

Installing the Main Roof Rafters, Ridgeboard, and Studs (Figure 5 and Diagram 1)

Step 1: Cut eight roof rafters, complete with bird's-mouth notches, and four rafters without bird's-mouth notches from six 2 x 4 x 10 footers, as in Figure 5. Cut the 1- x 6-inch ridgeboard to length: 6 feet.

Step 2: Lay out the position of the roof rafters on both sides of the 1- x 6- x 6-foot ridgeboard, and on the top plates of the side walls (the rafters should sit directly over the wall studs). See Diagram 1.

Step 3: Tack four main rafters in place along the top plate of a side wall.

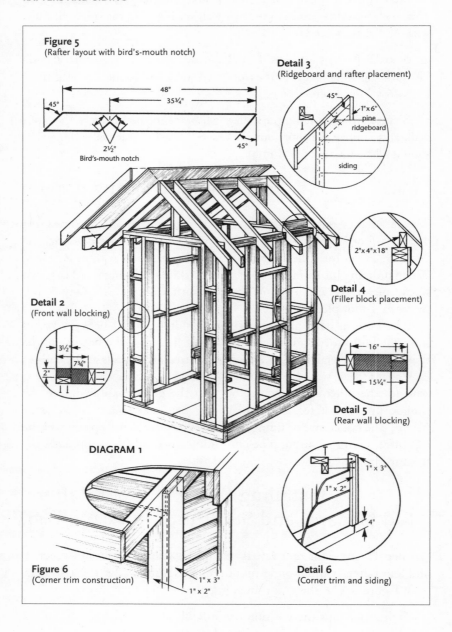

Figure 5
(Rafter layout with bird's-mouth notch)

48"

35¾"

45°

45°

2½"
Bird's-mouth notch

Detail 3
(Ridgeboard and rafter placement)

45°

1"x 6"
pine
ridgeboard

siding

2"x 4"x18"

Detail 4
(Filler block placement)

Detail 2
(Front wall blocking)

3½"

7¾"

2"

16"

15¼"

Detail 5
(Rear wall blocking)

DIAGRAM 1

Figure 6
(Corner trim construction)

1" x 3"

1" x 2"

1" x 3"

1" x 2"

4"

Detail 6
(Corner trim and siding)

Step 4: Tack the other four main rafters in place along the top plate of the other side wall. The ends should rest against each other.

Step 5: Slide the ridgeboard up between the rafter ends. Position one rafter from each pair on the layout lines. The top edge of the rafter end should be flush with the top of the ridgeboard. Move the other rafter from each pair slightly to one side so that you can nail directly through the ridgeboard into the rafter end (use 2-inch nails). Move the other rafters onto the layout lines and nail in place. Obviously, you will have to nail obliquely. Finish nailing the rafters to the top plates (yes, toenailing is the order of the day, always a bit of a challenge).

Step 6: Locate the gable-end studs on the front wall and rear wall top plates, and under the ridge board, and nail in place (Diagram 1).

Step 7: Square the roof frame, and install a temporary brace (diagonally, of course) on one side.

Installing the Siding on the Gable Ends

When you install the siding on the gable ends, simply extend the pieces slightly past the rafters. Once you finish nailing the siding in place, snap a chalk line that follows the rafter slope, and trim the ends with a circular, jig or handsaw.

Installing the Filler Blocks Between the Main Rafters (Diagram 1 and Detail 4)

Step 1: Cut six 18-inch pieces from a 2 x 4 x 10 footer. These are filler blocks for the spaces between rafters, top plates, and roof sheathing to keep out the elements and the beasties. Some outhouse builders could choose to put screen in this opening, but since this design has windows for ventilation, I decided to close this space to reduce cold-weather drafts.

Step 2: Position each filler block so that it will just contact the roof sheathing when in place (Detail 4). Nail to the top plates and to the rafters.

Installing the Roof Sheathing (Diagram 1)

Step 1: On each sheet of ⅝-inch x 4- x 6-foot plywood, locate and mark the lines for nailing to the rafters with chalk or pencil.

Step 2: Slide a sheet up onto the rafters (obviously, the side without the brace)—lines up. It should be flush to the ends of the rafter tails and to the ends and top edge of the ridgeboard. Adjust for square, and nail in place with 2-inch spiral nails, spaced about 6 inches apart.

Step 3: Remove the brace from the other side of the roof and nail the other piece of sheathing in place.

Installing Corner and Gable End Trim
(Figure 6 and Detail 6)

As noted earlier, normal variations during construction might result in slightly different measurements than those given. Always check your own building before cutting, or in this instance, leave the assembled corner long at the bottom, fit, mark, and then cut to the final length.

Step 1: Cut the corner trim pieces according to Figure 6, bearing in mind the note above. Observe that the 1- x 2-inch is cut at 45° across the edge, not the face.

Step 2: Pick a corner and pre-fit two trim pieces to determine the right match. When assembled correctly, the 1- x 3-inch piece should be flush to the underside of the roof sheathing, while the 1- x 2-inch should be flush to the underside of the rafter (Figure 6). Nail the two pieces together—2-inch galvanized finishing nails (you could glue them together as well, but that is not necessary structurally).

Step 3: Repeat for the other three corners.

Step 4: Nail the corner trim to the building—2-inch galvanized finishing nails.

Step 5: Cut the gable-end trim pieces from the 1- x 2- x 12-footer as in Figure 6. Trim to fit.

Step 6: Nail the gable-end trim pieces to the gable ends—2-inch galvanized finishing nails. The trim should be tight to the roof sheathing (Detail 3).

Installing the Remaining Four Rafters
(Diagram 1)

There should be four rafters that do not have a bird's-mouth. Install the rafters at the ends of the roof; each rafter end should be tight to the ridgeboard, and the face of the rafter end should be flush to the end of the sheathing. Secure with 2-inch nails or #8 x 2-inch deck screws. You should install each rafter separately so that you can nail or screw through the ridgeboard into two rafter ends. Fastening the other rafter end to the ridgeboard is a bit more difficult.

Installing the Fascia (Diagram 1 and photo)

Step 1: Cut to length and nail—2-inch finishing nails—the 1- x 6-inch pine fascia to the rafter ends on each side of the outhouse (see Detail 3 for alignment).

Step 2: Cut the two 1- x 6- x 10-foot pine boards into four equal lengths. Make a 45° cut at one end of each piece. These will be used on the rafter faces at each end of the building.

Step 3: Temporarily install all four fascia pieces with a couple of finishing nails (leave the heads sticking out for easy removal). The top edge of the fascia should be flush with the top of the sheathing, and each set should meet neatly in the middle (if necessary, a little judicious trimming with a small plane can provide you with that expert fit). Scribe lines on the end fascia pieces where they meet the fascia on the rafter ends (hopefully, that line is more or less plumb).

Step 4: Remove the fascia end pieces, cut to length, add a design—if desired—and nail back in place.

Building the Seat Box (Figure 7)

Step 1: Remove the temporary bracing from the inside of the outhouse.

Step 2: The front panel of the seat box measures 21⅝ x 48 inches, while the seat deck panel measures 24 x 48 inches. These are cut from the piece of 4- x 4-foot G1S (acronym for Good-One-Side) fir plywood.

Step 3: Cut the notches in each panel with a jig saw. The two rear notches are larger than necessary to permit maneuvering the deck panel into place as one piece.

Step 4: Place the front panel in the pit opening. The 3½- x 7¾-inch notches should allow it to rest on the bottom plates of the side walls; the top of the front panel should be flush with the tops of the side wall seat deck supports that you installed at the beginning of the project. The panel should be plumb when tight against the ends of the supports. If one or the other of these conditions is not satisfied, then the side wall seat deck supports will have to be removed and adjusted. Screw the front panel to the 2- x 6-inch floor joist, and to the ends of each seat deck support—#8 x 2-inch screws.

Step 5: Install the rear seat deck support if you have not already done so.

Step 6: Install the galvanized liners to the front and rear interior faces of the seat box (you will need several ⅝-inch or ½-inch screws to secure the liner to the front panel—it is only ¾-inch thick). Roofing nails are good for the rear liner.

Step 7: From a 2- x 4- x 10-foot board, cut two pieces 18½ inches long. Screw them in place, flush to the top edge of the front panel and flush to the top edge of the rear seat deck support (these will provide greater support around the hole).

Step 8: Slide the seat deck panel into place. Sounds easy enough, but I know that I had to resort to a few well-used expletives during this operation; you might have to enlarge one or more of the notches, or plane an edge or two. Screw the deck to the supports and to the front panel. The latter job will require a half-dozen #6 x 1½-inch screws—#8s might split the plywood's laminations. Cover the gaps between the edges of the notches and the studs with two 1- x 3- x 5-inch pieces of pine. Nail or screw in place.

Step 9: Round the top edge of the piece of 1- x 2- x 4-foot pine; a plane and sandpaper will do a nice job. Fasten to the front panel with #8 x 1¼-inch screws; the trim piece should be flush to the top of the seat deck panel.

Step 10: Locate the toilet seat on the seat deck. This is where personal preference plays a significant role. Once you have determined the sweet spot, so to speak, mark the location for the bolts, and trace a line around the inside of the toilet seat onto the deck. Remove the toilet seat and carefully trace a new line about ½-inch larger than the line you traced originally.

Step 11: Cut out the hole with a jig saw. Round the edge of the hole with sandpaper or with a router equipped with a round-over bit. Drill clearance holes for the bolts. Position the toilet seat, and secure with the bolts provided.

Step 12: Cut the ¾-inch quarter-round to length, and nail in place where the front panel meets the floor—2-inch finishing nails.

Step 13: If you intend to paint the interior, then caulk around the seat box with a paintable caulking.

Installing and Trimming the Windows
(Figures 8 and 9)

Step 1: Each window jamb consists of two 1- x 4- x 22½-inch pieces of pine, and two 1- x 4- x 18-inch pieces. Nail flush to the outside face of the siding.

Step 2: Cut a piece of window screen: 18 x 24 inches. Staple to the outside edge of the 1- x 4-inch jamb.

Step 3: Cut and install the 1- x 3- and 1- x 6-inch window trim with 2-inch finishing nails, as in Figure 8 and photo.

Step 4: There will be a ½-inch space between the edges of the jambs and the edges of the 2- x 4-inch window frames. This will provide room for the Plexiglass window panels. Inspect the surfaces of the sills; if they are a bit rough, sand smooth. Nail the ¼- x ¾- x 7⅞-inch plywood strips to the top and bottom edges of the 1- x 4-inch jambs with a few 1-inch finishing nails.

Step 5: Carefully drill clearance holes in two of the plastic panels (about 12 inches up, and ⅜-inch in from the edges). Select a 5/16-inch bit and countersink the hole so that the head of a #6 screw will be flush with the surface of the Plexi panel.

Step 6: Install a drawer-type knob on each of these panels. Using a metal file, carefully round the four corners of each of these panels (so the corners won't catch as the panel slides).

Step 7: Locate and install the stationary Plexi panels.

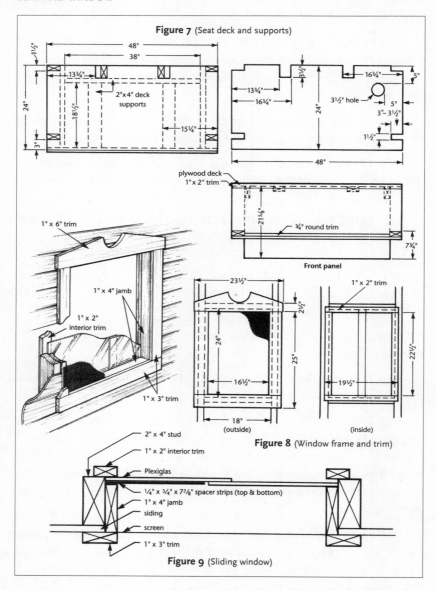

Figure 7 (Seat deck and supports)

Front panel

1" x 6" trim

1" x 4" jamb

1" x 2" interior trim

1" x 3" trim

Figure 8 (Window frame and trim)

2" x 4" stud

1" x 2" interior trim

Plexiglas

¼" x ¾" x 7⅞" spacer strips (top & bottom)

1" x 4" jamb

siding

screen

1" x 3" trim

Figure 9 (Sliding window)

Step 8: Screw the bottom and two side pieces of 1- x 2-inch trim to each window frame with #8 x 1¼-inch screws. These are flush to the surface of the jamb.

Step 9: Slide the movable Plexi panels down into place—knob in, and determine slidability; make corrections as necessary.

Step 10: When you are satisfied with the fit, screw the top trim pieces into place. With any luck, you should have a sliding window.

Installing the Vent Stack

Some learned sources have advocated the use of two vent stacks in an outhouse, though government specs only require one. Since our outhouse has never had much of an odor problem and doesn't even have a single vent stack, I was somewhat perplexed by the double stack theory. Now I didn't want this outhouse to look like the cab of an eighteen-wheeler but, nonetheless, the opinions of eminent vent scholars had to be respected. So I came up with a unique compromise. I added only one vent and equipped it with a mini whirly (similar to the larger ones on the roofs of countless homes and cottages). It offers, to use an expression of the 90s, a proactive venting system. They are pricey and a bit difficult to locate, but add a nice touch. Unfortunately, the whirly's collar measures 4 inches in diameter while the outside of the ABS vent pipe is only 3½ inches, so I did have to shim the pipe (another duct tape solution). According to regulation, I covered the top of the vent pipe with a piece of screen (this was secured by the duct tape).

Step 1: Locate the hole for the vent stack in the roof sheathing. Here's a suggestion: cut a short piece from the end of the 3-inch x 12-foot ABS pipe; make the cut at a 45° angle (or as close to 45° as possible). Position the piece against the sheathing—the underside, of course—so that it is plumb; it must also be 1½ inches from the rear wall and side wall top plates (this will align the hole, in the sheathing with the hole in the seat deck). Draw a line around the pipe.

Step 2: Cut the hole in the roof sheathing. You will need a round file to taper the top edge of the hole; otherwise the pipe will not slide through.

Step 3: Fit the pipe through the hole in the roof, and down through the hole in the seat deck (the cut end—i.e. the 45° end—should be in the pit). The pipe should extend to the bottom of the floor structure. You can secure it to the rear or side wall blocking with some pipe strap and a couple of screws.

Step 4: Cut the stack to length. It should extend about one or two inches above the peak of the roof.

Step 5: Caulk around the pipe where it passes through the seat deck.

Installing the Eave Starter, Paper, Roof Vent Flashing, and Shingles

Step 1: Cut the galvanized eave starters to a length of 75½ inches (each piece should extend 1 inch past each end of the roof). Install with roofing nails.

Step 2: Staple roofing paper to roof sheathing.

Step 3: Install roof vent flashing.

Step 4: Shingle roof and install whirly vent.

Trimming Out the Door (Figure 10)

Step 1: As in Figure 10, the header jamb consists of a 1- x 4- x 29½-inch length of pine, while the side jambs are 1- x 4- x 77¼-inch. Install flush to the outside face of the siding with 2-inch finishing nails; shim for plumb if necessary.

Step 2: The outside vertical trim is 1 x 3 x 79¼ inches (times two), while the horizontal piece is 1 x 6 x 36 inches (this is the piece leftover from the window trim). Nail all three trim pieces flush to the inside faces of the jamb.

Step 3: Cut the 1- x 2-inch door stop, but do not install at this time.

Step 4: Cut and nail the 1- x 2- x 28-inch trim piece into place at the bottom of the door frame opening. It should be flush to the surface of the plywood floor sheathing.

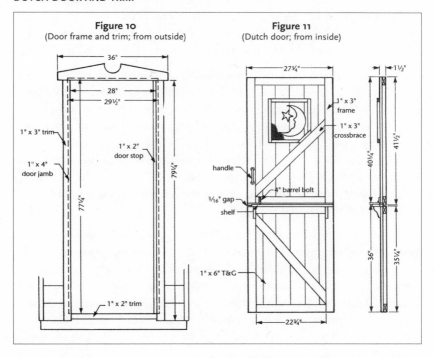

Figure 10
(Door frame and trim; from outside)

Figure 11
(Dutch door; from inside)

Building and Installing the Dutch Door (Figure 11)

A Dutch Door is not necessary, but makes for an attractive feature.

Step 1: The inner frame of the door is constructed of 1- x 3-inch pine. The bottom half consists of two pieces 35¼ inches long and two pieces 22¾ inches long. The top half consists of two pieces 40¾ inches long and two pieces 22¾ inches long. Assemble—face assemble, not edge—so that the shorter pieces are inside the longer pieces; the corners are simple butt joints, screwed and glued together. Make sure each frame is square before the glue sets. Don't add the bracing at this point.

Step 2: The outer frame of the bottom half is constructed of 1- x 2-pine: two pieces 32¼ inches long, and two pieces 27¾ inches long. The top half consists of two pieces 1 x 2 x 38½ inches, one piece 1 x 2 x 27¾ inches, and one piece 1 x 2 x 27¾ inches. The corners are simple butt joints—face assembly, not edge—screwed and glued together. Make sure each assembly is square before the glue sets.

Step 3: Screw (#8 x 1¼ inch screws) and glue the inner door frames to the outer frames. The top half of the outer frame is ¾-inch longer than the top half of the inner frame. There will be a 1-inch rim around the inside of each door half. The tongue-and-groove will be nailed to this rim.

Step 4: Cut the 1- x 6-inch tongue-and-groove to length for each door half. Generally, the back of 1- x 6-inch tongue-and-groove has a beveled channel that makes it look like 1- x 3-inch tongue-and-groove; this will be the side facing out. Start with the grooved edge of one length against the inside edge of the outer frame. Glue and nail each piece of tongue-and-groove with 1½-inch galvanized finishing nails, driven in at an angle. The last piece will likely be too wide to fit in the remaining space but you should only need to trim the tongue off, though a bit more fiddling may be required for a proper fit.

Step 5: Glue and screw (#8 x 1¼-inch screws) the cross-brace to the inside of the bottom half of the door. If desired, lay out a pattern for the cutout on the upper half of the door (according to outhouse tradition, the moon was the marker for a women's facility, while the sun or a star signified a rest stop for men; I figured that it would be easier and cheaper to adorn my privy with both symbols, rather than to build a separate outhouse for each gender). Staple a piece of screen over the cutout; it should be big enough to form a square or rectangle around the cutout. Cut trim to fit over the edges of the screen, and screw the trim in place. Glue and screw a cross-brace to the inside of the upper half of the door.

Step 6: Cut the 1- x 6-pine shelf for the bottom half of the door to length: 26¾ inches. I used the bottom of a coffee can for the pattern for the corners; trim with a jig saw.

Step 7: Glue and nail the shelf to the top of the bottom half of the door so that the leading edge of the shelf is flush with the inner frame (this will create a ¾-inch lip). The shelf is 1 inch shorter than the door; it should be positioned so that the 1-inch space is on the **opening side** of the door (this will allow the shelf to clear the door stop when the door is opened). The shelf needs brackets for stability; cut these from the remaining piece of 1- x 6-inch, and install with 2-inch screws.

Step 8: Since the regulations in some jurisdictions call for a self-closing door, spring-loaded hinges—the type often found on cottage screen doors—are appropriate for this job. Screw a pair to the frame on the bottom half of the door. I substituted #8 x 1¼-inch screws for the little ones included in the package. Install the bottom half of the Dutch door in the opening.

Step 9: Install two 4-inch T-hinges on the upper half of the door (the upper half is not self-closing, but when the bolt connecting the two door halves is in place, the whole door becomes a self-closing unit). Install the upper half in the door opening. That ¾-inch lip on the bottom of the upper half of the door should overlap the leading edge of the shelf on the top of the bottom half to create a simple weather seal.

Now, as anyone who has ever installed a door knows, it is never quite that straightforward. Most often, a little work with the plane is a fundamental requirement. The two halves created even more painstaking adjustments.

Step 10: Stick foam weatherstripping to the 1- x 2-inch door stop you cut earlier. Nail the door stop in place with 2-inch finishing nails. The door—both halves—should be flush to the outside of the trim.

Step 11: Install the 4-inch barrel bolt to the back of the upper half of the door as in Figure 11. When the door is closed, carefully mark the location of the bolt where it strikes the shelf. Open the door as a unit, and mark the new location of the bolt where it meets the shelf. An interesting phenomenon occurs as the door is opened: the bottom half actually travels farther away from the door frame in its opening arc than does the upper half. Drill the two holes with a bit slightly larger than the bolt. With a small chisel or a utility knife, remove the wood between the holes to create a slot. When the door opens and closes as a unit, the bolt can slide freely.

Step 12: Install door handles on the outside of the bottom half, and on the inside of the top half of the door. Add a screen door spring catch.

Step 13: I believe that keeping an outhouse clean and tidy, and therefore more attractive to all, begins with a paint job, inside and out. Consequently, this is also the occasion for the official christening; there could be no better time to sit and give serious contemplation to the decorating scheme you will choose for the new outhouse!

NOTE A good way to help minimize odors is to keep a bucket of wood-stove ash on hand; sprinkle the ashes liberally after each visit.

THE PERFECT PRIVY MATERIALS LIST

Lumber

MATERIAL	SIZE	QUANTITY
pressure-treated spruce	2" x 6" x 10'	3
"	2" x 6" x 8'	2
spruce	2" x 4" x 16'	1
"	2" x 4" x 14'	9
"	2" x 4" x 10'	10
"	1" x 3" x 8'	6
plywood spruce sheathing	5/8" x 4' x 8'	2
G1S plywood	5/8" x 4' x 4'	1
pine cove siding	1/2" x 6" thick	275 linear feet
pine	1" x 6" x 10'	2
"	1" x 6" x 7'	1
"	1" x 6" x 6'	3
"	1" x 6" x 4'	1
"	1" x 4" x 10'	1
"	1" x 4" x 7'	3
"	1" x 3" x 16'	1
"	1" x 3" x 12'	3
"	1" x 3" x 8'	4
"	1" x 3" x 7'	2
"	1" x 2" x 14'	1
"	1" x 2" x 12'	1
"	1" x 2" x 8'	3
"	1" x 2" x 7'	4
tongue-and-groove pine	1" x 6" x 6'	5
pine quarter-round	3/4" x 4'	1
pine trim	4' length	1
plywood strips	1/4" x 3/4" x 7 7/8"	4

APPROXIMATE COST: $1,000

Hardware

MATERIAL	SIZE	QUANTITY
galvanized ardox spikes	3 1/2"	5 lbs
galvanized ardox nails	2"	3 1/2 lbs
galvanized finishing nails	2"	1 1/2 lbs
"	1 1/2"	1/2 lb
roofing nails	3/4"	1 1/2 lbs
screws	#8 x 3"	25
"	#8 x 2"	50
"	#8 x 1 1/4"	100
"	#6 x 1"	2
"	#6 x 5/8"	6
fibreglass screen	24" x 60"	1 piece
Plexiglass panels	3/16" x 10" x 23 7/8"	4
drawer pulls		2
toilet seat assembly		1
galvanized eave starter	10'	2
shingles		2 bundles
roofing paper		
T-hinges	4"	2
spring-loaded hinges		2
foam weather-stripping	3/16" x 3/4"	1 roll
door handles		2
screen door spring catch		1
barrel bolt	4"	1
paintable caulking		1 tube
outdoor wood glue	150 mL	1
ABS pipe	3" x 12'	1 piece
roof flange (for vent pipe)	3"	1
end-cut treatment	small container	1
light galvanized sheet metal	21 5/8" x 41"	1
"	18" x 41"	1
"	18" x 20"	2
finishing nails	1"	12
whirly vent	4"	1

Three to remember:

1. Check with your municipality about regulations before you begin.

2. Dig the hole first.

3. Keep the vermin out!

CHAPTER 15

Basic Plumbing

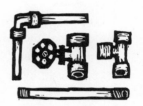

IT'S SHAMEFUL, REALLY, HOW OFTEN I HAVE TAKEN ADVANTAGE of my best friend's welding and metal-working background. Take my cottage plumbing system. Oh sure, I am passably able to do the work, but when someone at hand has a particular gift, it would be foolish to do a second-rate job yourself. For three or four years, it seemed inevitable that when we opened up in the spring, at least one copper water pipe would have a break in it (you'd think that after the second year, I might have blown the lines free of water, a standard procedure for some). It was Brian's job in those years to crawl under the cottage and to repair winter's damage. He had to contend with the black flies, dirt, and cramped quarters, while I had to manage my beer and hand him the occasional tool; surprisingly, he wouldn't agree that mine was the more difficult task. Eventually, the problems were resolved, and for some time now, opening up has proceeded without a glitch.

Basic plumbing and water system repairs are reasonably straightforward. Soldering copper pipe does require some skill, but it is a skill that can be acquired quickly. If you're starting from scratch (i.e. building a new cottage) and want to plumb the place yourself, then you will need your local building code and much more detailed instructions than this chapter can provide (invest in a good how-to book). We'll stick to the simple stuff: basic tools, soldering copper pipe, ABS pipe, and minor repairs. Make sure that any and all changes to an existing system comply with current regulations. In your area, permits and inspections may be required. In some jurisdictions, not having a permit may invalidate your insurance.

The Tools of the Trade

Typically, a professional plumber will have a wide range of specialty tools, but the average cottager needs only a few, as well as certain materials (see photo). Here's a suggested list:

- Tubing cutter.
- Hacksaw.
- Propane torch.
- Steel wool and/or emery cloth.
- Pipe wrench or a "constrictor"-type tool.
- Lead-free solder.
- Flux.
- ABS or PVC glue (PVC requires a primer as well).
- Teflon tape.
- Selection of ½-inch copper fittings.
- Selection of screwdrivers (mainly Phillips and standard slotted).
- Adjustable crescent wrench.

Tubing cutters make cutting copper pipe a breeze, and the mini cutter can be used in more confined spaces (so, if you can only afford one, buy the mini cutter—it's just a bit harder to turn). Naturally, a hacksaw will cut both copper and plastic pipe, but the cut ends obviously need more attention to achieve a good fit—a particularly important requirement for soldering.

If you haven't yet purchased a propane torch, or your old one needs replacement, do yourself a favor: buy a trigger-activated model. Ignition is hassle free, and you'll appreciate this feature when you're on your back under the old place and can barely move, let alone strike a match!

A pipe wrench is an all-tool; in other words, it is almost mandatory to include one in your tool collection. However, the "constrictor"-type tools shown in the facing photograph are

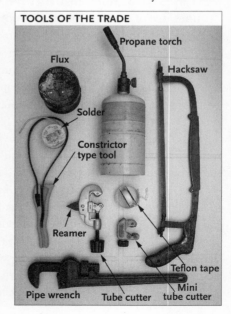

TOOLS OF THE TRADE

Propane torch
Flux
Hacksaw
Solder
Constrictor type tool
Reamer
Teflon tape
Pipe wrench
Tube cutter
Mini tube cutter

extremely versatile for removing or tightening plumbing fixtures, and will not mar surfaces. They are also perfect for removing water filters, oil filters, etc.

Copper Pipe

Though specialized plastic pipe continues to make inroads for the delivery of hot and cold water, copper pipe is still the material of choice. A cottage over ten years old will invariably have only copper pipe, generally ½-inch.

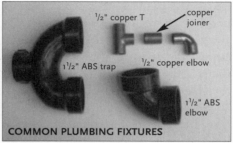

COMMON PLUMBING FIXTURES

These steps are essentially the same for repairing, replacing, and extending copper lines:

Step 1: Turn off the water supply when cutting into or extending the existing pressure system. Drain the system thoroughly.

Step 2: Cut the tube to length. Remember to include the depth of the fitting(s) in the overall measurement. Fit the tubing cutter over the pipe. Screw the cutting wheel tight to the pipe wall; make a rotation or two and retighten, a rotation or two and retighten until the wheel cuts through the pipe. Be careful not to overtighten, as this will dent the pipe. Some tubing cutters are equipped with a reamer; use this part of the tool to remove the lip on the inside of the cut end. If you had to use a hacksaw to cut the pipe, then you will have to file the burrs off; a round file, such as the type utilized for chainsaws, will work well for removing any burrs on the inside of the pipe.

Step 3: Polish the outside of the end of the pipe, at least 1 inch back, and the inside of the fitting with emery cloth—a type of sandpaper—or steel wool. This is a very important step, and must be completed carefully and methodically.

Step 4: Apply flux—an acid paste—to the end of the pipe and to the inside of the fitting. Twist the fitting around to make sure that the flux is evenly distributed.

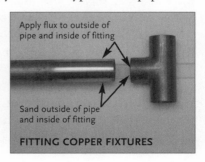

Apply flux to outside of pipe and inside of fitting

Sand outside of pipe and inside of fitting

FITTING COPPER FIXTURES

Step 5: Light the torch; adjust the gas flow so that the inner blue cone is about 2 inches long. Heat the fixture, *not* the pipe (remember, the pipe and fixture will get very hot so be careful, wear gloves). Move the flame back and forth over the fixture. Do not overheat (if you do, the solder won't adhere properly).

Step 6: Touch the end of the solder to the joint. This is the critical phase. If it melts, move the flame away; keep the tip of the solder against the joint. If the fitting and the pipe are the correct temperature, then the solder should, quite literally, be sucked into the joint (this is the it-takes-practice-to-get-it-right stage).

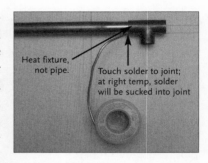

Heat fixture, not pipe.

Touch solder to joint; at right temp, solder will be sucked into joint

Rookies often believe that they have to apply solder all the way around the joint, but this is unnecessary if soldering is done properly. Turn the torch off.

Step 7: When the joint cools, wipe away excess flux with a rag. It takes very little time for the solder to solidify, so try not to move or bump it for a moment.

If you are soldering near combustible surfaces, remember to exercise caution; an old cookie sheet makes an excellent shield.

The steps described above will work every time, unless there is residual water in the line. Sometimes, older shut-off valves will permit a tiny trickle of water, but this can be enough to foil a cottage plumber. Though I have never tried it, I have often read or been told that stuffing a bit of white bread in the pipe will rectify this problem; the bread will absorb the water and once the system is turned back on, you can flush the bread out of the pipe (remember to remove the filter screen from the faucet!).

Support runs of copper pipe at three-feet (1-meter) intervals. Lay out the runs—i.e. slightly downhill—so that water can be drained completely from the system during close-up.

Try to make all pipes in the cottage accessible. I even incorporated a removable panel in the wall behind our shower, in case I had a problem with the shower pipes or fixtures.

If you are soldering a brass valve, take the valve apart, and remove the plastic and/or rubber components (otherwise, you'll burn or melt them). Once the joint has cooled, you can put the valve back together.

If you have to disassemble existing soldered joints, take extra care when cleaning the ends of previously soldered pipes or the insides of previously soldered fixtures. At times, they can be particularly challenging.

When soldering a fitting such as a T or an elbow, you will obviously have to solder one or two more joints of the same fitting; according to some sources, you can reduce the likelihood that the first part of the job will melt if you simply wrap a dampened rag around it. The temperature will remain low enough to prevent the solder from melting (don't set fire to the rag!).

Plastic Drain Pipe

ABS pipe—the rigid black stuff—is most often used in cottage country for drain/vent applications. It is much easier to work with than copper. ABS comes in two common sizes: 1½ and 3-inch. PVC pipe—the rigid cream-colored stuff—is also used, but the two are not interchangeable.

Step 1: Cut the pipe to length (remember to include the depth of the fitting). Even plumbers will use a hacksaw. Remove the burrs from both the outside and inside of the pipe with a file or emery cloth.

Step 2:. Dry-fit the assembly before gluing.

Step 3: Check the drain flow—the pipe's decline; about ¼-inch for every 1 foot of run is the general rule, though different jurisdictions may have different requirements.

Step 4: Apply the glue to both the pipe and the inside of the fitting. Slide the joints together with a twisting motion to distribute the glue evenly. Hold the joint together for a few seconds (make sure that the fitting is properly lined up on the final twist, because the glue sets up almost instantly; some kind of mark will help).

Once an ABS joint sets up, there is no taking it apart. If you screwed up, you'll have to cut the joint out and start over.

If you have several joints in the run, dry-fit the entire layout before gluing.

Basic Repairs

There may be times when you have to hire a pro to make repairs/replacements to cottage plumbing fixtures, but you should be able to deal with the most common minor problems.

Leaky taps—faucets—fall into that category. Compression models use washers or neoprene caps to seal the inlet while non-compression types use a brass or plastic ball, ceramic disk, cartridge or valve stems to stop the flow of water. Repairing either type is usually (quite a caveat, that!) an easy task.

It hardly seems worthy of mention, but the cardinal rule for repairing faucets is to *turn the water off first.* Proper layouts will have a shut-off valve for each faucet, but whoever plumbed your place may have only provided you with a main shut off.

Compression Faucet Repairs

Compression faucets may be indistinguishable from cartridge style faucets, i.e. both have a cold and hot water handle, so unless you are certain of which type you have in your cottage, do not purchase repair parts until after you disassemble the faucet.

Step 1: Remove the screw holding the handle (it could be concealed by a cap that must be removed first; use the tip of a knife to pry it off).

Step 2: Take the handle off. If it's stuck, you might have to purchase or borrow a special puller (Figure 2). Yes, I know a screwdriver might do it, but the likelihood of damage is increased.

Step 3: If there is one, remove the escutcheon—a decorative plate used to cover holes made during the installation of plumbing parts.

Step 4: Use a wrench to remove the stem-retaining nut and then remove the stem (Figure 3). At this point, you can determine whether the faucet uses washers or some other type of stem ending, such as a neoprene cap.

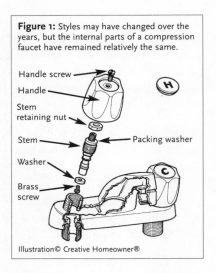

Figure 1: Styles may have changed over the years, but the internal parts of a compression faucet have remained relatively the same.

Handle screw
Handle
Stem retaining nut
Stem — Packing washer
Washer
Brass screw

Illustration© Creative Homeowner®

Figure 2: Avoid damage by using a special puller to remove handles from stems.

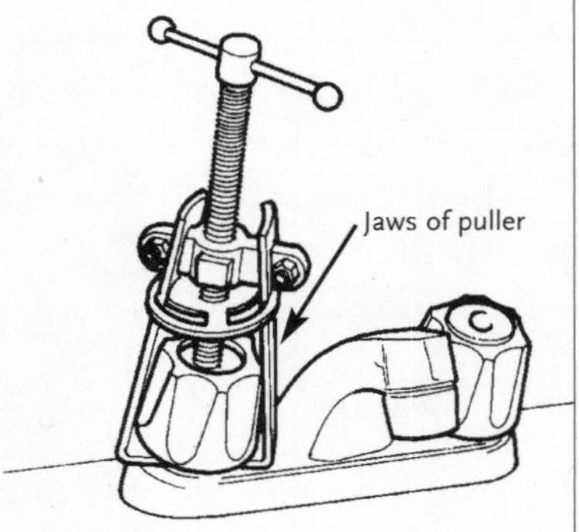

Jaws of puller

Illustration© Creative Homeowner®

Step 5: The washer or neoprene cap will be secured with a single screw. Undo the holding screw and replace the old washer *and* the screw.

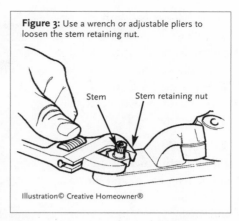

Figure 3: Use a wrench or adjustable pliers to loosen the stem retaining nut.

Stem   Stem retaining nut

Illustration© Creative Homeowner®

Step 6: If you have to replace a washer frequently, the seat inside the faucet against which the washer sits is probably damaged. You will feel roughness by inserting your finger into the hole and moving it against the seat. Roughness can be eliminated by rotating a valve-seat reamer against the seat for a few revolutions. If this doesn't cure the problem, use a valve-seat wrench to replace the seat. A faucet that doesn't have replaceable seats must be discarded if the problem persists.

To repair a leak around the handle of compression and non-compression faucets, the seal(s) have to be replaced. There are three variations, depending on the age of the faucet: O-rings, packing washers, or rope-style packing. Take the stem of the faucet to a plumbing supply outlet to get the correct replacement. O-rings and washers must be properly sized.

Cartridge Faucet

Cartridges are secured in two different ways. Inspect the outside of the handle for a clip that secures the cartridge, which is inside the handle, to the assembly. This is one style; pry out the clip and remove the Allen screw that is probably holding the handle. Remove the handle and cartridge, separate the two, and install a new, compatible cartridge.

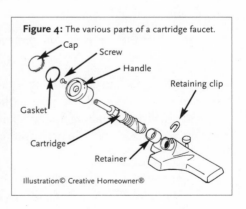

Figure 4: The various parts of a cartridge faucet.

Cap   Screw
Handle
Retaining clip
Gasket
Cartridge
Retainer

Illustration© Creative Homeowner®

With the other style of cartridge faucet, the handle is held by a screw that is under a cap (similar to a compression-style faucet). Pry off the cap, remove the screw, and take off the handle. You may encounter a retainer that houses the cartridge (Figure 4). Loosen this by turning it counterclockwise with adjustable pliers. Look for a retaining clip that holds the cartridge and remove that. Then grab the stem of the cartridge, pull it free, and replace it with a new one (Figure 5).

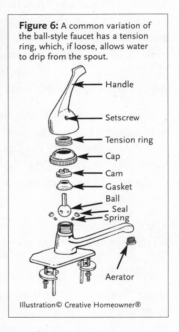

Figure 5: Grasp the cartridge stem with pliers and pull the part from the faucet body.

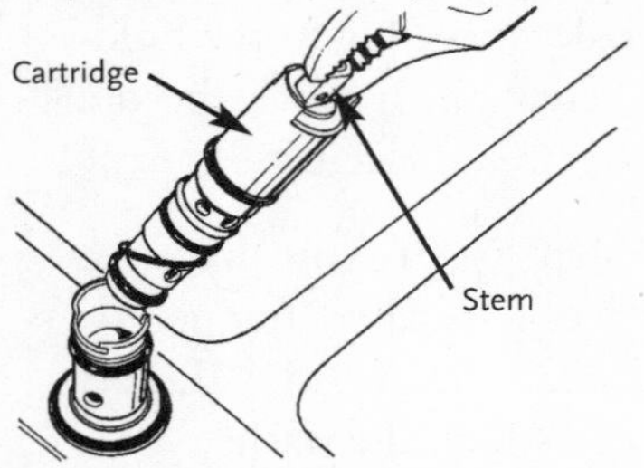

Cartridge

Stem

Illustration© Creative Homeowner®

Ball-Style Faucet

This type of faucet is common in kitchens, baths, and showers. Before purchasing a repair kit and taking the faucet completely apart, leaks can sometimes be eradicated by loosening the handle setscrew and removing the handle (Figure 6). Then use a ring spanner wrench (sold in the plumbing departments of home centers or plumbing supply stores) to tighten the adjustable tension ring. If doing this does not stop a leak, buy a repair kit and carry out the following:

Step 1: Wrap tape around the jaws of an adjustable wrench and use it to take off the cap and adjustable ring.

Step 2: Lift off the cam and remove the spout.

Step 3: Lift out the ball. Note that the slot in the ball slides onto a pin in the faucet body. When installing the new ball, make sure the slot and pin fit together (Figure 7).

Step 4: Use an awl to pry out the seat spring assemblies. Replace with those in the repair kit.

Step 5: In reassembling the parts, make sure the cam lug fits securely into its notch in the swivel base.

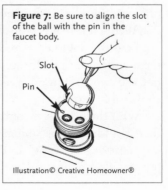

Figure 6: A common variation of the ball-style faucet has a tension ring, which, if loose, allows water to drip from the spout.

Handle

Setscrew

Tension ring

Cap

Cam

Gasket

Ball

Seal

Spring

Aerator

Illustration© Creative Homeowner®

Figure 7: Be sure to align the slot of the ball with the pin in the faucet body.

Slot

Pin

Illustration© Creative Homeowner®

Toilets consist of a bowl and the tank (Figure 8). Though they are reasonably simple mechanisms and generally very dependable, they are subject to malfunction from time to time.

When you flush the toilet and the waste does not go down, you have a bowl problem—it's plugged, baby! Hopefully, you won't have experienced a rather nasty flood; the water level will have simply risen to a very uncomfortable level in the bowl. Of the three methods suggested for unclogging a problem toilet bowl—plunging, chemicals, and augering—you should always reach first for the plunger. Chemicals often have little effect on a clogged toilet and an auger, unless carefully used, can damage the bowl. Ninety-nine percent of the time, repeated plunging will clear the obstruction. Once the obstruction has been cleared from the bowl, clean the plunger by swirling it in fresh water in the bowl before removing from the toilet.

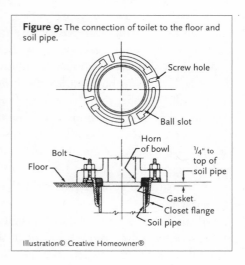

Figure 8: Toilet with tank attached.

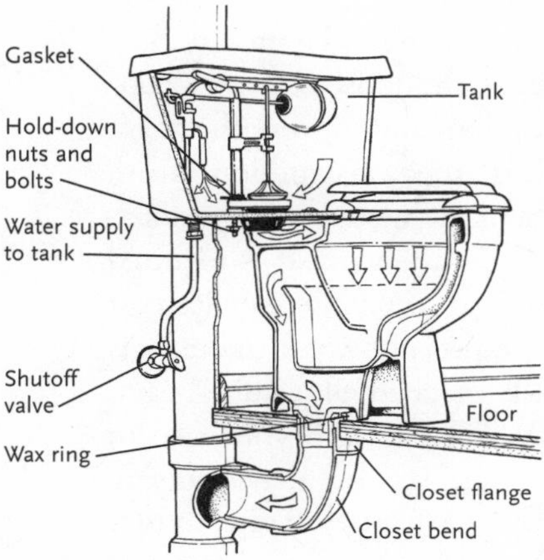

Gasket

Hold-down nuts and bolts

Water supply to tank

Shutoff valve

Wax ring

Tank

Floor

Closet flange

Closet bend

Illustration© Creative Homeowner®

Figure 9: The connection of toilet to the floor and soil pipe.

Screw hole

Ball slot

Horn of bowl

Bolt

Floor

¼" to top of soil pipe

Gasket

Closet flange

Soil pipe

Illustration© Creative Homeowner®

Feminine hygiene products can cause problems, not only in the toilet bowl but also in septic field beds. Despite my wife's objections, I installed a tasteful sign—at eye level when comfortably seated—that informed our washroom users of just what could be put down the cottage toilet, and feminine products are definitely not on that list!

In the rare event that the problem is in the drain, you have a couple of options. Your waste system should have a clean-out. This can simply be uncapped, and the obstruction augered out; of course, this is no job for the squeamish. It's messy and smelly! The other option is to remove the toilet from the closet flange (Figure 9 illustrates the most common connection) and to work the auger into the obstruction from there. Remember that a toilet, despite the work it is required to do, is really quite delicate; it is, especially when the tank is still attached, also quite heavy. Don't break it if you have to remove it. You may want to stuff a rag into the pipe to prevent sewer gases from entering the bath/washroom.

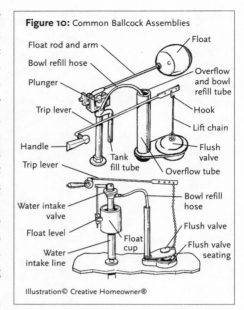

Figure 10: Common Ballcock Assemblies

Float rod and arm — Float — Bowl refill hose — Plunger — Overflow and bowl refill tube — Trip lever — Hook — Lift chain — Handle — Flush valve — Trip lever — Tank fill tube — Overflow tube — Water intake valve — Bowl refill hose — Float level — Flush valve — Water intake line — Float cup — Flush valve seating

Illustration© Creative Homeowner®

When you have to reinstall, care must again be exercised. Really, it is best to install the bowl and tank separately, but a good helper is also a practical approach. Wax ring gaskets are considered by most plumbers to be the best bet for a proper seal. The bowl must be set down absolutely straight on the bolts and wax ring. Rock the toilet slightly to seat the new ring properly. Do not over-tighten the bolts. Oh, I hope you remembered to remove the rag!

Tank problems are also reasonably simple to correct. There are a couple of common ballcock assemblies—the mechanisms that actually flush the toilet (Figure 10). If a toilet runs continuously, either the ballcock valve is not shutting off completely, or the flush or flapper valve is not sealing completely.

In the first case, adjust the float ball or float cup so that the level in the tank does not exceed the height of the overflow tube; the lower the float, the sooner the ballcock valve will shut off (a float ball can be adjusted by simply but carefully bending the rod to lower the float ball). Water may also leak into the toilet bowl through the flush or flapper valve. The chain that is connected to the trip lever and lifts the flush or flapper valve may be tangled or too tight causing an improper seal. There should be about ½ inch (12 mm) of slack in this chain. Residue in the flush valve seat may also cause an improper seal. Drain the tank, raise the flush valve, and clean the seat.

If water sprays out of the tank, quite likely the refill tube is not properly connected to the overflow tube. Water leaking from the bottom of the tank generally means that the gasket between the tank and the bowl may require replacement.

If the water level is set too high, it could leak down the overflow tube causing the toilet to run. Adjust the float to lower the water level.

If the toilet's flush cycle is insufficient, then there may be too much slack in the chain causing the flapper to close prematurely; adjust as necessary.

Electric Water Heaters are the most common type in cottage country. A typical electric water heater is pictured in Figure 11. While certain precautions are very necessary when dealing with electricity, some repairs to and/or replacement of an electric water heater are not that elaborate.

Water Won't Heat

Step 1: Check the circuit breaker at the main panel. If you find a tripped toggle, press to full "off" position and then snap to full "on." If the circuit is protected by a fuse, check to see if the fuse is burned out; if it is, replace with the same amp rating as the old one.

Step 2: If a fuse or tripped breaker is not the problem, and the fuse/circuit continues to blow/trip, then you will likely need an electrician.

Step 3: If the circuit seems okay, the trouble could be a malfunctioning element (see details in *Replacing an Element*).

Water Too Hot

This is most likely a thermostat problem. Check the thermostat and turn the setting down if it is too hot; a normal setting is between 110 and 140°F (45 to 60°C). If a thermostat adjustment doesn't work, it could be a malfunction, and again this could be a job for a pro.

Heater Pipes Leak

With the appropriate wrench, try tightening the pipe fitting at the leak point (your heater should be connected to your water system with threaded fittings—so the heater can be

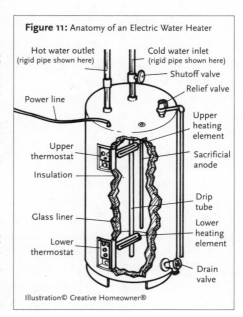

Figure 11: Anatomy of an Electric Water Heater

Hot water outlet
(rigid pipe shown here)

Cold water inlet
(rigid pipe shown here)

Shutoff valve

Relief valve

Power line

Upper heating element

Upper thermostat

Sacrificial anode

Insulation

Drip tube

Glass liner

Lower heating element

Lower thermostat

Drain valve

Illustration© Creative Homeowner®

easily replaced if necessary). Don't use too much pressure.

If tightening fails to stop the leak, turn off the power, turn off the water and replace the fitting.

If the heater is leaking around an element, the problem is probably a faulty element gasket. *Turn off the power* and the water supply and try tightening the thermostat bracket over the element (easy does it). If tightening doesn't work then you will have to replace the gasket (see *Replacing an Element*).

Replacing an Element
A faulty element can be the cause of no hot water.

Step 1: *Turn off the power* at the main panel, and turn off the water. Remove the thermostat/element protective access covers.

Step 2: Test the element for **continuity** (Figure 12). If the tester fails to light (or the ohms needle on dial-type testers does not indicate continuity), then you should suspect a faulty heating element.

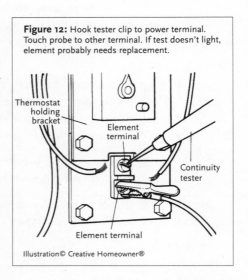

Figure 12: Hook tester clip to power terminal. Touch probe to other terminal. If test doesn't light, element probably needs replacement.

Illustration© Creative Homeowner®

Step 3: Drain the tank (obviously, you should not needlessly drain 40 or 60 gallons of hot water into your septic system; drain as you would at closing up: garden hose connected to outside hot water drain tap/faucet). If it's the top element, you don't need to drain the tank completely, but if it's the bottom one, then drain completely including the drain valve.

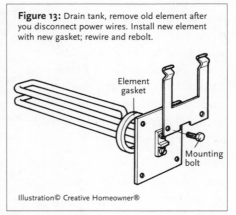

Figure 13: Drain tank, remove old element after you disconnect power wires. Install new element with new gasket; rewire and rebolt.

Illustration© Creative Homeowner®

Remove the bolts holding the thermostat bracket and the element. Let the thermostat hang by the connecting wires. Replace the old element with a new one of the same size, complete with a new gasket (Figure 13).

Step 4: Reattach the wires, position the new element and thermostat, and bolt in place (do not overtighten).

Step 5: Turn on the water and fill the heater tank. Check for leaks. When the tank is full, turn on the power. Be sure to repack the insulation around the thermostat, and mount the protective access cover.

Replacing a Heater
A leaking tank almost always requires replacing the water heater. It is a job you can do yourself, though let's not kid ourselves, it is no small job. A friend of mine lives by the dictum: *there are no small jobs*, a sign that should be hung in every cottage workshop! Always follow the manufacturer's instructions and recommendations for installation.

Step 1: *Turn off the power* to the heater at the main panel. Turn off the water and the shut-off valve at the heater if you have one. Completely drain the old tank (see page 160).

Step 2: Disconnect the water lines with an adjustable wrench, pipe wrench, or pliers (NOTE: use two wrenches when disconnecting copper pipe fittings to prevent twisting soldered joints).

Step 3: Remove the cover plate to the heater where the power line enters. Disconnect the wires. My father-in-law taught me to always label wires with a piece of masking tape; don't count on remembering which wire goes where, though the manufacturer's instructions may provide that information.

Step 4: Remove the old heater (get help; electric water heaters are heavy brutes). Clean the area under the old heater and place a drain pan where the new heater will go. Move the new heater into position; shim if necessary.

Step 5: Install the relief valve, drain pipe (if desired), and other fittings on the heater as per the manufacturer's instructions. Use teflon tape on plastic and copper fittings.

Step 6: Connect the water lines to the heater. If there wasn't a cold-water shut-off valve in the original layout, it would be a good idea to add one (you get a chance to solder!).

Step 7: Connect the power wires to the heater as per instructions. Remember that water heaters use 220 volts.

Step 8: Turn on the water valves and check for leaks. When the tank is full, turn on the power and set the thermostat.

General Advice for the Cottage Plumber

1. Buy a copy of Max Burns's *Cottage Water Systems*, and a good plumbing reference manual.
2. Clean your foot valve screen at least one a year, and install a sediment-type filter between your pump and pressure tank (I was called to a friend's cottage once to determine why the water pressure was low; turned out the filter was so clogged with junk that water was having a hard time getting through).
3. Consider low-flush or water-saving toilets to take some of the pressure off your septic system. There are those who argue that 1.6 gallons are not enough volume to provide a proper flush for solid waste, or that these toilets plug more often. We have used a low-flush toilet for many years and yes, there have been times when we had to flush the toilet twice to remove *some* waste, but those times have been relatively few. Consider also a water-saving shower head.
4. Check the aerator screen on your kitchen faucet and clean when necessary.
5. Clean the inside of your toilet tank at least once a season. Turn off the water, flush the toilet, add a small amount of detergent, and clean with a soft brush. While you're at it, clean out the small holes under the rim of the bowl and, if your toilet has a water discharge outlet at the bottom of the bowl—usually about ¾-inch in diameter—clean that out as well (sometimes mineral deposits can accumulate in this hole reducing the toilet's flush efficiency).
6. If you have to plunge a bathtub or bathroom sink, remember to stop-up the overflow with a rag; if you have to plunge kitchen sinks, plug the other sink.
7. Once every season, remove the sediment from the bottom of your electric water heater by draining a few gallons through the drain valve. Remember to first trip the heater breaker or remove the heater fuse in the main power panel!
8. Avoid drain cleaners; they are generally not septic system friendly.
9. Do not drain your traps in the fall as a way to protect against freezing. I know this from experience; traps are meant to prevent septic tank gas from entering the cottage. Use a non-toxic anti-freeze in your traps.
10. Trinket shelves above a toilet can create problems: larger objects can fall and break the tank lid or bowl, and smaller objects can fall into the bowl and get flushed down and stuck.
11. Be cautious when dumping buckets of dirty water down the toilet; a rag could inadvertently end up being flushed down and lodged.

12. Turn off the water pump and electric water heater when you leave the cottage for a few days. Remember to turn the hot water heater off if you have to make plumbing repairs and the system has to be drained; leaving the heater on could damage the elements if the tank is empty.

Three to remember:

1. Always turn the water off (and the power when working with electric water heaters).

2. Exercise caution when soldering; don't burn yourself or burn down the cottage.

3. Buy a good reference manual; if you're not sure, hire a pro.

Suggested websites for plumbing tips:

<www.doityourself.com>
<www.homerepair.about.com>
<www.fluidmaster.com>

CHAPTER 16

Critters—
The Unwanted

THE ALLURE OF COTTAGING, by definition, includes wildlife. Who ever tires of the call of the loon, of the antics of peanut-loving chipmunks, of identifying birds at the feeder, hearing an owl at night, or being dive-bombed by sweet-seeking hummingbirds? Our existence in an urban landscape is often devoid of natural encounters of the wild kind. And yet, as much as we may love wild creatures, there are some we may not care to entertain, especially if they are intent on moving in with us. They're okay, as long as they choose to remain in the great outdoors where they belong. Once they decide that cohabiting with people is a preferable arrangement, then cultures—critter and human—are bound to collide. It is a confrontation that only the prepared, the patient, and the determined have any hope of winning, or at least managing (of course it's cottagers I speak of; critters often seem to have an abundance of preparation and patience).

This list of unwanted cottage critters is not long, but it is one that I believe will receive universal approval.

Mice

Frankly, I find nothing redeeming in mice. Oh, I know that they are a dietary staple for countless predators in the forest, and thus have an almost sacred place in the food chain, but I really, really dislike them, plain and simple. When I built our cottage, I was determined to keep them out. My in-laws had not had a mouse in 30 years, so I reasoned that exclusion was indeed feasible. During construction, I took great pains to make sure that there were no access points for these furry little varmints. When I drilled holes in the floor for the plumbing, I made them *exactly* the size of the pipes. The cottage sits on properly constructed and well-drained piers; the place does not shift, and no cracks have appeared around door frames, windows or walls. Soffits are aluminum and well sealed. The dryer vent is covered by galvanized wire mesh (yeah, lint does collect but I can blow it out with my portable air-compressor—Reason Number 53 for owning one!). In short, I have prevailed. There has never been a mouse in our cottage. Not that I haven't had some scares over the years. Every once in a while I will mistake toast crumbs for mouse droppings, but that's only the machinations of an overly active mouse-paranoia. My vigilance has paid off—so far.

Not every cottager I know can make such a claim (and in fact, when I declare my cottage to be a mouse-free zone, some look at me with suspicion or even amusement—as if anyone could keep mice out of his/her cottage!). Mice are more or less constant visitors with many of my cottage friends. To be sure, older cottages do make deterrence a formidable task; among other reasons, seasonal movement and poorly fitting doors and windows provide mice with a choice of entry points. And even some newer cottages are plagued with mouse home invasions. So what's a cottager to do? First of all, you must know your enemy.

Deer Mouse

In Canada and the northern U.S., the most common intruder is the white-footed or deer mouse (*Peromysus maniculatus*). These guys have a hearty appetite: a mouse can eat about 2 pounds (a kilo) of food in six months. Mice are omnivores, and though they prefer cereals, seeds, and nuts, they are also attracted to foods high in fat and protein such as butter, meat, and sweets. Mice require less than an ounce (about three grams) of food a day, and can live without fresh water. What's worse for the cottager, a mouse is an incredible defecating machine, dumping about 9,000 droppings in six months. Their feces and urine contaminate food, cutlery, and linen, and mice and their parasites are implicated in the transmission of a number of diseases. The list is rather disturbing!

Mice are prolific breeders and a female, whose reproductive life begins at one-and-a-half to two months of age, can have eight to ten litters of 3 to 16 young annually. Even though the average mouse lifespan is one year, that still amounts to between 24 and 160 baby mice for the average female.

They are also excellent jumpers—leaping from heights of up to 7 to 8 feet (2.4 meters) without injury, or bounding up to 12 inches (30 cm). They can climb darned near anything, and, unfortunately, can squeeze through an opening about ¼-inch in diameter (6 mm).

Mice are rodents, and must gnaw to keep their front teeth worn down. This regrettable characteristic makes them even more unattractive house guests as they will chew through foam, wood, soft mortar, fiberglass insulation, rubber, and even electrical wiring (according to one source, mice are the cause of many fires).

The experts maintain that exclusion is the first line of defense. Of course, you would have to be simple-minded not to appreciate that preventing entry in the first place would dramatically reduce mice problems. It's not always easy, but here are some suggestions even the most mouse-savvy might not have considered:

- Dryer vents and other ventilation openings should be covered with heavy wire mesh (no bigger than ¼ inch/6 mm).
- Patch cracks in foundation walls.
- If there are gaps in the holes around pipes, or electric and telephone wires, stuff them with steel wool before caulking.
- Windows and doors must be tight-fitting; use metal weather-stripping under doors.
- Cupboard doors should have gaps no greater than the diameter of a pencil.

It is also important to make your cottage less appealing to Genghis Mouse and his hordes:

- Eliminate weed and other vegetative cover as well as debris and litter near the building.
- Keep garbage in containers with tightly fitting lids (this is good advice to deter all critters).
- Raise woodpiles off the ground, and keep them away from the cottage.
- Only deposit vegetation waste in the composter.
- Indoors, remove padded cushions from sofas and chairs, and store them on edge or separate from one another, off the floor.
- Remove drawers from empty cupboards or chests when closing up and re-insert them upside down.

- All dry foods should be kept in glass or metal jars with secure lids (keep the outsides of containers clean).
- Potatoes, onions, and other root vegetables should be kept in a rodent-proof cupboard or in the refrigerator.
- Properly store bird feed and dog and cat food (don't leave it out after Fido has dined).

Finally, we must consider the vexing question of eliminating mice in the cottage. I say vexing, because before the dawn of the animal rights movement, vegetarianism, and Mickey, everybody simply killed rodents—done. These days, it's not so simple. I try to keep an open mind about these things, although I have often, unjustly, been accused of a certain lack of sensitivity, but I can't seem to comprehend how love of God's creatures can possibly extend to mice. They're just like mosquitoes, to be dispatched quickly and finally. Yet, there are those who actually live-trap mice and release them into the wild, thereby sparing them an untimely demise. Accordingly, there are a number of live-trap mechanisms available, some capable of capturing over a dozen mice in a single setting. If these are used, then be advised that they must be checked periodically so that the mice do not starve or die of exposure. I may not be sensitive, but I am against the needless suffering of any creature.

Though some advocate the use of poisons or other mechanical systems such as glueboards (neither of these is a very humane option, according to the Canadian Federation of Humane Societies), in my opinion, the extirpation of mice can still best be achieved by the lowly snap trap. Here are some suggested procedures for deploying these snappy little house mines:

- Use enough traps to reduce mouse numbers quickly so mice will not become trap-shy.
- Mice rarely venture far from their shelter and food, so set traps no more than 6 feet (1.8 m) apart where mice are active.
- Traps should be placed against and perpendicular to baseboards, walls, and boxes where mice may travel, with the trigger close to the wall.
- Set them so the mouse is most likely to pass over the trigger.
- If traps are set parallel to the walls, they should be set in pairs with the trigger ends away from each other to intercept animals coming from either direction.
- Effectiveness can be increased by leaving the traps baited but not set for a few days.
- Inspect the traps and remove dead mice immediately.

- Relocate traps if bait does not disappear regularly.
- Reset traps in 2 to 3 weeks (this could eliminate any offspring).

It is important to handle dead mice carefully: to be safe, use gloves and wash your hands thoroughly after disposal. Clean up contaminated areas by using wet methods, includ-

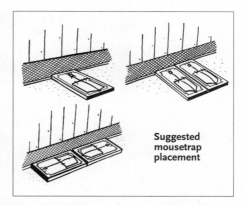

Suggested mousetrap placement

ing disinfectants such as bleach. Avoid sweeping and vacuuming when possible, or wear a dust mask to reduce exposure to fine dust particles.

Bats

Unlike mice, bats are truly beneficial. Unfortunately, they still make many cottagers uncomfortable. They appear to fly recklessly, but their erratic flight patterns are simply necessary hunting behavior. They are certainly not diving at us, but only trying to outmaneuvre their prey—insects. Contrary to the old axiom, "blind as a bat," bats actually have rather good visual acuity and do rely on their vision. But, as far as we know, they use echolocation to situate dinner. Our most common species, the Little Brown Bat (*Myotis Lucifugus*) is the most important predator of night-flying insects. Each bat eats up to half its weight every night, and that's a lot of mosquitoes—the bat's most important menu selection as far as cottagers are concerned! Moreover, bats are no more prone to rabies than other mammals.

Even though bats do not chew wood, insulation, or wiring, and even though a few bats in your cottage may go undetected, a colony can be difficult to overlook. The noise of baby bats and the smell might give it away. The Little Brown Bat—the species most readily adapted to living with people—prefers to roost in buildings in the summer months, so if they choose your place, then you are faced with the challenging task of posting an eviction notice.

Different methods have been used to discourage occupation, generally with less than satisfying results: lights in the attic, mothballs, and other noxious fumes are usually ineffective. Poisons have also been used to try to destroy bat colonies, but despite the questionable humaneness of this method, they often cause more problems than they solve: dazed bats can be picked up by kids and pets; dead bats may rot in corners and add to the smell; poisons could pose health hazards to cottage residents. The only sure way to eliminate a bat colony is to bat-proof the place.

Since bats can crawl through a hole the size of a quarter, any opening or crevice this size or larger must be blocked. Locate access and exit points by watching where they emerge at dusk, or by looking for droppings on the sides of the cottage (similar to mouse droppings, but found stuck to walls where mice cannot reach). A suggested method is to duct tape or staple a chute—such as a plastic bread bag with the bottom removed—over the exit for several days (bats don't leave their roost every night). This device allows bats to leave, but prevents entry. You can also staple a piece of aluminum screening over the hole; leave one edge unsecured so they can crawl out, but can't get back in. Once all the bats have emigrated, the entrances can be permanently sealed. Bats aren't easily discouraged, so expect them to persist: they will try to find other entrances. If they do, this means repeating the deportation process. Of course, the timing of eviction is important; this operation should be carried out before the end of June when the young are born, or after the end of July when the young can fly. Before blocking any entrances, check the bats' roosting area to determine whether or not young bats are present: babies are furless, while juveniles will not fly when disturbed.

What happens to homeless bats? Naturally, as one would expect, they will seek a new home (perhaps in your neighbor's attic). In the interests of continued friendships, and in view of the extremely beneficial role bats play in controlling insect populations, providing an alternative roosting site is an appropriate strategy. This goes not only for cottagers with bat problems, but for all of us—none of us is exempt from the dreaded and hated mosquito. May I suggest a bat house?

I have observed that commercially manufactured bat houses are more and more common in specialty outdoor stores. So you can buy one, but I have included bat house plans at the end of the chapter for those who like to build stuff. Plans are probably also available at your local library. In addition to somewhat conflicting advice about where to position bat houses, different sources have expressed somewhat contradictory opinions regarding construction considerations. The NWF (National Wildlife Federation) suggests that they greatly reduce the possibility of overheating on very hot days in areas where the *average* high temperatures in July are 85°F (29°C) or above (this would seem to eliminate much of cottage, camp, or cabin country). All agree that landing areas and roost partitions must be roughened (either scratched or covered with durable plastic screening).

When choosing a bat house location, sun exposure and heat absorption must be carefully considered. Bats in nursery colonies like it warm. Roosts will require plenty of solar heating in all parts of cottage country. Houses in cooler climates need to absorb much more solar heat. According to the NWF, they should be black where average high temperatures in July are 80 to 85°F (26 to 29°C) or less; dark (dark brown, gray, or green), where they are 85 to 95°F (29 to 35°C). To determine the average July temperature in your area, you can log on to the following Environment Canada site, and type in or choose a weather station site near you: <www.climate.weatheroffice.ec.gc.ca/climate_normals/index_e.cfm>. Another source suggests that wood preservatives will deter bats, so don't choose treated wood, and only paint or stain the exterior of the house.

According to the NWF, bats find houses mounted on poles or buildings (under the eaves, but still exposed to sunlight) more than twice as fast as those on trees. They claim that houses mounted on trees may not be as suitable because of the reduced exposure to sunlight, and perhaps because they are more vulnerable to predators. Others suggest that the houses can be mounted on trees, situated to receive morning sun and afternoon shade. They all seem to concur that bat houses should be mounted 15 to 20 feet (4.5 to 6 m) off the ground (though 10 to 12 feet [3 to 4 m] may be adequate).

As with much expert advice, there are contradictory points of view, and the ordinary cottager is left with choices that may have to be adjusted after some experimentation. Do what works for you!

Plans for the Johnson Bat House can be found at <www.npwrc.usgs.gov/resource/tools/ndblinds/johnbat.htm>

Raccoons

Raccoons, indigenous to virtually all of temperate North America, are one of the most adaptable wildlife species. About 39 inches (1 meter) long—including the tail, they can weigh from 15 to 45 lbs (7 to 22 kilograms) and can live 10–13 years. Females have one litter per year with an average of four to five kits. They are intelligent and curious opportunistic feeders and truly omnivorous. They also possess remarkable dexterity.

It was this dexterity that allowed an individual to gain entry to a friend's cottage a number of years ago. The family was awakened one very hot night in July by unusual noises in their cottage. When they ventured out to investigate, they discovered a rather large raccoon decimating the

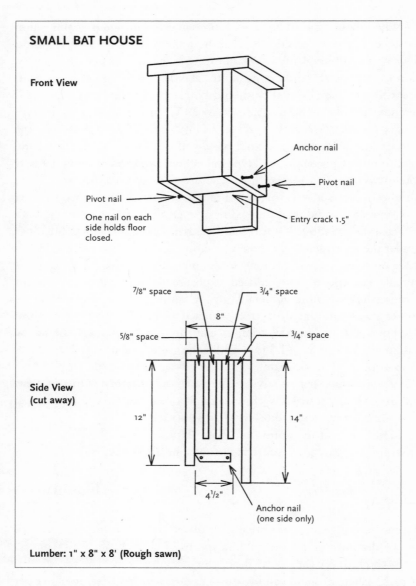

SMALL BAT HOUSE

Front View

Anchor nail

Pivot nail

Pivot nail

One nail on each
side holds floor
closed.

Entry crack 1.5"

7/8" space

3/4" space

8"

5/8" space

3/4" space

Side View
(cut away)

12"

14"

4 1/2"

Anchor nail
(one side only)

Lumber: 1" x 8" x 8' (Rough sawn)

kitchen. A concerted team effort with brooms managed to convince the felon to vacate. After cleaning up, the cottagers discovered that this varmint had come in through a window; they have that design that features horizontal sliders at the bottom. This particular window looks out over their deck, which is only about 18 to 24 inches (45 to 60 cm) below it. As you might expect, on hot nights they opened all of the windows in the cottage. Our intrepid raccoon discovered an open one, slid the screen back, and entered for a late night buffet. It didn't end that night; though there were no other frontal assaults that summer, for the next two years they had exactly the same problem (they weren't sure that it was the same B&E artist, but they remain astonished by the repeat performances). We have exactly the same window/deck layout at our cottage, and ever since their experience, we now close the downstairs sliders, making sure they are secured with the latch, before retiring for the night or leaving for the day.

The most frequent negative encounters with raccoons occur because of improper garbage storage. If raccoons discover an easy food source, they will return again and again. However, even though raccoons may be smart and agile, they aren't stronger than most people. If you can't pull the lid off a can, then they shouldn't be able to. We store our trash in a very heavy, old galvanized steel garbage can; I have chained it through the handles to the TV tower so it can't be tipped over, and a heavy-duty bungie cord keeps the lid secure. Alternatively, you can keep your garbage cans in a secure location, such as a shed (doors and windows must be closed tightly). And never, even though it is tempting, especially if a wee one makes an appearance, feed these bandits!

Occasionally, raccoons will take up residence indoors. As with most problems, proactive measures will minimize the chances of this taking place:

- Make sure that the eaves are in good condition, and that there are no weak areas or holes which would allow access to the attic.

- Screen bathroom, stove, and other vent and attic openings with heavy, galvanized ¼-inch (6-mm) wire mesh (remember the advice about keeping mice out?).

- Install chimney caps and make sure they are securely fastened (chimney caps are also a valuable fire prevention device).

- Trim overhanging tree branches and remove unused TV towers (hire a pro if conditions warrant).

- Keep pet doors locked at night, and keep pets indoors.

- Keep windows that can be easily accessed from the deck or ground locked at night.

- Check porches, decks and sheds for holes; if there are no animals inside, seal them up.

If raccoons do gain entry, there are suggested methods for persuading them to leave. First of all, determine where they are getting in, how many there are, and where they are denned up. If there is more than one point of entry, close all but one. It seems that raccoons do not like bright lights—they are nocturnal creatures—or loud noises. They may be encouraged to find other suitable accommodations if you simply place a battery-operated radio—tuned to a talk station and played loudly—and a battery-operated light (secured so it cannot be knocked over) in the occupied area. You might also spread cayenne pepper or a commercial product like Ropel™ around the entry and inside the hole. To determine the success of your efforts, stuff newspaper in the unsecured hole. If the ball of paper is pushed out the next day, put it back in and check again. Keep this up until the paper remains in the hole for at least 48 hours (this is a fairly reliable sign that the nest is no longer in use). Remove any debris, or deterrents, and secure the hole with galvanized mesh. One source suggests that before making this barrier permanent, you should do a food test to make doubly sure all of the animals have pulled up stakes: place a bit of peanut butter inside the hole so that only an animal inside can get at it (obviously, this means attaching the mesh in such a way as to be able to easily lift a corner). If it is untouched after several days, project "Get The Heck Outta My Place" has been successful. You can then permanently fasten the mesh (if the hole is near ground level, provide enough for an apron, and push it into the ground to discourage digging), and cover with something suitable. Remember that during the spring months the females will be giving birth, so eviction procedures might have to wait until the young are mobile enough to leave the den.

If the raccoons move into the chimney, never try to smoke them out, and if you get them to leave, clean the chimney before starting a fire.

Squirrels

One of the leading raiders of cottage country bird feeders, the squirrel is another intelligent and curious creature who might decide to become as permanent a fixture as your brother-in-law. Both the Eastern Gray Squirrel and the Red Squirrel, the two most common species, are members of the rodent family, and are primarily herbivores. Gray squirrels will store their food in various locations, while reds tend to stock the shelves where they live; thus, a sure sign of reds in the attic is a large store of pinecones, nuts, and fungi.

Preventive measures are similar to those required to keep mice, bats, and raccoons out. If a squirrel has gained entry, finding that hole can be difficult, because an opening the size of a golf ball will allow them to get in. The fascia board at the corners of the building is a common entry point. Removal must be effected during the day, when the squirrels are generally out and about. Cover the hole with the ever-popular galvanized mesh; extend it well beyond the hole to prevent the darlings from gnawing around the patch. Consider the inside-the-hole-food-test outlined in the raccoon segment. Eviction timing, as for other species, must be considered: babies are born and raised between March and May, and again between August and October. The light and radio routine—the same one you read about for raccoons—has also proven effective in convincing squirrels to leave, once the babies have matured enough to come out and hunt for grub. It is advisable to initiate these measures only when you have a few days at the cottage; if you detect animals trapped inside, you will be able to release them. An agitated squirrel near the hole might also suggest that some young ones haven't made it out. Once you are absolutely sure the den has been abandoned, seal the opening permanently.

Sometimes, squirrels will get trapped in chimneys. In this case, lower a thick, rough rope down into the opening so the squirrel can climb out (if you'd capped the chimney in the first place, of course, this never would have happened!).

Porcupines

Unless you leave the door open, a porcupine is not likely to move into your place. Generally, problems with porcupines occur because of their chewing behavior. For example, you don't have to go far to find evidence of their love for plywood; tell-tale sculpted profiles can be found on cottages, camps, cabins, outhouses, and sheds. This behavior is partly explained by their preference for certain substances—obviously something in plywood, and salt. They will often chew the handles of tools, and even the armrests on rocking chairs, anything that human sweat has come in contact with. It is also because, as members of the rodent family, they must chew to keep their continuously growing teeth from getting too long (they are the second largest member of this family; the largest is—you guessed it—the beaver).

To reduce the possibilities of porcupine troubles, remove debris that has accumulated under the camp or shed. If porcupines are currently dining on your buildings, you can staple galvanized mesh to the walls at ground level (a porcupine is only about 12 inches [30 centimeters] at the shoulder, so judge how high you will have to go up. Repellants can also be considered (the manufacturers claim that these are not poisons, but simply have a taste that is very disagreeable to chewing animals).

Wild animals must be treated with respect, and under most circumstances, should never be handled; remember that a cornered animal may attack (if you are bitten, you should seek medical attention). It must also be kept in mind that the procedures described in this chapter are suggestions only, and in no way do I mean to imply that these are the only ways to handle difficulties with cottage critters. Prevention is best achieved through good maintenance, and is really the smartest approach.

In some rare cases, a death sentence, as repulsive as that might seem, may have to be considered as the last option (unless you want to hire a professional). Poisons are illegal in controlling wildlife in some jurisdictions, and frankly, I would never recommend their use. If you are considering shooting, you should consult local authorities first. If you aren't a relatively good shot, get someone who is to do the deed. A wounded animal dies a miserable death.

> **TIP:** *Cooling the cottage at night.* My father-in-law taught me this one. Close every window in the cottage except the one in your bedroom, and one on the other side of the cottage on the same level, if possible. Put a fan—preferably a big square type—in the window of the empty bedroom, facing *out*. The fan blows hot air out through this window, and draws cool night air in through your window. Works remarkably well.

Three to remember:

1. Cover all vents with galvanized screening.
2. Check exterior of cottage for access points.
3. Secure garbage containers and lids.

CHAPTER 17

Making Maple Syrup

MAPLE SYRUP IS PART OF OUR HERITAGE. I've consumed enough to know that it's in my *blood*. And frankly, there is no substitute for the real thing. Every year, I buy a 4-quart (4-liter) can or two from a well-known gentleman entrepreneur up in our neck of the woods (there's a photo of Bill Auld's operation at the end of the chapter). Heck, it's good stuff; I imagine you could get addicted to it—heaven knows it's almost as expensive as illicit drugs!

But if you cottage in maple tree country, then, instead of buying it from a local or the hardware store, there is no reason why you couldn't make your own syrup. And these days, cottagers are spending more and more time up at the lake. Late March into early April—the syrup-making season—is actually a great time to be in the woods. It could be fun. But let's not kid ourselves; though it is not some monumental intellectual challenge, making maple syrup does entail a fair bit of work and organization.

A friend of mine fits the profile of my intended audience: he's a cottager, he's retired, and he always wanted to make maple syrup. The difference is, Moe Gauthier actually did it. In his typical "it-can't-be-that-hard" style, he researched the subject, gathered the necessary hardware, and started production. Naturally, I was intrigued and had to have a look at his setup. I was impressed. From his initial efforts, suggestions, and reference material, this chapter was hatched.

Making maple syrup requires planning. Before the snow flies, you have to plot your campaign. Naturally, you must have access to maple trees, either your own or someone else's (with permission, of course). Hard or sugar maples make the best maple syrup; other varieties can be tapped, but they don't have the same sugar content, and the syrup isn't as good (and, according to some, even birch trees can be tapped). It can be particularly difficult to differentiate between hard (sugar) and soft (silver) maples, so it is best to do so before the leaves fall (Figure 1 includes four species found in northeastern North America).

Tag the trees you would like to tap with flagging tape; bear in mind that you will have to get to these trees when the snow could be three feet deep. For each quart (liter) of syrup, you will need one tap. It is suggested that no tree less than 10 inches (25 cm) in diameter should be tapped, and that trees between 10 and 17 inches (25 to 43 cm) should have only one. Bigger trees can accommodate more than one spile, but be reasonable. If we use an arbitrary figure of, let's say 10 quarts (liters), then you

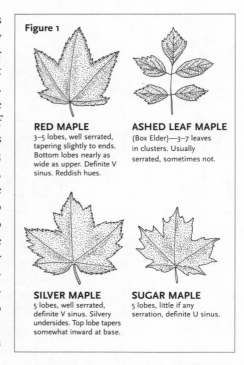

Figure 1

RED MAPLE
3–5 lobes, well serrated, tapering slightly to ends. Bottom lobes nearly as wide as upper. Definite V sinus. Reddish hues.

ASHED LEAF MAPLE
(Box Elder)—3–7 leaves in clusters. Usually serrated, sometimes not.

SILVER MAPLE
5 lobes, well serrated, definite V sinus. Silvery undersides. Top lobe tapers somewhat inward at base.

SUGAR MAPLE
5 lobes, little if any serration, definite U sinus.

would need, at most, 10 trees.

If you are going to boil the sap down over a wood fire, then you will have to have a source of good, dry firewood on hand (at least a face cord or more for ten quarts [10 liters]: a face cord measures 16 inches wide x 4 feet high x 8 feet long; a full cord measures 4 x 4 x 8 feet). Make sure it is covered and in proximity to the theater of operations. Boiling down requires a roaring fire, so even pine and cedar will do (both species burn fast, and so more wood will be required). You will also need containers to

collect the sap, and containers in which to store it. You can locate these during the winter.

Instead of relying on commercial metal sap buckets, you can make your own. The photographs show a common two-kilogram coffee can (an aluminum pie plate provides the cover to keep out snow or rain), and a plastic jug adapted to fit over a spile. Coffee cans—save the plastic lids—can also be used to store the syrup (5 cans should be adequate for storage). You will also need 10 **spiles** or sap spouts, and these can be purchased at many cottage-country hardware stores, at specialty outlets, and even over the Internet.

Sap storage must also be considered. Plastic barrels, the ones used for bulk foods and often seen for sale at produce markets, would be ideal (cleaned thoroughly); some even have handles and a lid. Garbage cans can be used too (plastic ones should be suitable for water storage—make sure they won't contaminate the sap). You will need an evaporator pan: a large surface area and shallow depth are ideal (say, 4 x 14 x 17 inches / 10 x 35 x 43 cm). Two would be even better (see explanation below). A common kitchen skimmer and filters (again, sometimes available in cottage-country hardware stores or from maple syrup specialty stores, or online) are also essential. A proper thermometer is a good investment as well.

Evaporators

This is supposed to be fun and *cheap*. Small-scale evaporators can be purchased, but you don't need something fancy to boil the sap down; in fact, you can simply do so on a gas barbeque. But if we stick to the stricture on cost, then a wood-fired evaporator fits the bill. The simplest structure could be made out of rocks, but cin-

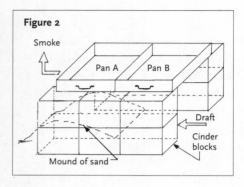

Figure 2

der blocks are preferable because you can make the firebox quickly, and to exact specifications—i.e. the size of your evaporator pan(s). The problem with cinder blocks is that they may crack when heated. The very simple evaporator in Figure 2 could be built in about 10 minutes; I would suggest some experimentation in good weather—maybe one tier of blocks would do; improvise, that's the cottage way! Mound some sand near the back; this creates an arched firebed and will direct the flame toward the bottom of the pan, as in the illustration. The configuration of this evaporator allows for two pans: raw sap is consigned to pan A, while pan B is designated for the trickier, final boiling down. The two-pan system is more efficient, though single-pan evaporation can be managed quite effectively.

The downside to this design is possible smoke-flavoring of the syrup—no chimney or damper, and an inability to properly control the draft. A makeshift draft of sorts could be fashioned out of a couple of extra blocks at the opening, and a little ingenuity could create a kind of chimney out of additional blocks at the rear. Build a fire and you're in the maple syrup business. Naturally, other variations of the cottage evaporator can be constructed from oil drums, old woodstoves, and discarded water pressure tanks, to name a few.

The Process

Sap starts to run in the spring; making maple syrup begins when the temperature at night falls below freezing, and rises above freezing during the day—late March to early April. As an amateur, you might want to set one tap fairly early as a kind of flow meter: sap starts to run, so do you! Choose a location for your tap, and drill a 7/16-inch (11-mm) hole, angled slightly up—Newton's principle—in about 2½ inches / 60 mm (the depth isn't too critical, as long as you get into good wood; keep the bit turning as you back it out to remove the shavings). Tap the spile lightly with a hammer to set it. Hang your bucket and move on to the next tree. The rest is up to Mother Nature, and with any luck she'll cooperate, yielding plenty of the necessary raw material. If you can't boil the sap right away, you will need to store it in a cool place—not a problem early on, but it can become one as the season progresses. Sap can spoil, so storage time should be brief: no more than 48 hours, as bacteria in raw sap propagates quickly.

Once you have collected enough sap, fill both pans to a depth of 2 to 3 inches (50 to 75 mm), and then start a fire (under the pans, of course!). As the sap boils, skim off the scummy foam that collects around the edges. Naturally, the level in each pan will begin to fall. Ladle boiling sap from A into B to bring the level back up in B, and add fresh sap to A to maintain the liquid level. If you can, invent a method to dribble fresh sap into A, such as a coffee can with a hole punched in it suspended above the pan; adding a large quantity of cold sap to Pan A will kill the boiling cycle.

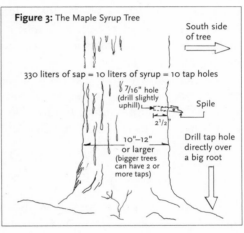

Figure 3: The Maple Syrup Tree

South side of tree

330 liters of sap = 10 liters of syrup = 10 tap holes

7/16" hole (drill slightly uphill)

Spile

2½'

10"–12" or larger (bigger trees can have 2 or more taps)

Drill tap hole directly over a big root

Eventually, you will run out of fresh sap or patience, and want to finish up for the day. You can simply add snow or fresh water to Pan A; don't let it boil dry over the flames, or you may have to throw the pan away. Turn all of your attention to Pan B. As the bubbles begin to get smaller, test the batch using a common metal spatula: the liquid should apron, or slide off the spatula in apron-like sheets, not drops as the sap becomes syrup. If you have a thermometer, the temperature should be about 7°F (4°C) above the boiling point of water. Since the boiling point of water is affected by pressure and altitude, determine that reference marker on the day you boil. As you approach real syrup, the batch can very suddenly rise up in the pan and boil over if you aren't careful. A time-honored, rapid-response remedy is to touch the surface with a bit of butter or bacon, and the boiling will settle. Better kill the fire!

You should probably steer clear of trying to finish the batch over the open fire. The object is to get *close*, and to then transfer your treasure to whatever receptacles you have gathered, and immediately complete the final boil-down over a better regulated heat source (such as the stove in the cottage, or the barbeque). If you overboil, simply add boiling water—or warm sap if possible—to the batch; underboiling can mean a greater risk of spoiling.

Moe Gauthier uses a single pan on his converted woodstove; he wisely chooses to do the final-boil down separately. Once the sap gets close to syrup, he scoops it out into a pot, and boils down in the kitchen, or on a little gas stove set up in the woodshed near his "Sugar Shack." He doesn't use a thermometer, or a spatula to gauge the apron effect. He just waits until it begins to boil over, and then he takes it off the stove and bottles it. It might not pass professional inspection, and I'm certainly no connoisseur, but it tastes darned good!

Pull the spiles when you've made enough syrup, the novelty has worn off, the syrup is getting darker or less sweet, the sap becomes cloudy, or after the sap simply quits running. Do not collect any sap after the maples have started to bud. The holes will heal by themselves.

Storage

The containers you saved for storage should be thoroughly cleaned. Pour the hot syrup—about 180–190°F (80–90°C)—into the cans or jars (if you are using glass jars, make sure they won't break). The syrup must be filtered to remove the niter, and any other gunge that may have collected in it during the boil down. Commercial filters are recommended. They need to be moistened with hot water before you start the filtering process, and should be rinsed out between pourings. If you choose the coffee can/plastic lid containers, seal the lids with freezer or duct tape. It is best to store your syrup in the freezer; this lessens the chance of it going bad. If a batch does get a bit moldy, it's no big deal: skim the mold off, and re-heat to 180–190°F (80–90°C). *Voilà!*

Obviously, the next thing to do is whip up a mess of my "Best Damned Pancakes in the Known Universe" (see page 203), cover generously in your own hot maple syrup, and enjoy.

Three to remember:

1. Organize long before the snow flies.

2. Tap only bigger, healthy trees.

3. Final boil down = controlled conditions.

Bill Auld's Maple Sugar Shack

CHAPTER 18

Coexisting with Small Engines

At the end of my son's third year at university, he landed a job at a summer camp near Parry Sound, Ontario. We were pleased with this, because it was reasonably close to our cottage, and we would be able to pick him up on his days off to join us. He would be responsible for maintenance tasks. While packing for the trip to camp, he mentioned that he would love to know something about small engines, because the camp had go-karts, and he might be expected to service them. Certainly, I am no expert when it comes to internal combustion engines, but I understand how they work—for the most part, I can service them, I can carry out basic troubleshooting techniques, and I can effect some simple repairs. However, I realized that I had been negligent in passing along any of this knowledge to my son. What should I have explained to Matthew? What should I have shown him?

Two Stroke, Four Stroke

Essentially, I could have explained that all small engines work on the principle that a rewind cord is pulled to start the combustion process (unless, of course, a battery-powered starter motor is substituted). Revolving magnets in the flywheel work with the ignition armature and the spark plug to produce a spark in the combustion chamber. The carburetor draws in a precisely regulated fuel and air mixture to form a vapor that is fed into the combustion chamber. When vapor is introduced to spark, ignition—basically a mini explosion—occurs. Ignition leads to a rapid expansion of the air/fuel mixture; expansion of the burning gases forces the piston to move down through the cylinder. The piston is attached to the crankshaft in such a fashion that the crankshaft turns. Momentum carries the piston back toward the top of the cylinder. Intake and exhaust valves open and close to let fresh combustible vapor in and spent gases out. If you're lucky (and have looked after your stuff), then one or two pulls will get the process working on its own: the vapor/intake/spark/power/exhaust cycle will self-perpetuate (see illustrations at the end of the chapter: Parts of the Small Engine—front and side views).

Small engines come in two styles: two stroke and four stroke (outboards are also available in two and four stroke). The difference is in the intake/exhaust cycle, and is perhaps a bit esoteric for most readers. The distinction that most of us are familiar with is that oil and gas must be mixed for a two-stroke engine, while oil and gas are added separately to a four-stroke (cars and trucks are almost all equipped with four-stroke engines). Oil lubricates the moving parts of both types of engine, but is introduced differently. It is actually this characteristic of the two-stroke that has earned it a bad rap; because the oil is mixed with the gas, the two-stroke engine produces far more pollution than a four-stroke. Manufacturers have responded to pressure from legislators and environmental groups and have moved to replace two-stroke engines for many traditional two-stroke applications (e.g. the lawnmower).

Maintenance

I would also have told Matthew that, like most things, proper maintenance is the fundamental first step in small engine care, regardless of the type. I realize that time at the cottage is precious, and caring for the outboard, the mower, the blower, the trimmer, the power washer, the generator, or gas water pump may not be a priority; most of us have the notion that if it works, don't worry, be happy! However, you can save yourself a good deal of aggravation and money for parts and repairs if you follow a regular maintenance schedule. The following includes generic maintenance instructions; you should always consult your manual for special instructions for your model. Remember to service more frequently if you use a small engine heavily, or under dusty or dirty conditions.

Before and/or after each use:

- ⚑ If the engine is a four-stroke model then you should check the oil.
- ⚑ Remove debris around the muffler (obviously not a concern for most outboards).
- ⚑ Check the overall condition of the engine and the system it operates.
- ⚑ Use only fresh, clean fuel, and wipe up any spills before starting.
- ⚑ Clean the exterior surfaces.

Each season:

- ⚑ Service the air cleaner/filter assembly.
- ⚑ Clean the fuel tank and line; replace the in-line fuel filter in the outboard.
- ⚑ Clean the carburetor float bowl, if equipped. (If you drain the fuel from the tank at the end of every season, you should be able to avoid cleaning fuel tank, line, and float bowl; gummy residue from old fuel can cause a lot of problems. Many outboard engines are equipped with a special orifice; a lubricant can be sprayed directly into the cylinders via this orifice.)
- ⚑ Inspect the starter cord for wear (if you can't find a starter cord, it's either broken, or you have electric start!).
- ⚑ Clean the cooling fins on the engine block (another excuse to buy that compressor!).
- ⚑ Check engine compression (a special tool is required to obtain accurate compression readings).
- ⚑ Inspect the muffler.
- ⚑ Replace the spark plug; set the gap with proper feeler gauges (see photograph on page 189).
- ⚑ Check the engine mounting bolts/nuts.
- ⚑ Inspect the ignition armature and wires (clean legs and magnet with 400/600 grit wet/dry paper).
- ⚑ Adjust the carburetor if necessary.
- ⚑ Inspect springs and linkages; lubricate linkages.
- ⚑ Change the oil in four-stroke machines.

Checking and Changing
the Oil in Four-Stroke Engines

Fresh oil has the appearance of liquid honey. Heat and dirt particles in the crankcase gradually cause the oil to darken. Dirty oil loses much of its ability to protect engine components; therefore, manufacturers often recommend changing the oil every 25 hours—a season of normal use (for a new engine, you should change the oil after the first 5 hours of operation). Despite this advice, this means that, for most cottagers, the oil is likely to get a change every couple of years!

1. Make it a habit to check the oil level before every use of a small engine; checking while the engine is cold produces the most accurate reading. If it's low, top up the level.

2. To prevent dirt and debris from falling into the crankcase, wipe the area around the cap prior to removal.

3. If the engine is equipped with a dipstick, pull out the dipstick, wipe off with a clean towel, insert the dipstick all the way in, pull out, and check the oil level. Do this at least twice to get a proper reading. The oil level should never be above the FULL line or below the ADD line.

4. Use only the type of oil specified in your owner's manual.

5. Change the oil when the engine has been run for several minutes (i.e. warmed up).

6. Disconnect the spark plug lead and secure it away from the plug. This prevents accidental startup.

7. Clear debris from the drain plug—prior to removal—to prevent it from getting into the crankcase.

8. If your engine has an oil filter, replace it as well (lightly oil the filter gasket with clean oil). Install hand tight.

9. Add only the required amount of oil. Check the oil level.

10. Reconnect the spark plug lead and run the engine at idle to check for leaks.

11. Dispose of the oil properly.

Checking and Servicing Spark Plugs

The electrodes on a spark plug must be clean to produce the powerful spark required for ignition. If you have to yank repeatedly on the rewind rope to get the old mower running, then chances are the villain could be a dirty plug. Fortunately, a spark plug is easy to service and cheap to replace.

1. Disconnect the lead from the plug and remove any debris to avoid getting it in the combustion chamber.

2. Use an appropriate socket to remove the plug.

3. Clean deposits from the electrodes with a wire brush or 400/600 paper (tougher deposits may require a knife or scraper).

4. Inspect the plug for cracks in the porcelain or electrodes that have been burned away (replace immediately if either condition exists).

5. Use a spark plug gauge to measure and set the gap between the two electrodes (see illustration). Check your manual for the appropriate gap. When set correctly, the gauge will drag slightly as it is pulled through the gap.

Checking and setting spark plug gap

6. Reinstall the plug; *do not overtighten.*

7. Attach the lead to the plug.

A spark tester (see photo) offers an inexpensive, easy way to diagnose ignition problems, without the bother of removing the plug to examine it.

Spark tester

1. Attach the spark plug lead to the long terminal of the tester; attach the alligator clip to the plug.

2. Pull the rewind cord, and look for a spark in the tester's "window."

3. If you see a spark jump the gap, the ignition system is functioning.

A dirty plug, or a plug with an improperly set gap may not allow the spark to jump the gap between the electrodes consistently. This will result in spark "miss" and decreased performance. The spark tester can also be used to determine spark miss.

Servicing Air Cleaners

An air cleaner is an engine's first line of defense against dirt. If an air cleaner is not maintained, then dirt and dust will gradually make their way into the carburetor and engine.

Many types of air cleaners are used in small engines, and most contain a foam or pleated-paper element (some contain both).

To service a foam air cleaner:

1. Remove and inspect the air cleaner once per season; replace if it is torn or badly discolored.

2. A dirty foam element air filter can be cleaned in warm soapy water. When it is dry, add a *small* amount of clean engine oil to the element; squeeze the element to spread the oil throughout, and then squeeze out any excess into a paper towel.

3. Inspect the gasket, and replace if necessary.

4. Reassemble and install.

To service a pleated-paper or dual-element air cleaner:

5. Remove cover, and separate the pre-cleaner (if equipped) from the cartridge.

6. Tap cartridge gently on a flat surface to remove loose dirt. Inspect the element and replace if dirty, wet or crushed.

7. Inspect the pre-cleaner (if equipped). Check your manual; the pre-cleaner may or may not need lubrication.

8. Clean cartridge housing with a dry cloth.

9. Reassemble and install. Make sure that any tabs are in their slots on the engine housing.

Troubleshooting

The following troubleshooting charts have been borrowed from Briggs and Stratton's guide: *Small Engine Care and Repair*. Obviously, many of the procedures require instructions from specific small engine manuals (these are denoted by *).

IF THE ENGINE WON'T START

Ask this question:	If the answer is yes:
Is the fuel tank empty?	Fill fuel tank; if engine is still hot, wait until it cools before filling tank.
Is the shut-off valve closed?	Open fuel shut-off valve.
Is the fuel diluted with water?	Empty tank, replace fuel and check for leaks in fuel tank cap.
Is the fuel line or inlet screen blocked?	Disconnect inlet screen from engine and clean using compressed air. Do not use compressed air near engine.*
Is the fuel tank cap clogged or unvented?	Make sure cap is vented and air holes are not clogged.*
Is the carburetor blocked?	Remove spark plug lead and spark plug; pour teaspoon of fuel directly into cylinder; reinsert spark plug and lead; start engine; if it runs shortly before quitting, overhaul carburetor.*
Is the engine flooded?	Adjust float in fuel bowl, if adjustable; make sure choke isn't set too high.*
Is the spark plug fouled?	Remove spark plug; clean contacts or replace plug.
Is the spark plug gap set incorrectly?	Remove spark plug; reset gap.
Is the spark plug lead faulty?	Test lead with spark tester, then test engine.
Is the kill switch shorted?	Repair or replace kill switch.*
Is the flywheel key damaged?	Replace flywheel key, then try to start engine; if it still won't start, check ignition armature, wire connections or points.*
Are the valves, piston, cylinder or connecting rod damaged?	Perform compression test. If test indicates poor compression, inspect valves, piston and cylinder for damage and repair as needed.*

IF THE ENGINE RUNS POORLY

Ask this question:	If the answer is yes:
Is the fuel mixture too rich?	Adjust the carburetor.*
Is the air filter plugged?	Replace the air cleaner.
Is the engine dirty?	Clean the engine.*
Is the oil level low?	Add oil to the engine. NOTE: Never add oil to the gasoline for a four-stroke engine.*
Are any shrouds or cooling fins missing or broken?	Install new parts as needed.*
Is the fuel mixture too lean?	Adjust the carburetor.*
Is there a leaky gasket?	Replace the gasket.*
Is the fuel tank vent or fuel tank screen plugged?	Clean the fuel tank vent and fuel tank screen.*
Does the combustion chamber contain excess carbon?	Clean carbon from the piston and head.*
Is the flywheel loose?	Inspect the flywheel and key; replace as needed.*
Is the spark plug fouled?	Clean the spark plug.
Is the spark plug faulty or gap incorrect?	Replace the spark plug or adjust the spark plug gap.
Are the breaker points faulty?	Install a solid-state ignition.*
Is the carburetor set incorrectly?	Adjust the carburetor.
Is the valve spring weak?	Replace the valve spring.
Is the valve clearance set incorrectly?	Adjust the valve clearance to recommended settings.

Remember to *use the correct tools and always work safely.*

- ⚡ Keep an approved fire extinguisher near your work area (or in your boat).
- ⚡ Disconnect the plug wire to prevent accidental starting when servicing.
- ⚡ Avoid contact with hot engine parts.
- ⚡ Never strike the flywheel with a hammer or hard object.
- ⚡ Disengage the cutting blade, wheels, or other equipment, if possible.
- ⚡ Remove fuel from the tank, and close the fuel shutoff valve before transporting.
- ⚡ Keep your feet, hands, and clothing away from moving engine and equipment components.
- ⚡ Use eye and hearing protection.

Check out <www.smallengineadvisor.com> on the Web; it offers hundreds of service tips.

Three to remember:

1. Always read your engine and equipment manual for the proper service and maintenance schedules and procedures.

2. Regular maintenance and service will save you a lot of aggravation (and money) in the long run.

3. Practice safe work habits.

PARTS OF THE SMALL ENGINE front view

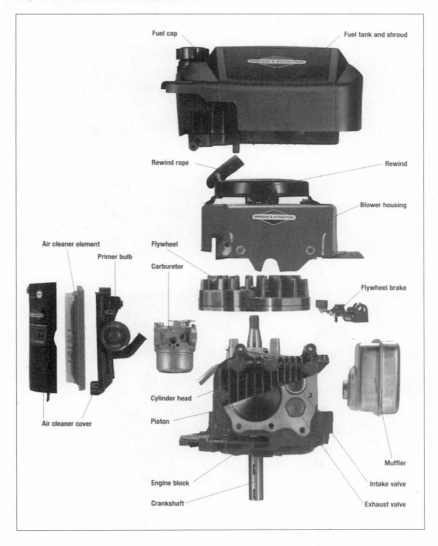

Fuel cap

Fuel tank and shroud

Rewind rope

Rewind

Blower housing

Air cleaner element

Flywheel

Primer bulb

Carburetor

Flywheel brake

Cylinder head

Piston

Air cleaner cover

Muffler

Engine block

Intake valve

Crankshaft

Exhaust valve

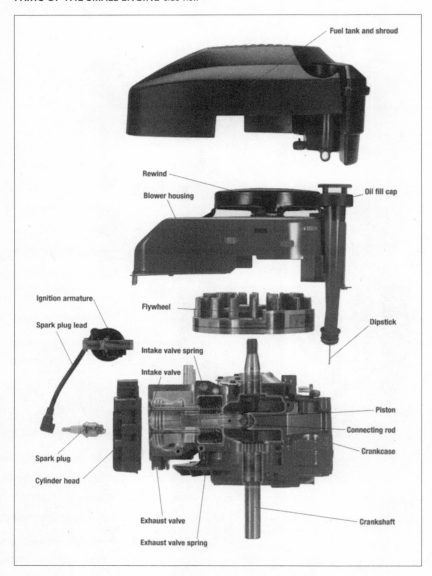

Fuel tank and shroud

Rewind

Blower housing

Oil fill cap

Ignition armature

Flywheel

Spark plug lead

Dipstick

Intake valve spring

Intake valve

Piston

Connecting rod

Crankcase

Spark plug

Cylinder head

Exhaust valve

Crankshaft

Exhaust valve spring

CHAPTER 19

Fishing—
From the Lake
to the Plate

THIS IS GOING BACK SOME—though surely older readers will remember—but Ron Popeel, that quintessential TV marketing giant, once peddled a product called the Fishin' Magician™. Obviously, the folks at Popeel had never met my next-door lake neighbor. Jim Muncy is the real fishin' magician, and his success rate, especially for walleye and small mouth bass, is legendary (truthfully, he is only interested in pickerel, but he will keep bass if the former aren't biting). To be sure, he has a natural gift, but he also attributes his achievement to study, a tried and true methodology, and modern technology. In particular, he credits a now out-of-print little book titled *Lunkers Love Night Crawlers* for shaping his fishing system (regrettably, his only copy was stolen at a college interest course he hosted—says something about the legendary dishonesty of fishermen!).

Jim, on the right, shares his expertise with fishing buddy Tim.

Jim does not own the typical treasure-trove tackle box; most lures, in his opinion, are meant to attract the fisherman, not the fish. He swears by the simplest of rigs: sinker, hook, and a fresh dew worm. The hooks are #6, while the sinker is a Water Gremlin™ split shot—PSS®-3—secured to the line about 12–18 inches (30–45 cm) from the hook (see diagram). The dew worm is hooked about ¾ inch (18 mm) from the end, so it will look as natural as possible to the fish (though how the heck the fish knows what a dew worm is supposed to look like has never been fully explained to me!).

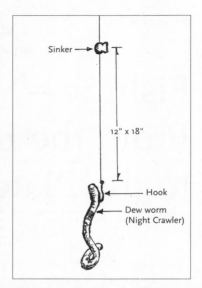

He also stresses the use of fresh worms; he changes them regularly when he's fishing, never allowing them to get limp or damaged (the fact that he buys worms in flats of 500, and stores them in a "worm fridge" out in the shed might give you some idea of the depth of his faith in this particular bait).

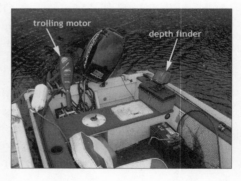

Other than the essential boat, outboard motor, and fishing rod (Jim prefers the open-face spinning varieties loaded with 6- or 8-pound test), a depth finder and an electric trolling motor must be part of your equipment inventory. The depth finder allows you to locate and mentally map shoals, while the trolling motor lets you work them. Jim does not still fish (i.e. anchored in one spot), and he maintains that typical shoreline trolling is not very fruitful. At this point in his fishing career, he can find just about every productive rock structure in our lake, but he still relies on the depth finder to maintain the appropriate depth: about 12 to 20 feet (3 to 6 m). He works the edges of the shoals, trolling back and forth. He also prefers to fish from the back of the boat, always trolling in reverse (some trolling motors have more power in the forward mode, so depending on the model, Jim has even rotated the head to accommodate his style). In this manner, fishing lines are less likely to become tangled in the trolling motor prop. He suggests that the worm should be about 16 inches (40 cm) from the bottom, and he will regularly gauge the depth by simply releasing the line, letting the sinker hit bottom, and then reeling in. If he doesn't get a hit in the first few minutes, he moves on, never staying very long on any unproductive structure.

Hooking and landing a fish must also be managed systematically. If you get a strike, release the bailer immediately and let the fish run with the line. Jim maintains that walleye are much smarter than the average fisherman supposes, and will grab the bait and take off with it, sometimes running for 20 or 30 feet (6 to 9 m) before actually swallowing. After a measured time—dictated, unfortunately, by experience—engage the bailer and carefully test to see if the fish is still there. If it demonstrates that it still has an interest, then set the hook with a quick, firm yank. Reeling in a good-sized fish requires a bit of patience, and Jim rarely relies on the reel's drag when landing the big ones, preferring instead to back reel when the fish decides it doesn't want to get in the boat just yet. Once you get the fish close, use the landing net; if it's a keeper, load it in the live well. If it's not, get the hook out quickly, and release the fish. Jim suggests that if the hook is deeply embedded, just cut the line as close to the hook as possible and the fish's corrosive digestive system will take care of the rest. (see notes at the end of the chapter).

Cleaning Them

Okay, you've landed some keepers, and now you have to clean them. One of the most common ways to clean a fish is to fillet it. Though the procedure is reasonably simple, it does take practice.

1. Lay the fish on a flat work surface (preferably on some clean newspaper). Insert the tip of a sharp thin filleting knife into the dorsal surface just slightly back from the head. Keep the blade as close to the spine as possible, Figure 1.

2. Cut to the rib cage and then back toward the tail—keep the knife blade parallel to the spine. At the end of the rib cage, push the knife tip through to the anus, Figure 2.

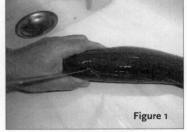

Figure 1

3. Continue to cut through to the end of the tail, keeping the blade flat against the spine, Figure 3.

4. Make a slightly angled incision just behind the gills, cutting through to the spine and rib cage. It should intersect with the initial cut, Figure 4.

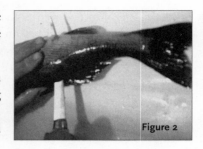

Figure 2

5. Lift the corner, and carefully cut the fillet away from the rib cage. Keep the knife close to the bones. Note that you will have to cut through a small row of lateral bones about half way down the rib cage (the neophyte will sometimes mistake these for the main ribs and cut right out through the middle of the fillet); these will be removed later. See Figure 5.

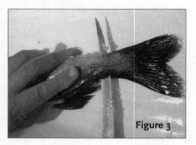

Figure 3

6. Once you clear the rib cage, cut the fillet clean of the guts by making an incision down the middle of the belly from the anus, Figure 6.

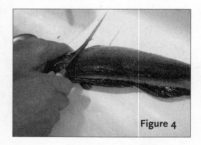

Figure 4

7. Flip the fish over and repeat the process (this is a bit more challenging, as you have less fish to work with). Hopefully, you will now possess two lovely fillets. In turn, lay each one out, firmly secure the tip, and slide the knife under the flesh and along the inside surface of the skin, Figure 7. You can buy filleting boards, and they make this

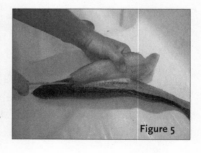

Figure 5

task a good deal easier. My father-in-law made his own. Why buy it, if you can make one for next to nothing? It consists of a scrap piece of ¾- x 6- x 18-inch plywood; the legs are four short pieces of dowel. He bent the nose of one leg of an old welding clamp, and this device holds the fillet securely in place. In fact, he cleaned all of his fish on this board, and this made washing-up rather simple.

8. If you run your thumb up the center of the fillet, you will find that row of lateral bones you cut through in Step 5. Cut this strip out, being careful to remove the bones, but as little flesh as possible (Figure 8).

9. That's it. Wash the fillets and dispose of the carcass.

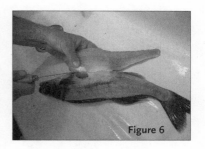
Figure 6

Cooking Them

Jim's wife, Pat, cooks up the best mess of fish in the world. Her recipe is probably not unique, but it is the standard by which we measure all others. An invitation for fish dinner—which generally just consists of heaps of deep-fried fish, a tossed salad, and potato chips or potato salad—is always a summer highlight, and an occasion to disregard calorie counts and cholesterol intake. Here's a cottage tip: if you're not much of fisherperson yourself, always curry favor with a fisherperson by offering to help with any task; in this way, the fisherperson will feel compelled to invite you to fish fries.

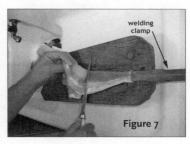
welding clamp
Figure 7

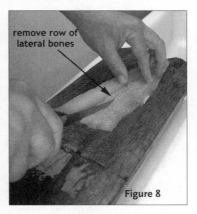
remove row of lateral bones
Figure 8

The coating ingredients consist of flour, cracker crumbs, and eggs. Pat advises crushing the crackers in a zip-lock bag; it is a much neater method. Add some milk to two or three eggs (depends on the quantity of fillets you'll be cooking), and beat gently. Lay out some sheets of waxed paper to work on.

Once all of the ingredients have been prepared, wash the fillets one last time. Shake off any excess water; however, the fillets need to be moist. Dredge the fillets in flour (Step 1) then dip into the egg mixture (Step 2) and coat in the cracker crumbs (Step 3).

The final step is the most important. Pat deep-fries her fish (you can't beat the flavor) in canola oil, and she never uses the oil more than twice. She prefers a heavy, cast-iron Dutch oven, but will use an electric

Step 1

Step 2

Step 3

Step 4

deep fryer (in the photo, the fish is cooking in a borrowed propane-fired model—keeps the splatter and smell outside). The oil is ready when a drop of water sizzles. It is important to maintain adequate heat, otherwise, the fillets will absorb too much oil; if the oil starts to smoke, then it is too hot. CAUTION: *never leave the oil unattended!*

The fillets are cooked when they float to the surface and are a delicious golden brown. Remove and place in a paper towel-lined serving platter. Serve to an appreciative group of diners.

Enforcement staff at the Ontario Ministry of Natural Resources in Parry Sound, Ontario, suggested that if you're fishing for the meal value, you should keep a fish that has been deeply hooked, if it is a legal species and the appropriate size. They did concur with Jim that cutting the line and leaving a deeply embedded hook was better than trying to remove it.

If you are practicing catch and release methods, you should be fishing with barbless hooks.

Three to remember:

1. Learn from successful fishermen.

2. Consider the long-term health of the fishery in your lake and the lakes you fish in.

3. If you don't fish, curry favor with someone who does.

Loaves
and Fishes

COTTAGES AND FOOD GO TOGETHER, and since cottages and guests also seem to go together, cottage dwellers often find themselves having to prepare meals for somewhat larger groups, perhaps at very short notice. It creates a bit of a dilemma because we certainly don't want to spend too much valuable holiday time at the sink, stove, or barbeque, and yet we want to serve up good fare. Hot dogs, corn, and burgers have their place in the grand scheme of casual victuals, but bad weather and/or a desire to be a bit more creative might require substitutions. Most of us have a couple of standby recipes for these occasions, and every cottager will have a few good cookbooks to consult, but additional options are always welcome.

In this chapter, I offer a few simple meal prep suggestions that are great tasting, easy enough to prepare, and can be readily adjusted for a crowd. I have also tried to keep the average weekend home larder in mind. No point including recipes that require hard-to-come-by ingredients. And I have opted for the two-meal-a-day regimen: brunch and dinner. There is no way any guest should expect three squares: hit 'em hard at about 10 a.m. and again at 6 or 7 p.m., with maybe a snack mid-afternoon. Let them pay for a resort if they want breakfast, lunch, and dinner!

Strata-Various 1-2-3
(These are super easy and mighty tasty.)

- 3 cups (750 mL) cubed white bread (it's one meal so forget the multigrain)
- 1 cup (250 mL) finely diced ham
- 1 cup (250 mL) shredded Swiss cheese
- 2 green onions, thinly sliced on diagonal
- 2 cups (500 mL) cooked broccoli florets
- 5 eggs, beaten (if you must, make them Omega eggs to balance the negative effects of white bread)
- 1½ cups (375 mL) milk
- ½ tsp (2 mL) each, salt and pepper

Preheat oven to 350°F (180°C). Lightly oil a 10-inch (25-cm) pie plate or shallow casserole dish. Spread bread cubes evenly in dish.

Spread ham, cheese, green onions, and broccoli over bread cubes. In a bowl, whisk eggs with milk, salt, and pepper. Pour over bread mixture.

Bake in center of preheated oven for 30 to 40 minutes or until set and golden. Let rest for 10 minutes before slicing and serving.

Serves 4 to 6.

Variations:

California: Substitute leftover chicken for ham, Monterey Jack cheese for Swiss, and add 2 seeded, chopped tomatoes for broccoli.

Stampede: Substitute chopped cooked steak for ham and cheddar cheese for Swiss. Add 1 tsp (5 mL) chili powder to milk mixture if you want to heat it up.

Florentine: Skip the meat. Squeeze the water from 1 pkg (340 g) thawed frozen chopped spinach. Substitute mozzarella cheese for Swiss and 2 seeded, chopped tomatoes for broccoli.

Uptown: Substitute smoked salmon for ham and asparagus tips for broccoli. Add 1 tsp (5 mL) chopped fresh dill or ½ tsp (2 mL) dried dillweed to the egg mixture.

The Best Damned Pancakes in the Known Universe
(These pancakes are about 3 to 4 times the size of Aunt What's-Her-Name's, and are situated culinary-wise somewhere between a traditional pancake and a crêpe.)

- 1½ cups (375 mL) flour
- 4 tbsp (60 mL) icing sugar
- 2 tsp (10 mL) baking powder
- 4 eggs
- 2 cups (500 mL) milk
- dash of vanilla extract or 1 tbsp (15 mL) rum
- 1 lb (450 g) bacon, cooked and fat reserved

Combine flour, icing sugar, and baking powder in a large bowl; mix thoroughly. Beat eggs, milk, and vanilla extract in a separate bowl. Add to dry ingredients and beat until relatively smooth.

Naturally, pancakes must be served with bacon. Lightly grease a pan with ½ tsp (2 mL) of the reserved fat before each pancake is cooked. Scoop about ⅔ cup (80 mL) of the mixture for each pancake (should create a pancake about 8 inches/25 cm in diameter—tip the pan to spread the mixture out if necessary).

Add blueberries or raspberries—if available—to provide an unforgettable taste experience. Cover with real maple syrup.

Serves 4 people, or 6 kids (not teenagers).

Good Solid, Delicious Dinner

Sweet and Sour Meatballs
(My mom makes these; the bonus is that these meatballs do not need to be browned.)

- 2 lbs (900 g) lean ground beef
- 1 cup (250 mL) bread crumbs or oatmeal
- 1 beaten egg
- ½ tsp (2 mL) salt
- ½ cup (125 mL) milk or cream

Mix ingredients in a large bowl, and then form into meatballs (about 24). DO NOT BROWN. Just place the balls in a 9- x 13-inch (2 L) ovenproof dish. In another bowl (or wash the first one, if you will), mix the following ingredients for the sauce:

- ¾ cup (175 mL) water
- ¾ cup (175 mL) vinegar
- 1½ cups (375 mL) brown sugar (firmly packed)
- 1 tsp (5 mL) dry mustard
- 1 cup (250 mL) ketchup

Pour the sauce over the meatballs. Heat oven to 350°F (175°C). Place the dish in the oven; bake uncovered for 1 hour. Turn the meatballs after the first half hour. Delicious. Serve with rice or noodles and a salad.

Feeds 6 normal people (not teenagers!).

Cabbage Casserole
(Kinda like cabbage rolls, but a lot less bother.)

- 1 lb (450 g) ground beef
- 1 cup (250 mL) diced onions
- 1 tsp (5 mL) salt
- dash pepper
- ¼ cup (60 mL) rice
- 1 small can (250 mL) tomato soup
- 1 can water (the soup can)
- 1 tbsp (15 mL) brown sugar
- 1 tbsp (15 mL) lemon juice
- 3 cups (750 mL) shredded cabbage

Lightly brown the beef with the onions—drain off the fat. Add the salt, pepper, rice, soup, water, brown sugar, and lemon juice. Mix well.

Arrange the shredded cabbage on the bottom of a greased casserole dish. Pour the meat mixture over the cabbage.

Heat oven to 350°F (175°C). Cover and bake for 1 hour.

You can add crumbled bacon bits and/or mushrooms to vary the flavor. Serve with mashed potatoes and a salad.

Feeds 4–6.

Gramaroni
(This recipe—couldn't be simpler—got its name because my mother-in-law, Beth Abbott, used to make this for the kids—big and small—at the cottage, and it continues to be a family favorite.)

- 4 cups (1 L) uncooked macaroni elbows
- 4 cups (1 L) grated cheddar cheese (medium or old)
- salt

Add the macaroni to boiling, salted water. Cook *al dente*. Drain.

Preheat oven to 400°F (200°C).

Sprinkle one-third of the grated cheese on the bottom of a casserole dish (best if the dish is lightly sprayed with a nonstick product). Add half of the macaroni. Spread one-third of the grated cheese over the macaroni. Add the remaining macaroni. Spread the remainder of the grated cheese on top. Place, uncovered, in oven. Bake for 30 to 35 minutes, or until cheese on top is a crispy shade of brown.

Feeds 4–6 adults or 3 teenaged boys.

Roman Fritatta

- 1 tsp (5 mL) vegetable oil
- 1 small onion, peeled, halved and sliced
- 1 pkg (300 g) thawed, well-drained frozen chopped spinach or 1 cup (250 mL) cooked, chopped spinach
- ¼ cup (60 mL) golden raisins
- ¼ tsp (1 mL) cayenne pepper
- 10 eggs, beaten
- ¼ cup (60 mL) milk
- ½ tsp (2 mL) Dijon mustard
- ½ tsp (2 mL) each, salt and pepper
- 1 cup (250 mL) shredded mozzarella cheese or four-cheese blend
- 1 tbsp (15 mL) toasted pine nuts

Preheat oven to 375°F (190°C). Lightly grease a 9-inch (23-cm) glass pie plate or casserole. Heat oil in a nonstick skillet set over medium heat. Add the onion and cook, stirring often, for 5 minutes. Add the spinach, raisins, and cayenne pepper. Reserve.

Whisk eggs with milk, mustard, salt, and pepper. Stir in onion mixture and cheese, then pour into prepared pie plate or casserole. Sprinkle pine nuts over the top.

Bake in center of oven for 25 to 30 minutes or until set in the center and golden brown. Let stand for 5 minutes before slicing.

Serves 6 to 8.

Swiss Steak

(A solid choice. I wonder if the Swiss really had anything to do with this?)

- 2 lbs (900 g) round steak (about ¾-inch / 18-mm thick)
- 1 tsp (5 mL) salt
- pepper
- 2 tbsp (30 mL) all-purpose flour
- 2 tbsp (30 mL) vegetable oil
- 1 small onion, sliced
- 2 cups (500 mL) tomato juice
- 1 tsp (5 mL) Worcestershire sauce
- 1 tbsp (30 mL) chopped celery
- 1 tbsp (30 mL) chopped green pepper
- ¼ cup (60 mL) sliced mushrooms

Leave steak in one piece or cut into bite-size pieces. Season with salt and pepper; sprinkle with flour. Heat the oil in a heavy frying pan. Brown meat on both sides; brown onions. Add remaining ingredients and stir well. Cover and cook slowly on top of the stove for 1 hour or bake in a moderate oven (325°F / 160°C) for 1¼ to 1½ hours or until tender. Add more liquid if necessary, to keep meat from sticking.

Serves 4–6, depending on appetites.

Chicken Cacciatora

(Now here's a retro recipe!)

- 1 cut-up chicken—3 to 4 lb (1.5 to 2 kg)
- ¼ (60 mL) cup all-purpose flour
- ¼ (60 mL) cup olive oil
- 2 medium onions, sliced
- 1 clove garlic, minced
- 2½ cups (725 mL) canned tomatoes
- 1 can tomato sauce—5½ oz (170 mL)
- 1 tsp (5 mL) salt
- 1 tsp (5 mL) oregano
- ½ tsp (2 mL) celery seed
- ¼ tsp (1 mL) pepper
- 1 bay leaf
- ¼ cup (60 mL) dry white wine (optional)

Coat chicken pieces with flour; brown in olive oil. Remove chicken from skillet, add onions and garlic; sauté until tender but not brown.

Combine remaining ingredients (except wine). Return chicken to skillet and pour sauce on top. Cover and simmer 45 minutes; stir in wine (if using). Cook uncovered, turning chicken occasionally, about 20 minutes or until chicken is tender and sauce is thick. Skim off excess fat and remove bay leaf. Serve with rice or noodles.

Serves 4 to 6.

Super But Simple Soups
(good substitutes for dinner)

Hamburger Soup
(Now this will fill you up!)

- 2 tbsp (30 mL) olive oil
- 1 lb (500 g) lean ground beef
- 1 onion, chopped
- 3 cloves garlic, minced
- 3 cups (750 mL) sliced mushrooms
- 2 stalks celery, chopped
- 3 cups (750 mL) beef stock
- 3 cups (750 mL) water
- 2 carrots, chopped
- 1 large potato, peeled and diced
- 2 cups turnip or rutabaga, diced
- ½ tsp (2 mL) dried thyme (or 2 tsp/10 mL fresh)
- 2 tbsp (25 mL) fresh parsley
- ½ cup (125 mL) barley
- 1 28 oz (796 mL) can of tomatoes, chopped
- ½ cup (125 mL) red wine
- 1 tbsp (15 mL) Worcestershire sauce
- salt and pepper to taste

In a large saucepan, heat 1 tbsp (15 mL) oil over medium heat. Add ground beef and sauté for 5 minutes (meat is no longer pink). Drain and set aside. Heat remaining oil in the saucepan. Add onion, garlic, mushrooms and celery; sauté for 4 minutes.

Return beef to saucepan. Add stock and water, carrots, potato, turnip, thyme, parsley, barley, tomatoes with juice, wine, and Worcestershire sauce; bring to a boil. Reduce heat, cover, and simmer for 30 minutes or until barley is tender. Stir occasionally. Season with salt and pepper.

Serves 8.

Mom's Chicken and Rice Soup
(Obviously, if it has "Mom" in it, it's gotta be good!)

- 1 tbsp (15 mL) butter
- 1 tbsp (15 mL) olive or safflower oil
- 2 leeks, white and light green parts only, sliced
- 1 onion, chopped
- 2 stalks celery, sliced
- 4 cups (1 L) chicken stock
- 4 cups (1 L) water
- ½ cup (125 mL) white wine (optional)
- 2 bone-in chicken legs or bone-in chicken breast pieces, skin removed
- 2 bay leaves
- 1 tsp (5 mL) chopped fresh thyme or ¼ tsp (1 mL) dried thyme
- ⅓ cup (80 mL) long-grain rice
- 2 carrots, scraped and sliced
- ½ cup (125 mL) frozen peas, partially thawed
- ¼ cup (60 mL) chopped, fresh parsley
- salt and freshly ground pepper to taste

In a large saucepan, heat butter and oil over medium heat. Add leeks, onion, and celery; sauté for 4 minutes. Add stock and water, wine, chicken pieces, bay leaves, and thyme; bring to a boil. Reduce heat, cover, and simmer for 40 minutes. Remove from heat.

Remove chicken pieces from the saucepan and place on a cutting board. When cool enough to handle, remove meat from bones and discard bones. Cut chicken into bite-sized pieces and return to saucepan.

Add rice, carrots, and peas; cover and simmer for 20 minutes or until rice is tender. Discard bay leaves.

Stir in parsley and season with salt and pepper.

Serves 4 to 6.

Note: One large onion can be used to replace leeks. If substituting noodles for rice, add 1 cup (250 mL) dried noodles and cook for 10 minutes or until tender but firm.

Reasonably Fast and Easy Sweets

Butterscotch Brownies
(Another Abbott cottage favorite.)

- ½ cup (125 mL) butter
- 1 cup (250 mL) brown sugar
- ½ tsp (2 mL) vanilla extract
- 1 egg, beaten
- pinch of salt
- ¾ cup (175 mL) all-purpose flour
- 1 tsp (5 mL) baking powder
- ½ cup (125 mL) chopped walnuts (you could substitute pecans)

Melt butter; add sugar, vanilla, beaten egg, and salt. Stir in flour and baking powder. Add walnuts. Pour into lightly greased 8- x 8-inch (20- x 20-cm) pan. Preheat oven to 350°F (175°C). Bake for 30 minutes. Ice with a plain butter icing if desired. Cut into squares.

Don't worry about putting the leftovers away!

Makes about 16 brownies.

Pineapple Ambrosia

- 1 cup (250 mL) drained pineapple chunks
- ⅔ cup (150 mL) whipping cream
- 2 tsp (10 mL) lemon juice
- 2 tbsp (30 mL) sugar
- 8 large marshmallows cut in 4 pieces (or 32 little mallows)

Chill pineapple chunks. Pour cream into a chilled bowl; add lemon juice and beat until stiff. Fold in sugar and marshmallows; chill. Fold chilled pineapple chunks into whipped cream mixture when ready to serve. Serve immediately.

Note: any fresh or frozen fruit may be used instead of pineapple chunks. If frozen berries are used, keep in refrigerator until almost thawed.

Serves 4 to 6.

Rolled Oats Cookies
(Now is this simple or what?)

- ½ cup (125 mL) butter or margarine
- 1 cup (250 mL) brown sugar
- 1 tsp (5 mL) vanilla extract
- 2 cups (500 mL) rolled oats

Melt butter; add sugar, vanilla, and rolled oats. Mix thoroughly. Press into a greased 8- x 8-inch (20- x 20-cm) pan and bake at 325°F (160°C) for 25 minutes. Cut into squares while hot.

Makes about 16 cookies.

Fruit Crumble

- fruit of any kind, about 2–3 cups (500–750 mL)
- ½ cup (125 mL) butter
- ½ cup (125 mL) brown sugar
- ¾ cup (175 mL) all-purpose flour
- ¼ tsp (1 mL) cinnamon
- ¼ tsp (1 mL) cloves (optional)

Cover bottom of an 8- x 8-inch (20- x 20-cm) square cake pan with a 1-inch (2.5 cm) layer of any fruit prepared in the usual way (if canned fruit is used, drain thoroughly). In a separate bowl, cream butter and add brown sugar gradually, creaming well. Add flour and spices and mix to a crumbly consistency. Spread crumbled topping over fruit and bake in a moderate oven (350°F/175°C) for 40 to 45 minutes or until fruit is cooked. Serve plain or with whipped or ice cream.

Serves 6 to 8.

The Cottage Bartender

LET'S BE FRANK: we tend to drink more at the cottage. It comes with the territory. We have more free time, the weather is more conducive to the consumption of spirits, and our social interactions generally witness a dramatic increase. While only some people actually know and entertain their city neighbors, most of us are generally quite familiar with our fellow weekenders and their families, so invitations for cocktails are as plentiful as black flies at a pump priming. Even random encounters—someone pulls up to the dock, or drops in to borrow a ladder—are prefaced with the universal cottage salutation: "Can I get you a drink?" or "Come on up for a beer!" Overnight guests may also be more common, and their appetite for booze is regulated (or perhaps unregulated) by the knowledge that they don't have to drive.

Naturally, cottage projects are much better lubricated with alcoholic beverages; you wouldn't dare work too long without offering a sudsy brew at a suitably measured time into the task. Offers of aid would dry up in a heartbeat if the word got out that you hadn't offered Harold a cold beer(s) while he helped you with the deck railing. If you own a cottage, camp, or cabin you must have a reasonable assortment of beer, wine, and spirits on hand, even if you don't imbibe all that much yourself.

There are even folks who will keep specific types of drinks or brands on hand just because a cottage acquaintance prefers it; such is our commitment to proper cottage etiquette! On the other hand, there are those, shall we say, clever cottagers who will keep different varieties available for less generous reasons: the choice of refreshments will depend on who you are and how frequently you just "drop in." The ever-thirsty brother-in-law may only be offered an ordinary beer, while the expensive import might be reserved for more honored guests (a wise strategy indeed).

Cocktails

At the cottage, that extended leisure time also offers us the opportunity to experiment a bit more with the drinks we serve. We concoct mixtures that might not be considered at home, and we may even develop a reputation among our friends as the best at a particular specialty. I'm particularly proud of my Bloody Caesar, while an acquaintance up the lake serves a to-die-for Margarita.

If you like to prepare mixed drinks, here's a list of conventional recipes garnered from friends, bartenders, and other sources (I've taken the liberty of making minor alterations to some of the recipes, keeping the reality of most cottage liquor cabinets in mind). I've also added some distinctive formulae for those who might fancy something a bit unusual. A good bar should be equipped with a cocktail shaker, a mixing or bar glass, and a good blender. However, at the camp, we often make do with what we have; the results are often just about the same: a good drink!

Your own cocktail formulation may be different from the ones suggested here.

Bloody Caesar—*the cottage classic.*
The Caesar has the distinction of being a uniquely Canadian invention, and even our American friends have come to recognize the superiority of the Caesar over the Bloody Mary—there simply is no comparison.

Wet the rim of a tallish glass (plastic is okay) with a slice of lemon.

Invert the glass, and rotate it in a dish of Mott's Rimmer™ to coat the rim (I tend to favor a less generous coating, so I often shake off some excess).

Squeeze the juice from the lemon slice into the glass, and add the slice. Combine, in the prepared glass:

- 1½ oz (45 mL) vodka (for a Virgin Caesar exclude the vodka)
- 6–8 oz (180–250 mL) Mott's Clamato Juice™ (I have used generic brands, but call me a brand snob; the others just don't cut it)
- a dash or two of Worcestershire sauce
- a couple of drops of hot sauce
- ¼ to ½ teaspoon (1–3 mL) horseradish

Stir thoroughly, throw in some ice and a stalk of celery (optional).

Though it quickly leads to a less than steady gait, a great way to enjoy Caesars is to chase them with cold beer: take a drink of the Caesar, savor, swallow, and then chase with a swig of your favorite suds.

Margarita—*a taste of Mexico at the lake.*
Wet the rim of a glass with a wedge of lime—cocktail glass, or any wide-brimmed, stemmed glass recommended.

Coat the rim by rotating the glass in a dish of salt.

In a blender, combine:

- 2–3 ice cubes
- 1½ oz (45 mL) tequila
- 1½ oz (45 mL) Cointreau
- 2 oz (60 mL) lime juice (or juice of large fresh lime)

Blend until ice is slushy. Pour into prepared glass. Add the lime wedge.

Strawberry Daiquiri / Banana Daiquiri—*the fruit makes it good for you.*

- 6 large, fresh strawberries, or ½ banana (sliced)
- 1½ oz (45 mL) rum
- 1 oz (30 mL) lime juice
- 2 tsp (5 mL) sugar (if you want it sweeter, add a bit more)

Mix with plenty of ice in a blender and serve in a stemmed glass

Piña Colada—*for the Latin lover.*
In a blender, combine the following:

- 2 oz (60 mL) rum
- 2 oz (60 mL) coconut milk (the real thing, if you can get it)
- 2 oz (60 mL) pineapple juice, or a couple of tbsp (30 mL) crushed pineapple
- several ice cubes

Blend at high speed for one minute. Serve in a stemmed glass.

Hey, we're at the cottage, so you can, of course, cheat with Margaritas, Piña Coladas, and Daiquiris. Prepared mixers can be found in most supermarkets. Follow the directions on the container—you'll need only rum and, with half the bother, you can create great drinks.

Manitoulin Island Ice Tea—*all the booze you need, or want, in one drink.*
Combine the following in a stemmed glass:

- ½ oz (15 mL) vodka
- ½ oz (15 mL) tequila
- ½ oz (15 mL) rum
- ½ oz (15 mL) gin
- ½ oz (15 mL) Triple Sec
- ½ oz (15 mL) lemon juice

Stir gently. Add a dash of cola, ice, and garnish with twist of lemon or lime. Serve.

After drinking, provide guest with a comfortable place to collapse.

The Fuzzy Navel—*better than an ordinary breakfast drink.*
In a tall glass, combine:

- 1½ oz (45 mL) peach schnapps
- 4 oz (120 mL) orange juice (or more to suit your taste)

Stir, and add several ice cubes.

Sea Breeze—*or lake breeze if you prefer.*

- 5 crushed ice cubes (use a piece of granite, or the blender)
- 1 oz (30 mL) vodka
- 1½ oz (45 mL) cranberry juice
- 1½ oz (45 mL) grapefruit juice
- lime slice to decorate

Add the vodka, and cranberry and grapefruit juices to the crushed ice. Stir well and decorate with slice of lime.

Mai Tai—*an old favorite.*

- lime slices
- sugar (caster sugar if you have it, but who the heck has it?)
- 1 oz (30 mL) rum
- ½ oz (15 mL) lime juice (fresh, if possible)
- ½ oz (15 mL) orange juice
- 3 crushed ice cubes
- cherries, pineapple, or orange slices for garnish

Wet the rim of a tall glass with a slice of lime; dip into the sugar to coat. Add rum, lime, and orange juices; mix well. Add the crushed ice. Decorate with cherries, a pineapple slice, or an orange slice. Serve with a straw.

Acapulco—*isn't the lake better than Mexico in the summer?*

- crushed ice
- 1 oz (30 mL) tequila
- 1 oz (30 mL) rum
- 2 oz (60 mL) pineapple juice
- 1 oz (30 mL) grapefruit juice
- 1 oz (30 mL) coconut milk (canned)

Crush the ice, and add with the other ingredients to a cocktail shaker. Shake until a frost forms. (Obviously, if you don't have a cocktail shaker, then you'll have to cover the top of the glass with your hand; it is indeed acceptable to lick your hand immediately after shaking.) Alternately, you could crush or chop the ice in a blender, and then add the ingredients to the blender container. Pour into tallish glass and serve.

White Russian/Black Russian—*no Revolution here, Comrade!*
For a White Russian, combine the following in a glass:

- 1 oz (30 mL) vodka
- 1 oz (30 mL) Tia Maria
- 1 oz (30 mL) light cream

Mix, add ice, and serve.

For a Black Russian, combine the following in a glass:

- 2 oz (60 mL) vodka
- 1 oz (30 mL) Kahlua

Mix, add ice, garnish with a chocolate stick (optional), and serve.

Sex on the Beach—*seems appropriate for life at the cottage.*

- ½ oz (15 mL) vodka
- ½ oz (15 mL) peach schnapps
- 1 oz (30 mL) cranberry juice
- 1 oz (30 mL) orange juice
- 1 oz (30 mL) pineapple juice (optional)

Mix, add ice, and garnish with a maraschino cherry. Serve in a tall glass with a straw. What follows is up to you!

Gin Sling—*didn't we drink these in college?*

- 1 oz (30 mL) cherry brandy
- 3 oz (90 mL) gin
- juice of ½ lemon
- 4 oz (120 mL) soda water

Mix with ice in a tall glass, top with soda water, and add stemmed cherries for decoration (optional).

Tequila Sunrise and Sunset—*for those lazy summer mornings and late summer evenings.*
For the Sunrise:

- 1 oz (30 mL) tequila
- 3½ oz (105 mL) orange juice
- 2 tsp (10 mL) grenadine

Mix the tequila and o.j. in a glass with ice. Slowly pour in the grenadine and allow it to settle. Just before serving, stir once. Decorate glass with orange slice.

For the Sunset:

- 1 oz (30 mL) tequila
- 1 oz (30 mL) fresh lemon juice
- 1 oz (30 mL) fresh orange juice
- 1 tbsp (10 mL) clear honey

Mix the first three ingredients in a cocktail glass. Drizzle the honey into the glass so that it falls to the bottom in a layer. Add ice.

Algonquin—*included because it reminds me of the famous park!*

- 1 oz (30 mL) dry vermouth
- 3 oz (90 mL) rye
- 1 oz (30 mL) pineapple juice

Mix with ice in a cocktail glass.

Honeydew—*simply tastes great.*

- 1 oz (30 mL) gin
- ½ oz (15 mL) fresh lemon juice
- 1 dash Pernod
- 2 oz (60 mL) honeydew melon diced
- champagne

In a blender, combine the gin, lemon juice and melon. Blend for 30 seconds. Pour into a large wine glass. Top up with champagne.

Wine

We also seem to go through a good deal more wine when we entertain at the lake. In fact, we—and our guests—consume at least two cases during the summer months. This can get to be expensive, so unless you're a wine snob, you might consider making your own (I do!) Most of us are too busy to actually bottle it at home, so you can do it the easy way: choose a reputable wine-making franchise and produce it on their site. It's a simple, fun, fast undertaking, and you get a very good product for a much, *much* better price. I go with a couple of buddies so we get a better selection. Simply order the wines you want for the summer (or year round for that matter), and then return to bottle a couple of months later. You can even get fancy enough to have your own labels made up. That'll impress the guests!

The wine-maker at the establishment that I frequent indicated that his best-selling whites included Chardonnay and Sauvignon Blanc, while his best-selling reds were Cabernet Sauvignon and Merlot. However, a couple of his favorites are Rosso Grande—a red—and Bella Bianco—a white. He also suggested that fruit wines are great for the summer and recommended Tropical Fruit Riesling and Raspberry White Zinfandel.

Beer

Cottage time could also be the time to experiment with new beers. Used to be that beer selection was a relatively simple matter; there weren't that many brands or styles to choose from in Canada. The emergence of craft beers and micro-breweries in the 1980s changed all that, and adventurous cottagers should take advantage of this sometimes bewildering sudsy cornucopia.

To help you choose a good beer, on October 20th, 1998, *Market Place*, a Canadian Broadcasting Corporation production, aired a program called The Great Canadian Beer Challenge. The producers assembled a panel of beer experts to determine the best Canadian beers in four categories. The panel's mission was to review and compare 28 of Canada's beers, "...from Whitehorse to St. John's, from Vancouver to Toronto and Edmonton to Montreal—and a few stops in between." They went on a national beer hunt, starting with the local beer store for national products and then, without regard for provincial trade barriers or liquor control laws, they gathered products from all over Canada. The selection of beer included: national brands, regional brews, and tiny local microbreweries. They didn't include every province, but they did include every region with an established bottling brewery.

The timing of the tests was crucial. Tests were conducted on a mid-summer morning, between 10 a.m. and noon, a time of day that has been proven to be the height of taste awareness.

The producers created a 20-point/5-star rating system, and used the Blind by Format Category test system. Lagers were served at temperatures of 50 to 54°F (10 to 12°C), while the ales were served at temperatures of 54 to 60°F (12 to 16°C).

Here are the results:

Lagers

COMPANY	BRAND	RATING
Creemore Springs—*Ontario*	Premium Lager	★★★★ (14)
Whistler Brewing—*B.C.*	Premium Lager	★★★★ (13)
Granville Island—*B.C.*	Island Lager	★★★ (11)
Molson—*Cross-Canada*	Canadian	★★★ (11)
Brick—*Ontario*	Premium Lager	★★ (8)
Labatt—*Cross-Canada*	Blue	★★ (8)
Moosehead—*N.S. and N.B.*	Lager	★★ (8)
Sleeman—*Ontario*	Silver Creek Lager	★★ (8)
Great Western—*Sask.*	Premium Lager	★★ (6)
Brasal—*Quebec*	Hopps Brau	★★ (6)

Ales

COMPANY	BRAND	RATING
McAusian—*Quebec*	St. Ambroise Pale Ale	★★★★ (16)
Chilkoot—*Yukon*	Pale Ale	★★★★ (15)
Niagara Falls—*Ontario*	Gritstone	★★★★ (15)
Wellington County—*Ontario*	Original County Ale	★★★★ (14)
Big Rock—*Alberta*	Traditional Ale	★★★★ (13)
Quidi Vidi—*Newfoundland*	1892 Traditional Ale	★★★ (11)
Molson—*Cross-Canada*	Export	★★★ (10)
Labatt—*Cross-Canada*	50	★★★ (10)
Okanagan Springs—*B.C.*	Pale Ale	★★★ (10)
Moosehead—*N.S. and N.B.*	Pale Ale	★★★ (10)

Specialty Beers—Fruit and Spice

COMPANY	BRAND	RATING
Unibroue—*Quebec*	Blanche de Chambly	★★★★ (15)
Alley Kat—*Alberta*	Aprikat Apricot Ale	★★★★ (14)
Kawartha Lakes—*Ontario*	Raspberry Wheat Beer	★★★★ (13)
Bowen Island—*B.C.*	Original Hemp Cream Ale	★★★ (11)

Strong Beers

COMPANY	BRAND	RATING
Seigneuriale—*Quebec*	Seigneuriale	★★★★ (16)
Big Rock—*Alberta*	McNally's Extra Ale	★★★★ (13)
Molson—*Cross-Canada*	Brador	★★★ (10)
Labatt—*Cross-Canada*	Wildcat Strong	★★ (8)

The judges rated each beer's aroma and initial impression out of five points, the taste out of ten, and overall enjoyment out of five, for a total score out of 20.

One to remember:

DRINK RESPONSIBLY; DON'T DRINK AND DRIVE (CAR OR BOAT)

Websites:
<www.thestarwineconnection.com>
<www.worldofbeer.com>
<http://members.rogers.com/douglas.j.steele/BreweryLinks.html>

CHAPTER 22

A Children's Treasure Hunt

> "Here be buried the cremated remains of Ole Pete Moss.
> (We burned the durned scoundrel ourselves.)
> Born: ???
> Died: July 10, 1802.
> His ashes be put in a tabaccy can.
> (Don't be foolish enuff to hunt for it,
> 'Cause the rumors of treasure be false,
> And the remains be curssed)."

WITH THE DISCOVERY OF AN OLD "HEADSTONE" bearing this ominous epitaph, another annual Treasure Hunt began at our cottage. This tradition was innocently launched in 1985, when I planned a simple hunt for my then five-year-old son Matthew and his cousins; I never imagined that it would become an eagerly anticipated yearly event, but I have organized one every year since.

As the years progressed, the hunts had to be tailored to the ages of the kids involved; the treasure hunts became more elaborate, requiring hours of planning (including a good deal of time spent simply wandering around seeking interesting possibilities) as I tried to improve on the previous year's hunt. And you know, I have enjoyed these hunts every bit as much as the kids (and maybe even more!).

The headstone that kicked off 1992's quest, created for seven-year-old Katie and her following—and believe me, there is always an entourage—was made from a scrap piece of ¼-inch plywood. It was spray-painted gray, and the epitaph was "engraved" with a black magic-marker (in a suitable script). I put the first clue in an old tobacco can that I found in the cottage workshop, and filled it with ashes from the wood-stove—hence the "cremated remains" referred to in the epitaph. I placed the headstone in a pile of earth from a recent excavation, and hid the can in the pile (the ruthlessness of treasure hunters is boundless; upon the discovery of Pete's remains, the ashes were rather unceremoniously and irreverently dumped without the proper regard generally afforded the dead). That initial starter pitch is always a challenge, and over the years, I have had bottles with notes in them "blow ashore," antique-looking letters, and any number of other leaders that the kids accidentally stumble on to get the treasure hunt started.

Most of my clues are contained in horrible poems offering instructions or a message that must be deciphered: "The end of your search is drawing near / The treasure is worth it, do not fear / I always loved flowers, I must confess / And *meadowsweet* was the one I loved the best. / Walk along the shore towards the dock / But don't walk past the great big rock / In the sand where you dig / A clue is there, not small but big." In this case, the kids had to consult our flower book to find out what mead-owsweet looked like, so I was able to sneak a little botany into the hunt.

Nonsense rhymes are also useful: "Once upon a time / There was a rhyme / It was made of lemon-lime / No it was not slime / But I'll give you a dime / If you can be mine / Along the straight line / With a ball of twine." The underlined letters spelled out the location of the next clue: (IN THE) CULVERT. Jumbled letters also make good clues, and the complexity of the jumble can increase with the age and abilities of the hunters.

In all, there were nine clues in that hunt, written on scraps of bark or carefully scorched paper (for that aged look). The best gimmick was a stroke of inspiration that grew out of a reconnaissance mission during which I had discovered an empty vireo's nest. I carefully cracked a regular brown egg, removed the contents, washed the inside of the shell, placed a clue inside and resealed the egg with a thin bead of hot glue. To find the egg, the treasure hunters had to "...count 35 paces heel to toe / West along the road you must go / Look to the north and there you will spy / A little lodging for our friends who fly / Don't be a chicken now and get crackin' / Time's a wastin' and treasure you're trackin'."

For the final clue in that hunt, I drew a detailed map of the treasure site on cardboard—an X indicated where the loot was buried—and then cut the map into large puzzle pieces. It took the five kids...rather the five treasure hunters...almost half a day to locate the spoils—about $15-

worth of gold-foil–covered chocolate coins.

Over the years I have used various hiding places and techniques, tailored to the kids' abilities. I have hidden clues on top of our dock's flotation billets (yep, the kids had to swim under the dock to find the plastic peanut butter container). I screwed the lid of a can to the underside of our dock ramp so I could conceal a clue there. I have used rocks, flowers, and trees as references (I once hid a clue under a flap of birch bark, and used a colored tack to secure the flap—that was a tough one to find). Clues have been hidden in rock piles, hollow logs, culverts, an old boot, and abandoned birds' nests; treasure hunters have had to make use of the compass, crude maps, the dictionary, field guides, diagrams, riddles, rhymes, and other adults (I give them—often an older adult—the next clue if the kids can decipher who it is they must ask). Once, I hid a clue behind a loose stone in a bit of a retaining wall that my father-in-law had built many years before; there was a convenient hollow in behind the rock, and I placed several loaded mousetraps in the way (the clue alluded to "danger"). In her eagerness to get at the clue, one of Katie's friends pulled the rock away and quickly reached in for the paper before she realized the traps were there. Fortunately, for her and for me, the traps went off without snagging any of her fingers (I caught heck for that one—both from the kids and their mothers!). I also make sure that clues force the kids to travel all over, so the physical tour increases the hunt time. Finally, I designed and built a simple "treasure chest" (plans below), and I generally use foil-covered chocolate coins as the booty.

Treasure hunts are great fun, and worth the work. Perhaps the hardest part for the hunt designer is to not jump in too quickly to help. After all, the hunters should have to work for their rewards.

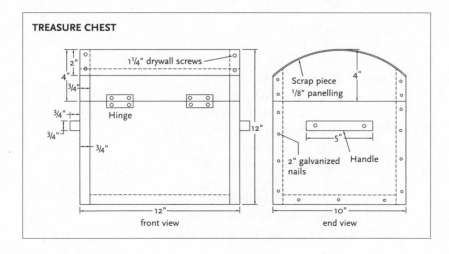

TREASURE CHEST

2"
4"
3/4"
1¼" drywall screws
3/4"
Hinge
3/4"
3/4"

12"

Scrap piece
⅛" panelling
4"
5"
Handle
2" galvanized nails

12"
front view

10"
end view

Here are some more clues that you might find useful as a framework for a hunt:

1. Deer, deer, we
   Certainly are on
   The horns of a dilemma.
   (The clue was hidden behind an old rack of antlers that hung on the shop wall.)

2. Oh Virginia Meadow Beauty
   Stately flower that thou art
   Growing among the rocks
   How do you survive?
   Your loveliness will guide these treasure hunters
   In their quest!!!
   (Again, a botany lesson was used to guide the seekers.)

3. On Uncle Tim's lot
   Stands a pretty little pine
   Whose needles number X
   —by the way, X is the square root of the unlabeled side on the right-angled triangle pictured to the right.

   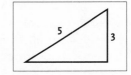

       Now cast about for the big "O".
   (The answer is obviously 2, the number of needles on a red pine, and near this pine was a big "O" drainpipe; the clue was stuffed in the end.)

4. Long ago I made my fortune in lumber
   The forests here'bouts I did plunder
   They said to put my money in the bank
   But I declined, said no thanks.
   I hid it so no one but me
   Could find it and wealthy be.
   As I neared the end of my days
   I tried to spend it all in so many ways
   But there was just too much to spend
   So with a treasure hunt my life would end.
   Someday I knew this tree would be cut down
   And the first clue to my wealth found.
   Good things must be earned
   So you'll have to work I do declare
   If my goodies you'd like to share.
   You'll have to know your trees by the by,

Whose mighty crowns crowd the sky.
Look ye first for a big old basswood
Long, long, long has it stood.
There is a large crevice at its base
And there you shall find the next place.
Fare thee well.
(This was an opening gambit. I had cut a big maple down and it had a hollow stump. I put this clue in an old can, jammed the can into the hollow, and then yelled for the kids, excited with my discovery.)

5. It's not the CPR,
   But it is at the end of the line.
   (My father-in-law built a marine railway of sorts and the clue was hidden down near the water.)

6. love did I birds the Ah
   To fe_d them w_s a j_y.
   So I bu_lt them a l_tt_e re_t_ur_nt.
   Pole a of top on
   Filled w_th se_d_ tr_ats.
   Around root and now there go so
   Another clue will there be found.
   (In this one I included missing letters and jumbled sentences! The clue was IN THE BIRD FEEDER.)

7. On this shore is a place west of here
   Where you can go up
   And you can go down
   But you go nowhere special.
   Isn't that weird!
   (A neighbor had a stairway built to negotiate a particularly steep incline, hence the reference to "nowhere special"; a clue was hidden under one of the stairs.)

8. Red bars
   Red leaf
   Flapping away
   Up high
   Down low
   In a space
   Toward the lake.
   (A neighbor flies the Canadian flag; a clue was hidden in a hollow at the base of the flag.)

9. The colors of light there are three
   When I paddle, I feel so free.
   (This clue was hidden in the stern of a red canoe.)

10. Aye, aye searchers,
    Hey, that's two ayes!
    Or is that eyes?
    I have two eyes,
    You have two eyes,
    She has two eyes.
    Eyes to see with,
    But there are other eyes.
    Eyes to hold.
    On the shore there are two eyes;
    Line them up (looking east)
    For the glory gold!
    (Two eyebolts drilled into the rock hold our dock in place; by lining the two eyebolts up and looking through them—facing east, the kids could see a hiding place among the rocks where a clue was hidden.)

Three to remember:

1. Tailor the hunt to the kids' abilities.

2. Just about everything around you can be used as a clue.

3. Don't jump in to help too soon!

CHAPTER 23

The Library

IN EVERY COTTAGE, CAMP, OR CABIN you will find a selection of books. There will be trashy and classic novels, reference texts for such things as flowers and birds, and an assortment of manuals, among others. It seems that we have more time to read at our retreats, we often take an interest in identifying the fauna and flora that surround us, and occasionally we need to consult a reference text for a new card game, or the rules to crokinole.

A cottage library, like any library, is a reflection of the person(s) who has collected the books; it is unique in some way. The list of titles that follows is my idea of the, if not definitive, at least essential cottage library; the titles have been gathered from numerous sources (personal knowledge, friends and acquaintances, snooping, bookstore owners, etc). Undoubtedly, most cottagers will have one or more of these books already. Undoubtedly, every cottager could add to this list. And undoubtedly, some cottagers and learned critics might disagree with me on a particular choice(s). However, this is one of the joys of writing: I get to decide!

Field Guides

At the lake, most of us are able and eager to nurture our naturalist alter egos. We want to identify and know something about the plants and the animals around us. For years, I have had a great interest in wild flowers, and I have also prided myself on being able to name many of the birds.

In bookstores in cottage communities this fascination with flora and fauna is evident from the collection of field guides offered for sale: there are manuals for birds, mammals, trees and plants, wild flowers, reptiles and amphibians, mushrooms, edible plants, insects, stars and constellations, rocks, etc. The selection can be a bit overwhelming. Some, of course, are better than others.

A Field Guide to the Birds of Eastern and Central North America by Roger Tory Peterson, published by the Houghton Mifflin Company (<www.hmco.com>) is widely accepted as one of the most reliable birding books available. There are over a dozen birding books in the Peterson series: everything from *A Field Guide to Hummingbirds of North America,* to *A Field Guide to the Birds' Nests.*

Another highly recommended bird book is the National Audubon Society volume, *The Sibley Guide to Birds* by D.A. Sibley, published by Alfred A. Knopf, a division of Random House (<www.randomhouse.com/knopf/nature/>).

More regionally specific books are available from publisher Lone Pine Books (<www.lonepinepublishing.com>), and include such titles as *Ontario Birds* and *West Coast Birds,* both by Chris Fisher. The former describes 125 common species found in Ontario, while the latter describes 90 varieties of the West Coast.

Peterson's *A Field Guide to Mammals* by W.H. Burt and R.P. Grossenheider (Houghton Mifflin Company) and National Audubon Society's *Field Guide to North American Mammals* (Alfred A. Knopf) are both excellent field resources. Lone Pine offers regional guides such as *Mammals of Ontario, Mammals of Alberta, Mammals of the Rocky Mountains,* etc. Armed with these, you should easily be able to distinguish between a black bear and a raccoon!

National Audubon Society's *Field Guide to North American Wildflowers,* and *Newcomb's Wildflower Guide,* by Lawrence Newcomb (published by Little and Brown, <www.twbookmark.com>) present two different approaches to wild flower identification. The former uses color plates while the latter uses a key system to find a match among the mostly black-and-white illustrations. I have the Audubon book.

Trees in Canada by J.L. Farrar, published by Fitzhenry and Whiteside is also a valuable asset, and is one of the most comprehensive books ever written about Canadian trees (<www.fitzhenry.ca>).

Up North: A Guide to Ontario's Wilderness from Blackflies to the Northern Lights by Doug Bennett and Tim Tiner, was first published by Reed Books Canada. *Up North Again: More of Ontario's Wilderness, from Ladybugs to the Pleiades* is the sequel and is published by McClelland and

Stewart Inc. Both of these books address subjects from the natural world: birds, mammals, amphibians, creepy-crawlies, reptiles, the heavens, Mother Earth. While highly informative, the books are also very entertaining. For example, in the original, the authors have devoted a segment to black flies. Shaded columns for each subject list fascinating facts; for the black fly they include the odd but amusing subtitle: "Number of the 10 biblical plagues of Egypt that were insect based: 6." Two great books that should be on the shelf.

Ontario Rocks by Nick Eykes, published by Fitzhenry and Whiteside, provides a useful reference book for would-be geologists.

Though it seems somewhat alien to me, many cottagers enjoy gardening (don't trees and rocks make a great garden?). If you're one of these, obviously it would be worthwhile to make your garden not only beautiful, but also a popular spot for birds, squirrels, butterflies, and other wildlife to visit. *The New Gardening for Wildlife—A Guide for Nature Lovers*, by Bill Merilees and published by Whitecap Books (<www.whitecap.ca>), deserves the consideration of cottage gardeners.

Reference Texts

At the cottage, there seem to be more issues that have to be arbitrated by an authority, or there are problems that can only be fixed by referring to the appropriate source. My wife and I are rabid Scrabble™ players and fancy ourselves as reasonably proficient; sometimes we'll play three games a day; my desire to play is partly fueled by the belief that so much cerebral activity will surely guarantee an old age free of dementia. Many of our games are decided by slim margins—two or three points. Her family had employed a particular scoring system for years, a system that had heretofore never been questioned. Having lost a close one, I finally challenged her notion of the final score, and *The Games Treasury* proved that I was right (it doesn't happen often, so I savored it for the better part of a week).

The Games Treasury by Merilyn Simonds Mohr is published by Chapters Publishing Ltd., and is distributed by Firefly Books. If you attempted to play every game explained in this book (over 300), you would need more cottage summers than are allotted to a regular lifetime. This volume has them all—card games, board games, games with playing pieces, indoor and outdoor games, manufacturers, games organizations—and they're presented in a very readable manner; good illustrations are also provided where needed.

A somewhat less expensive, but no less functional, guide is *Hoyle's Rules of Games*, edited by A.H. Morehead and G. Mott-Smith (revised and updated by P.D. Morehead) and published by the Penguin Group (<www.penguinputnam.com>).

A dictionary is another mandatory book, and if you are Canadian then the *Canadian Oxford Dictionary* is the required reference while American cottagers will likely opt for *Webster's*.

Some Scrabble aficionados will only play the game if the contestants agree to use a dictionary as the only true Holy Grail of acceptable words. Others, however (and that would include my wife and me), turn to *The Official Scrabble Players Dictionary* published by Merriam-Webster, Inc. This volume is endorsed by the National Scrabble Association, and includes words that will make you a cottage champ: xi: a Greek letter; xu: a monetary unit of Vietnam; qua: in the capacity of; qaid: caid (a Muslim leader); and countless other game makers. If it isn't in this book, then you can't use it on the board, no way, no how! By the way, my wife calculated the final score in this manner: the first player to go out got to add the value of the letters remaining on the other player's board, while that player must also subtract the value of those letters. The final score was thus calculated. It certainly seemed like a case of double jeopardy, and it was: the first player to go out does *not* get to add the value of the letters remaining on the other player's board; that player must subtract the value of those letters, and the final score is thus tabulated.

If you are a cottager, especially a water-access cottager, then a first aid course should be part of your skills repertoire (see the chapter on basic first aid). Because of my affinity for outdoor adventures, I have a copy of the St. John Ambulance *Official Wilderness First-Aid Guide* by Wayne Merry, published by McClelland and Stewart. It provides an excellent overview of first aid, and many of the so-called wilderness scenarios apply to many typical cottage situations.

A really good atlas is another worthwhile cottage library investment. How many times, when you're listening to the CBC, or in a discussion, have you wanted to know just where someplace was, exactly? *Geographica's Family Atlas*, published by Whitecap Books, is a superbly illustrated atlas that is suitable for every member of the family.

How-to books are among many cottagers' favorites, and one of these is Max Burns's *Cottage Water Systems* published by Cottage Life Books, and distributed by Firefly (<www.fireflybooks.com>). Burns covers every aspect imaginable, from pumps to septic systems. Cottage Life also publishes *Docks and Projects, How to Buy a Cottage,* and *Summer Weekend Cookbook.*

This book is one that I need! I can barely tie my shoes. *Knots* by Gordon Perry provides easy-to-follow instructions for selecting and tying over 100 knots. This is another Whitecap publication.

Cookbooks

Generally, we have a bit more time at the lake to experiment with culinary creations. My wife works long hours, so I am the head chef at our place during the off-season, and since I work as well, many of our meals are the freezer-to-stove/microwave-to table variety. However, once we settle in at the cottage, Lynn becomes a regular Mme. Benoît (complete with the French accent); she loves her cookbooks, and is constantly referring to them to prepare great meals.

The culinary version of the Bible is, unquestionably, *The Joy of Cooking* by Irma S. Rombauer, Marion Rombauer, and Ethan Becker, published by Scribner. Certainly, cottage cooks will have other cookbooks on the cupboard shelf, but if you only have room for one, then *The Joy of Cooking* should be it! There is, in fact, a whole series of *Joy of Cooking* books.

Recently, we purchased a copy of the much acclaimed *The Silver Palate* by Julee Rosso and Sheila Lukins, Workman Publishing. The Chicken Marbella recipe is one of our favorites.

On the shelf reserved for similar publications, we have a well-used copy of the *Five Roses Guide to Good Cooking.* Whitecap Books publishes this old standby—the 24th edition—as part of its line of best-selling Classic Canadian Cookbooks.

Children's Books

Occasionally, time can drag for kids at the lake. Good cottage books supply hours of games and activities, while others simply provide the pleasure of a good read.

The Kids Cottage Book written by Jane Drake and Ann Love is published by Kids Can Press Ltd. This original work was followed by *The Kids Campfire Book* and the *The Kids Cottage Games Book*, both written by Drake and Love and also published by Kids Can Press Ltd. All three are illustrated by Heather Collins. The first book is an eclectic collection of inside and outside games, hiking and camping activities, crafts, etc. The *Campfire Book* is self-explanatory: fire-building, campfire games, songs, and recipes. The most recent installment is an up-dated compilation of fun stuff for kids to do at the lake. These three books are well written and full of great pictures; they will definitely appeal to kids and to parents searching for ways to get children off their butts and away from electronic games.

The *I Spy* series of picture riddle books written by Jean Marzollo and photographed by Walter Wick, is published by Scholastic. In these books, the reader (young and not so young) is challenged through riddles to find objects hidden in the pictures. Mr. Wick actually creates a miniature set that he photographs for the scenes (in *I Spy Treasure Hunt*, he required the help of an assistant and three freelance model makers; one set alone required an elaborate 16 x 16 foot HO scale [1:87] stage). I have spent countless hours with my nephews searching for objects, and all three of us have delighted in a difficult discovery.

A couple of classic storybooks include *Blueberries for Sal* by Robert McCloskey, published by Puffin Books, and *Paddle to the Sea* by Holling Clancy Holling, published by the Houghton Mifflin Company.

Kids' Canadian Atlas, published by Whitecap is a beginner's guide to understanding what maps are and how they work. It presents the basics of geography in a fun and exciting way (I have taught Grade 9 geography, and this is no mean feat).

Up North at the Cabin by Marsha Wilson Chall, with illustrations by Steve Johnson, is a marvelous read, and the paintings are incredibly evocative of the cottage experience. It is published by Lothrop, Lee, and Shepard Books of New York.

Periodicals

Cottage Life magazine is published by Quarto Communications. This ultimate cottage publication features great general interest pieces, how-to articles, recipes, photo contests, advice columns, and just about everything any cottager would need to know. Many subscribers actually have every edition neatly saved in *Cottage Life* binders. I am honored to have written for this magazine for quite a number of years. The *Cottage Life* staffers also host an annual *Cottage Life* Show that is attended by tens of thousands of people from Canada and the U.S.

Harrowsmith Country is published six times a year by Malcolm Publishing. As the name implies, most of the pieces are devoted to country living: gardening, ecology and the environment, building, fauna and flora, etc.

Food and Drink, published by the Liquor Control Board of Ontario, appears six times a year in LCBO outlets and, unlike most magazines, is free (in spite of that, it is an excellent magazine). *Food and Drink* provides recipes, both food and beverage, as well as interesting short pieces.

Canadian Geographic is published six times a year by Canadian Geographic Enterprises on behalf of the Royal Canadian Geographical Society (<www.canadiangeographic.ca>). As you would expect, most of the pieces center on Canadian issues.

Miscellaneous

At the Cottage by Charles Gordon, published by McClelland and Stewart, is a funny look at our obsession with the summer place.

The title is a bit unusual, but the content of *How to Shit In The Woods* by Kathleen Meyer, published by Ten Speed Press, makes for a fascinating, and obviously humorous, read.

Cottage Country Canoe Routes by Kevan Callan, published by Boston Mills Press, describes canoe routes in Central Ontario.

Vinyl Café Unplugged, Home from the Vinyl Café, and *Stories from the Vinyl Café* by CBC broadcaster Stuart McLean, published by the Penguin Group, traces the often humorous and quirky life, adventures, and misadventures of Dave and Morley and their family and friends. My wife complained repeatedly when I read these; I would stay up late, reading in the living room, and my laughter kept her awake. Mr. McLean is a Stephen Leacock Award winner.

From Ink Lake is a collection of Canadian short stories selected by renowned author Michael Ondaatje (the Vintage Canada edition, published by Random House).

Mensa Puzzle, Challenge 3 is the third in a series of puzzle books. This addition contains over 350 fiendish brainteasers (published by Carlton, and available from Whitecap).

The *Backroad Mapbooks* series by Mussio Ventures Ltd. are softcover publications that provide detailed information and maps for freshwater fishing, paddling routes, multi-use trails, wilderness camping, and winter recreation (<www.backroadmapbooks.com>). At the time of writing, editions included: Near North Ontario, Eastern Ontario, Ontario Cottage Country, Algonquin Region, Central Alberta, Southwestern Alberta, Southwestern British Columbia, Central B.C., Kamloops/Okanagan, Vancouver Island, the Kootenays, and Cariboo.

Even though we love life at the lake, there are many creatures that we do not care for. *Living Things We Love to Hate* by Des Kennedy (foreword by David Suzuki) details flora and fauna that have historically been given a bum rap.

Most cottagers I know own a pet (or perhaps the pet owns them). *Caring for Dogs and Cats* published by the Australian Women's Weekly, and available from Whitecap Books, offers advice on all aspects of pet care.

Leisure reading is one of the great rewards of spending time at the cottage. Most of us do not have the luxury to read whatever we want during the rush of daily living, or to ignore the clock if the next page of a good book beckons. An interesting collection of reading material will always be appreciated by family, friends, and neighbors. Who knows? Next time I'm over I might borrow a book or two.

CHAPTER 24

Closing Up

COTTAGERS KNOW THAT CLOSING UP IS THE MOST MELANCHOLY TIME of the year—worse even than the income tax deadline. Summer's done, another cottage season finished. Unlike opening up, there is none of that excitement or anticipation when you close: just work. But despite the gloom, it's work that must be done properly, or you'll pay for it in the spring in more ways than one, so it behooves you to develop a systematic approach. Every cottager's closing-up routine is a custom operation, but virtually all have similar requirements. And one of the best ways to make sure that everything gets done is to create a checklist. Get it photocopied, stick it on a clipboard, and hang it up for use in the fall.

The Water System

The fundamental priority during close-up is the water system: this includes the pump, water lines from the lake to the pump and from the pump to the cottage, interior (and exterior) plumbing, and all water appliances. Water is a curious substance; unlike most other compounds, water begins to expand as it freezes (expansion occurs between 39 and 32°F / 4 and 0°C). That unique characteristic is the kicker for cottagers because expanding water exerts a force great enough to split granite. If water remains in constricted areas in your plumbing, this expansion can cause serious water system damage.

Step 1: Water system shutdown generally starts at the pump. You will first turn the power off; don't forget to pull the water heater fuses or hit the breaker (an empty water heater could be damaged if the power is left on). Remove the intake line from the pump; quick connects make removal and connection a positive, easy experi-

Figure 1

quick connect

ence (Figure 1). Years ago, we spent a lot of needless time and energy removing the line itself from the lake; then, one fall we simply decided to leave it in. It was a rational decision, not one born of frustration or laziness, as you might expect. Naturally, despite our faith in the theory, we worried that as the water froze in the line it would split, or that lake ice would drag the line out of the water as the ice was blown on shore during break-up. However, we've never had a problem, either way. And the bonus is that priming in the spring is no longer a black fly–swatting, yelling, cursing, frenzied nightmare; generally, the intake line needs topping up only, while the pump has to be filled once or twice to start operating.

Step 2: Next, the line from the pump to the cottage has to be removed; quick-connects can be used here as well (Figure 1). The pump itself must be thoroughly drained, and the plug at the bottom of the pump housing (Figure 2) should be removed (if you have an air compressor—as if you needed another excuse to buy one—blow any residual water out of the pump as well). During storage, prop the pump up so the intake points down.

Figure 2

pump drain plug

Step 3: Meanwhile, back at the cottage. Most likely, you will have devised some method to drain the water from the hot and cold lines, as well as the hot water tank. Open all the taps in the cottage. Some cottagers won't trust Sir Isaac Newton's rules and insist on blowing the lines clear as a guarantee that no water can possibly linger in a pipe. Don't forget to drain the toilet tank (just keep the lever depressed during that last flush), and remove or service any water filters, softeners, or purifiers.

Step 4: Every trap will need anti-freeze—the RV kind, as will the toilet (the appropriate quantity is generally defined on the container). If you didn't get every drop out of the toilet tank, then splash some in there as well. Washing machines and dishwashers may also require anti-freeze as part of the winterization procedure. Make sure that the water cooler is well drained too.

The checklist outlined below is a suggested starting point; your own may include other water system-related procedures not summarized here, or you may be able to exclude certain items.

- Water heater breaker to the off position.
- Water pump breaker to the off position.
- Remove intake/output lines from pump.
- Winterize pump.
- Open taps in cottage:
  - Kitchen sink taps
  - Bathroom sink taps
  - Bathtub taps
  - Washing machine taps
  - Outside taps.
- Drain cottage lines.
- Drain toilet tank.
- Anti-freeze for:
  - Kitchen sink trap
  - Bathroom sink trap
  - Bathtub trap
  - Toilet trap.
- Anti-freeze for (continued):
  - Washing machine drain trap
  - Toilet tank.
- Winterize washing machine.
- Winterize dishwasher.
- Remove water filter, clean housing.

General Maintenance

This includes all of the necessary closing-up chores, both indoors and out. Some may not be absolutely essential, while others certainly require your attention at this time of the year.

Inside jobs:

- Pack up all perishable foodstuff and load in vehicle for trip home.
- Pack up all products that cannot be exposed to freezing (e.g. paint).
- Pack up all spirits.
- Check oven.
- Check microwave.
- Clean waste, recycling, and compost containers.
- Clean fridge (and defrost line); leave door ajar.
- Empty and clean tea/coffee pots.
- Load all liquid cleaning agents into a plastic bin.
- Load all remaining liquid foodstuffs (e.g. cooking oil, vinegar) into a separate plastic bin.
- Check and secure all windows (including storm doors).
- Critter-proof the premises.

Obviously, some of these tasks have been incorporated because, at one time or another, something unpleasant has happened to merit their inclusion on the closing-up list. We no longer want to forget to check the oven because we do not wish to discover another smelly treasure. Moldy tea bags and coffee filters are less than attractive in the spring, and a burst plastic jug of some cleaning agent is much better contained in a plastic bin.

Other jobs have been added by virtue of necessity: they should be done, so why not do them in the fall? Tedious drudgery must be associated with closing up; opening up should be fun, and should only include absolutely necessary tasks like putting the dock in, and hooking up the water. Opening up is the time for camaraderie, the Stanley Cup Playoffs, red meat, card games, the stuff of beer commercials. Where was I? Oh yeah, closing up.

Outside jobs

- Check garbage pail.
- Clean eavestroughs (gutters).
- Rake leaves.
- Service boat (as per manual), and store for winter.

- ⟁ Service ATV (as per manual).
- ⟁ Service snow machine (as per manual).
- ⟁ Clean and store other watercraft and toys.
- ⟁ Take flag down.
- ⟁ Check roof and make any necessary repairs.
- ⟁ Move dock and dock ramp (if ice is a problem).

As you leave, casting a last, sad look around, remember to:

- ⟁ Check the woodstove.
- ⟁ Turn the main breaker to the off position.
- ⟁ Lock all doors.

Finally, we include a space at the end of our checklist for comments: these generally include must-do jobs, repairs, or parts requirements for the next year.

Glossary
of Common
Construction Terms

Don't you just hate it when you want to build something and you're standing there at the counter in the building center but you can't for the life of you name the actual part, other than to refer to it as the piece of wood nailed between two floor joists.

Well, here's a list for you.

Armed with this knowledge, you should be able to approach that same counter with a renewed sense of confidence; that salesperson's know-it-all little grin will vanish when, cupping your chin thoughtfully, you ask him / her just what is the **rough opening** for the sliding glass door you ordered, and what **lintel** size will be required?

You will be accorded a measure of respect you have secretly craved; as a fledgling member of the fraternity/sorority of builders you will be able to talk of cripples without the fear of appearing politically incorrect!

The following list is not exhaustive, but it does provide most of the common construction terms (naturally, there will be some differences in regional terminology).

Anchor bolt: an L-shaped bolt embedded in the top of a concrete wall or in the perimeter of a concrete foundation slab (obviously, thread side up) so that framing members can be secured to the wall or slab.

Baseboard: trim where wall and floor meet.

Beam: a wood or steel member used to support a floor, deck, or roof system.

Bearing wall: any wall that supports a vertical load (as opposed to a partition wall that is not load bearing); bearing walls cannot be removed or altered without regard to the role they play in supporting said load.

Bird's-mouth: a notch cut in a rafter so that the rafter sits squarely and securely on the top plate of a wall; it consists of a seat cut and a plumb cut.

Blocking: short pieces of framing material nailed between wall studs for support and to prevent fire from spreading through the walls.

Board foot: in North America, the imperial unit is still king in the construction industry; the old board foot is the volume of a piece of wood measuring 1 foot long, 1 foot wide, and 1 inch thick.

Bottom (or sole) plate: usually 2- x 4- or 2- x 6-inch, this is the horizontal bottom member that the wall studs are nailed to; it, in turn, is nailed to the floor.

Brace: a piece of lumber generally nailed to a wall section, roof truss, etc., and to some other structure (i.e. the floor) to provide temporary support to the wall section or roof truss.

Bridging: solid or cross bridging—usually 2- x 2-inch—pieces nailed between floor joists to prevent warping or twisting under load.

Butt joint: one piece of lumber placed end to end against another piece of lumber.

Cantilever: An unsupported floor extension that can carry a load; the size of the joists generally determines the length of the cantilever.

Carriage bolt: a heavy bolt with a domed head; a square shape below the head permits the bolt to "bite" into wood when tightened.

Casing: finish trim used around door and window openings.

Collar tie: a horizontal piece of lumber attached to opposite roof rafters to provide support to the rafters. These are used in "stick" frame roof construction where trusses are not required or needed.

Compound cut: a cut consisting of two angles; compound cuts are often required in the construction of certain types of roofs.

Corner bead: generally, a metal strip used to reinforce and protect an exterior corner in drywall applications.

Cripple: the short studs required above window and door lintels (if necessary), or below the sill of a window.

Crown: most lumber is not perfectly straight; the crown is the high side of the curve (looking along the edge).

Door jamb: the vertical sides of a door frame.

Door sill: the horizontal piece at the bottom of an exterior door frame.

Door stop: a thin piece of material nailed or screwed to the door jamb; it "stops" the door from opening too far (i.e. usually no more than halfway through the opening).

Dormer: a framed area that projects from a sloping roof; a dormer creates an external recess in the roof space.

Dress: to smooth one or more sides of a piece of rough lumber.

Eave: the part of the roof that projects past the exterior wall.

Fascia: the vertical edge of a roof around the face of eaves and roof projections.

Finished size: the overall dimensions of a completed project.

Flashing: wide strips of sheet metal most often installed in roof valleys to aid in shedding water.

Footing: the widened section, usually of concrete, at the base or bottom of a foundation wall, pier, or column.

Forms: A series of panels that, when assembled and erected, hold concrete in place until cured, forming foundation walls.

Framing: the rough lumber assembly of a house, including the flooring, walls, roofing, partitioning, and beams.

Front elevation: an artist's drawing of what the front of a building will look like.

G1S: this is an acronym for Good-One-Side, and refers to plywood-type materials that have a finished face.

Gable: the triangular upper part of a wall closing the end of a roof.

Grade: the finish level of the land around a house.

Gusset: a piece of metal or wood applied to one or both sides of a joint to increase the joint's strength.

Hip roof: a roof consisting of four surfaces that slant in to meet at the peak (sometimes referred to as a "cottage" roof).

Jackpost: an adjustable steel post used to support a beam.

Jack stud: a vertical framing member, usually 2- x 4-inch or 2- x 6-inch that supports the ends of a lintel (sometimes referred to as a trimmer stud).

Joist: one of a series of horizontal wood members that support either a floor or a ceiling.

Joist hanger: a manufactured metal stirrup designed to support the end of a joist; hangers must be used when a joist cannot be supported by a wall or a beam.

Kiln dried: a reference to lumber that has been placed in a heated environment to reduce the moisture content.

Lag bolt: a heavy bolt-like screw (i.e. it has a head that can be turned by a wrench or socket, and a threaded shank).

Laminated wood: a number of pieces of wood joined together by glue, nails, or screws to form one stronger piece.

Ledger board: a piece of lumber attached to the wall of an existing structure; it provides a starting point for the addition of structures such as a deck.

Level: horizontally true (as determined by instruments such as a spirit level, water level, or laser level).

Lineal foot: a unit of measure pertaining to length; used when ordering a quantity of lumber that does not have standard lengths (for example, if you order 150 lineal feet of 1- x 2-inch pine, random lengths—could be a combination of 7-, 8-, or 10-footers—will be selected by the shipper to make up the order).

Lintel: a horizontal structural member that supports the load over an opening such as a window or door (sometimes referred to as a header).

Miter: an angled cut, most often at 45°.

Mortar: a mixture used to create a bond between concrete blocks or bricks.

Molding: trim pieces (wood, plastic, metal) that give a finished appearance.

Nominal size: the dimensions by which a piece of lumber is commonly known, but which may vary from the actual size (for example a 2 x 4 actually measures 1½ inches by 3½ inches).

On center (o.c.): the distance from the middle of one wood member measured to the center of the neighboring wood member (for example, wall studs are often 16 inches o.c.).

Parging: a special mortar mixture that is applied to the outside foundation walls in the same manner as plastering.

Pier: a column, usually made of concrete blocks or poured concrete designed to support other structural elements.

Plumb: vertically true.

Quarter round: molding or trim formed from a quarter-section of a circle.

Rafter: one of the sloping wood members, usually a 2-inch nominal thickness that forms the framework of a roof.

Rebar: steel reinforcing rods, placed in concrete to add strength.

Retaining wall: a wall designed to withstand pressures created by lateral forces that result when earth or water push against it.

Ridge: the line at the high point of a roof.

Ridgeboard: a horizontal framing member running the length of the roof, used to attach rafters at the peak.

Rim joist: the outermost floor joist that extends around the perimeter of the foundation wall.

Riser: the vertical board extending from one tread to another in stair construction.

Roof pitch: a term used for identifying the slope of a roof; essentially it compares the rise of a roof over a 12 foot run (e.g. a roof with a 4/12 pitch would have a 4 foot rise over a 12 foot run).

Rough opening: the dimensions, both horizontal and vertical, of an opening within which a finished window or door will be placed.

Shake: a wood shingle, usually cedar, used as a roofing material.

Sheathing: a material used to cover wall studs, creating the exterior walls, or roof rafters, creating the roof.

Shed roof: roof with one surface only, higher at one end.

Sill: the board anchored to the top of the foundation wall that the floor system sits on.

Slab: a pad, usually of concrete, used to support a building without a foundation.

Soffit: the finished undersurface of the roof overhang or eaves; it is often perforated to increase ventilation in the roof space.

Span: the horizontal length from one beam support to another; building codes provide span tables (maximum unsupported spans for a particular lumber size).

Stair stringer: the supporting sides of a set of stairs.

Strapping: wood material, such as 1- x 3-inch or 1- x 4-inch, applied to walls, ceilings, or roofs; coverings such as drywall or steel roofing are then attached to the strapping.

Stud: a vertical framing member, usually 2- x 4-inch or 2- x 6-inch that extends from the bottom plate to the top plate (studs are often pre-cut to 92½ inches allowing for the double top plate and the single bottom plates to bring the finished wall height to 97 inches).

Subfloor: The covering—either plywood or a composite material—of the floor joists that serves as the basis for the finish floor material.

Toenailing: nailing at an angle.

Top plate: the horizontal top member of a wall; the wall studs are nailed to the top plate. A **double top plate** is nailed to the top plate; it is used to tie intersecting walls together.

Tread: the part of a stair on which you step.

Truss: an engineered and pre-manufactured roof component that incorporates the rafters and ceiling joists into a single unit.

Underlay: a layer of smooth plywood that is applied over the subfloor sheathing before certain types of flooring, such as vinyl, are installed.

Vapor barrier: a polyethylene—plastic—material used to prevent the passage of air, vapor, or moisture into any insulated wall or ceiling; it is applied to the heated side of the room.

Weeping tile: a perforated plastic pipe, placed around the perimeter of the footings to collect and channel water away from the footings.

Sources

Going for a Walk in the Woods
Material for this chapter was borrowed, with permission from: *The Psychology of Wilderness Survival* (fifth edition) by Dr. G.F. Ferri, printed by Skyway Printing, Hanover, Ontario.

Dr. Ferri assumes no liability for my rendition.

Thanks to Dr. Ferri and his staff for reviewing this chapter and making several recommendations. <www.survivalinthebushinc.com>.

First Aid at the Lake
Thanks to Deborah Hennig—a registered First Aid/CPR provider for the Workplace Safety Insurance Board of Ontario, and a CPR Instructor Trainer for the Heart and Stroke Foundation of Ontario— for allowing me to reproduce material from her company's manual (*VITALITY©*), and for reviewing this chapter for errors. Ms. Hennig was also a First Aid Instructor for the Metro Toronto Ambulance Service.

The King of Cottage Country—The Black Bear
Material for this chapter was borrowed, with permission from the following sources:

© Her Majesty the Queen in Right of Canada. All rights reserved. Source: *Black Bear*, Hinterland Who's Who series, Environment Canada, 1993. Reproduced with the permission of the Minister of Public Works and Government Services, 2002. <www.cws.ca>.

Bear Facts by the Federation of Ontario Naturalists <www.ontarion-ature.org>.

Ontario Ministry of Natural Resources. *Living with Black Bears in Ontario—A guide to co-existing with black bears.* Toronto: Queen's Printer for Ontario, 2000.

The booklet is available in hard copy from the OMNR, or from their website: <www.mnr.gov.on.ca/MNR/bears/>.

The Chainsaw

Excerpts from this chapter first appeared in an article in *Harrowsmith* Magazine and, later, in the *Harrowsmith Reader.*

Illustrations and some references used with permission of Blount Inc., Oregon Cutting Systems Division. Blount assumes no liability for this rendition.

Tree Felling—The Good, the Bad, and the Ugly

Excerpts from this chapter first appeared in an article in *Harrowsmith* Magazine and in the *Harrowsmith Reader.*

Thanks to Ian Grainge for permission to reprint the illustrations that accompanied the Harrowsmith article.

Some material used with permission of the Ontario Forestry Safe Workplace Association, and excerpted from their publication, *The Cutting Edge.* OFSWA assumes no liability for my rendition. *The Cutting Edge* is available from OFSWA at (705) 474-7233, or through their website: <www.ofswa.on.ca>.

A special thanks to John Murray of OFSWA for reviewing this chapter and providing technical recommendations.

Firewood and Wood Fires

Material for this chapter was borrowed, with permission from *Renewable Energy—A Guide to Residential Wood Heating,* published by National Resources Canada in cooperation with Canada Mortgage and Housing. NRC assumes no responsibility for my rendition.

Wood-Heating Appliances

Material for this chapter was borrowed, with permission from *Renewable Energy—A Guide to Residential Wood Heating,* published by National Resources Canada in cooperation with Canada Mortgage and Housing Corporation. NRC assumes no responsibility for my rendition. Visit their website for the complete guide: (<www.canren.gc.ca/prod_serv/index.asp?CaId=103&PgId=576>), or pick up a copy from woodstove retailers.

Thanks to Dave Martin of Napoleon Stoves in Barrie, Ontario for reviewing this chapter.

Oil Lamps—Operation and Maintenance

Material for this chapter was borrowed, with permission from: *Aladdin, the Magic Name in Lamps* by J.W. Courter; the book, a very fascinating read, is available from the author:

J.W. Courter
3935 Kelley Rd.
Kevil, Kentucky 42053

Thanks to Mr. Courter for reviewing this chapter for technical accuracy. Mr. Courter also very kindly sent me a copy of his book; it's headed to the cottage library.

Thanks also to the Aladdin Mantle Lamp Company for allowing me to reprint illustrations and information from their operating brochures. <www.aladdinlamps.com>.

Thanks to Mr. Stan Walker for spending an afternoon discussing lamps; it was time enjoyably spent. His shop, Cottage Kitsch, stocks a wide selection of parts.

Cottage Kitsch
Box 70
Kearney, ON
P0A 1M0
1-877-867-0666
sales@cottagekitsch.com

Using a Water Level

Thanks to Tim Abbott for explaining and demonstrating this device.

The Deck

A version of this chapter first appeared on the *Cottage Life* magazine website: <www.cottagelife.com>.

Thanks to the staff at Switzer's Tim-BR Mart in Orillia, the Orillia Home Hardware, Marcel Rousseau of McPhee's Paints, and to Kelly Smith, Deputy Chief Building Official, City of Orillia for reviewing and editing this chapter.

The Outhouse

A version of this chapter first appeared in *Cottage Life* magazine in August 1999. It proved to be, according to magazine staff, one of the most popular building projects featured.

Thanks to Terry Dovaston for granting permission to use his excellent illustrations, and thanks to J. Michael Lafond for granting permission to reprint the photograph featured on page 147.

Basic Plumbing

Text and illustrations taken from its Booklets are reprinted with permission from Creative Homeowner®.

Creative Homeowner® books are available wherever books are sold: 800/631-7795 <www.creativehomeowner.com>.

Thanks to Tim Bakke of Creative Homeowner for reviewing this chapter.

Critters—The Unwanted

I would like to thank the organizations that allowed me to borrow from their publications for this chapter. They do not assume responsibility for my interpretation. Material for this chapter was borrowed, with permission from the following sources:

Mice
- Canadian Federation of Humane Societies <www.cfhs.ca>.
  Urban Wildlife Series—*Mice and Rats*
- Alberta Department of Agriculture, Food, and Rural Development (<www.agric.gov.ab.ca>) *Mice and Their Control*—fact sheet

Bats
- The Nova Scotia Department of Natural Resources' publication *Conservation*, Volume 14, Number 1, Spring 1990; *Building for Wildlife: Living With Bats*, by Matt Sauders (<www.gov.ns.ca>).
- National Federation of Wildlife (<www. nwf.org>).
  Keep the Wild Alive—Building a Bat House

Raccoons
- Canadian Federation of Humane Societies (<www.cfhs.ca>)
  Urban Wildlife Series—The Raccoon
- Toronto Humane Society
  (<www.torontohumanesociety.com>)

Squirrels
- Canadian Federation of Humane Societies
  Urban Wildlife Series—The Squirrel

Making Maple Syrup

Material for this chapter was borrowed, with permission from: *Backyard Sugarin'* by Rink Mann, published by the Countryman Press, PO Box 748, Woodstock, Vermont 05091 (the picture of the maple leaves was printed, with permission, from page 17).

Thanks to the folks at Atkinson's Maple Syrup Supplies for reviewing this chapter, and for providing technical comments. E-mail address: sales@atkinsonmaple.com; website: <www.atkinsonmaple.com>.

Coexisting with Small Engines

Material for this chapter was borrowed, with permission, from the Briggs and Stratton Company guide: *Small Engine Care and Repair—a step-by-step guide to maintaining your small engine* (<www.briggsandstratton.com>).

Thanks to Cherie Burns, Briggs and Stratton, for arranging to have this chapter reviewed, and for providing resources from Briggs and Stratton.

Thanks also to Jeff Henderson, senior Transportation teacher, Orillia District Collegiate and Vocational Institute, for providing suggestions and constructive criticism.

Fishing—From the Lake to the Plate

Thanks to Pat and Jim Muncy and to Tim Abbott.

Loaves and Fishes

Some recipes were borrowed from *For the Love of Soup* compiled by Jeanelle Mitchell, published by Whitecap Books; *Five Roses: A Guide to Good Cooking*, published by Whitecap Books; and *Pantry Raid* compiled by Dana McCauley, published by Whitecap Books.

The Cottage Bartender

Some cocktail recipes were borrowed, with permission from *150 Classic Cocktails*, published in Canada by Whitecap Books.

Some cocktail recipes were borrowed, with permission from *New Classic Cocktails* by Allan Gage, also published by Whitecap Books.

Results of The Great Canadian Beer Challenge were borrowed, with permission, from the CBC website: <www.cbc.ca/consumers/market/files/food/beer_challenge/taste_results.html>

Thanks to Don Corrick of WINE NOT™ in Orillia, Ontario for his suggestions for wine making.

Thanks to our cottage friends who were kind enough to sample and evaluate the drink recipes.

A Children's Treasure Hunt

A version of this chapter first appeared in *Cottage Life* magazine.

The Library

Thanks to Charlotte Stein, owner of Parry Sound Books for her opinions about books that should be included in a cottage library.

Glossary of Common Construction Terms

Thanks to David Bond, author of *The Complete Guide to Planning & Contracting Your Home or Cottage* (distributed by Home Hardware Stores Limited) for allowing me to borrow many of these terms from the Glossary.

Index